MICROSOFT® OUTLOOK® 98 FOR WINDOWS® FOR DUMMIES®

MICROSOFT® OUTLOOK® 98 FOR WINDOWS® FOR DUMMIES®

by Bill Dyszel

IDG Books Worldwide, Inc.
An International Data Group Company

Foster City, CA ♦ Chicago, IL ♦ Indianapolis, IN ♦ New York, NY

Microsoft® Outlook® 98 For Windows® For Dummies®

Published by
IDG Books Worldwide, Inc.
An International Data Group Company
919 E. Hillsdale Blvd.
Suite 400
Foster City, CA 94404
www.idgbooks.com (IDG Books Worldwide Web site)
www.dummies.com (Dummies Press Web site)

Library of Congress Catalog Card No.: 98-85133

ISBN: 0-7645-0393-6

Printed in the United States of America

10 9 8 7 6 5

1O/QY/RS/ZY/IN

Distributed in the United States by IDG Books Worldwide, Inc.

Distributed by Macmillan Canada for Canada; by Transworld Publishers Limited in the United Kingdom; by IDG Norge Books for Norway; by IDG Sweden Books for Sweden; by Woodslane Pty. Ltd. for Australia; by Woodslane (NZ) Ltd. for New Zealand; by Addison Wesley Longman Singapore Pte Ltd. for Singapore, Malaysia, Thailand, and Indonesia; by Norma Comunicaciones S.A. for Colombia; by Intersoft for South Africa; by International Thomson Publishing for Germany, Austria and Switzerland; by Distribuidora Cuspide for Argentina; by Livraria Cultura for Brazil; by Ediciencia S.A. for Ecuador; by Ediciones ZETA S.C.R. Ltda. for Peru; by WS Computer Publishing Corporation, Inc., for the Philippines; by Contemporanea de Ediciones for Venezuela; by Express Computer Distributors for the Caribbean and West Indies; by Micronesia Media Distributor, Inc. for Micronesia; by Grupo Editorial Norma S.A. for Guatemala; by Chips Computadoras S.A. de C.V. for Mexico; by Editorial Norma de Panama S.A. for Panama; by Wouters Import for Belgium; by American Bookshops for Finland. Authorized Sales Agent: Anthony Rudkin Associates for the Middle East and North Africa.

For general information on IDG Books Worldwide's books in the U.S., please call our Consumer Customer Service department at 800-762-2974. For reseller information, including discounts and premium sales, please call our Reseller Customer Service department at 800-434-3422.

For information on where to purchase IDG Books Worldwide's books outside the U.S., please contact our International Sales department at 317-596-5530 or fax 317-596-5692.

For information on foreign language translations, please contact our Foreign & Subsidiary Rights department at 650-655-3021 or fax 650-655-3281.

For sales inquiries and special prices for bulk quantities, please contact our Sales department at 650-655-3200 or write to the address above.

For information on using IDG Books Worldwide's books in the classroom or for ordering examination copies, please contact our Educational Sales department at 800-434-2086 or fax 317-596-5499.

For press review copies, author interviews, or other publicity information, please contact our Public Relations department at 650-655-3000 or fax 650-655-3299.

For authorization to photocopy items for corporate, personal, or educational use, please contact Copyright Clearance Center, 222 Rosewood Drive, Danvers, MA 01923, or fax 978-750-4470.

is a trademark under exclusive license to IDG Books Worldwide, Inc., from International Data Group, Inc.

About the Author

Bill Dyszel writes frequently for leading computer magazines, including *PC Magazine, Windows Sources,* and *Computer Shopper,* while also working as a consultant to many of New York's leading firms in the securities, advertising, and publishing industries. His list of current and former clients includes Salomon Brothers, First Boston, Goldman Sachs, Ogilvy & Mather, KMPG Peat Marwick, and many others. He is currently preparing to write a book on his favorite gadget, the PalmPilot handheld computer.

The world of high technology has led Mr. Dyszel to grapple with such subjects as Multimedia (or how to make your $2,000 computer do the work of a $20 radio), Personal Information Managers (how to make your $3,000 laptop computer do the work of a $3.00 date book), and graphics programs (how to make your $5,000 package of computers and peripheral devices do the work of a 50-cent box of crayons). All joking aside, he has found that after you figure out the process, most of this stuff can be useful, helpful, and yes, even cool. He elaborates on that idea on his Web site (www.pcstudio.com) and in his speeches and seminars about making technology fun. He'll even send you his occasional e-mail newsletter about the things he finds enjoyable and useful; just drop a note to his e-mail address (BillDyszel@pcstudio.com).

Like many public figures with skeletons in their closets, this author has a secret past. Before entering the computer industry, Mr. Dyszel sang with the New York City Opera and worked regularly on the New York stage as a singer, actor, and writer in numerous plays, musicals, and operas. His opera spoof — *99% ARTFREE!* — won critical praise from *The New York Times,* New York *Daily News,* and the Associated Press when he performed the show Off-Broadway.

ABOUT IDG BOOKS WORLDWIDE

Welcome to the world of IDG Books Worldwide.

IDG Books Worldwide, Inc., is a subsidiary of International Data Group, the world's largest publisher of computer-related information and the leading global provider of information services on information technology. IDG was founded more than 30 years ago by Patrick J. McGovern and now employs more than 9,000 people worldwide. IDG publishes more than 290 computer publications in over 75 countries. More than 90 million people read one or more IDG publications each month.

Launched in 1990, IDG Books Worldwide is today the #1 publisher of best-selling computer books in the United States. We are proud to have received eight awards from the Computer Press Association in recognition of editorial excellence and three from Computer Currents' First Annual Readers' Choice Awards. Our best-selling ...For Dummies® series has more than 50 million copies in print with translations in 31 languages. IDG Books Worldwide, through a joint venture with IDG's Hi-Tech Beijing, became the first U.S. publisher to publish a computer book in the People's Republic of China. In record time, IDG Books Worldwide has become the first choice for millions of readers around the world who want to learn how to better manage their businesses.

Our mission is simple: Every one of our books is designed to bring extra value and skill-building instructions to the reader. Our books are written by experts who understand and care about our readers. The knowledge base of our editorial staff comes from years of experience in publishing, education, and journalism — experience we use to produce books to carry us into the new millennium. In short, we care about books, so we attract the best people. We devote special attention to details such as audience, interior design, use of icons, and illustrations. And because we use an efficient process of authoring, editing, and desktop publishing our books electronically, we can spend more time ensuring superior content and less time on the technicalities of making books.

You can count on our commitment to deliver high-quality books at competitive prices on topics you want to read about. At IDG Books Worldwide, we continue in the IDG tradition of delivering quality for more than 30 years. You'll find no better book on a subject than one from IDG Books Worldwide.

John Kilcullen
Chairman and CEO
IDG Books Worldwide, Inc.

Steven Berkowitz
President and Publisher
IDG Books Worldwide, Inc.

Eighth Annual
Computer Press
Awards ≥1992

Ninth Annual
Computer Press
Awards ≥1993

Tenth Annual
Computer Press
Awards ≥1994

Eleventh Annual
Computer Press
Awards ≥1995

Author's Acknowledgments

I'd like to thank all the wonderful people who helped me make this book entertaining and useful to the reader, especially John Pont, Elizabeth Kuball, Mike Kelly, Mary Corder, Mary Bednarek, Diane Steele, Darlene Wong, and the whole staff of IDG Books Worldwide that makes this series possible.

A special thanks also goes to my friend Mike Zulich for an unfailingly thorough and accurate technical review. Thanks to my friends, editors, and colleagues at *Windows Sources* magazine, *Computer Shopper,* and *PC Magazine*. Thanks to the people at Microsoft and Waggener Edstrom who also helped me figure things out, especially Rob Price. Above all, thanks to my personal cheering section, led by Leigh Williams.

Publisher's Acknowledgments

We're proud of this book; please register your comments through our IDG Books Worldwide Online Registration Form located at http://my2cents.dummies.com.

Some of the people who helped bring this book to market include the following:

Acquisitions, Editorial, and Media Development

Project Editor: John W. Pont

Acquisitions Editor: Michael Kelly

Copy Editor: Elizabeth Kuball

Technical Editor: Michael Zulich

Editorial Manager: Mary C. Corder

Editorial Assistants: Donna Love, Michael D. Sullivan

Production

Project Coordinator: Regina Snyder

Layout and Graphics: Cameron Booker, Lou Boudreau, J. Tyler Connor, Angela F. Hunckler, Jane E. Martin, Brent Savage, Janet Seib, M. Anne Sipahimalani, Deirdre Smith, Rashell Smith, Michael A. Sullivan

Proofreaders: Christine Berman, Kelli Botta, Vicky Broyles, Rebecca Senninger, Janet M. Withers

Indexer: Sharon Duffy

Special Help

Suzanne Thomas, Associate Editor

General and Administrative

IDG Books Worldwide, Inc.: John Kilcullen, CEO; Steven Berkowitz, President and Publisher

IDG Books Technology Publishing: Brenda McLaughlin, Senior Vice President and Group Publisher

Dummies Technology Press and Dummies Editorial: Diane Graves Steele, Vice President and Associate Publisher; Mary Bednarek, Director of Acquisitions and Product Development; Kristin A. Cocks, Editorial Director

Dummies Trade Press: Kathleen A. Welton, Vice President and Publisher; Kevin Thornton, Acquisitions Manager

IDG Books Production for Dummies Press: Michael R. Britton, Vice President of Production and Creative Services; Cindy L. Phipps, Manager of Project Coordination, Production Proofreading, and Indexing; Kathie S. Schutte, Supervisor of Page Layout; Shelley Lea, Supervisor of Graphics and Design; Debbie J. Gates, Production Systems Specialist; Robert Springer, Supervisor of Proofreading; Debbie Stailey, Special Projects Coordinator; Tony Augsburger, Supervisor of Reprints and Bluelines

Dummies Packaging and Book Design: Robin Seaman, Creative Director; Kavish + Kavish, Cover Design

◆

The publisher would like to give special thanks to Patrick J. McGovern, without whom this book would not have been possible.

◆

Contents at a Glance

Introduction 1

Part I: The Outlook Lookout 9

Chapter 1: This Is Your Life with Outlook 11
Chapter 2: Inside Outlook: Mixing, Matching, and Managing Information 25
Chapter 3: No Typing, Please! — Drag 'til You Drop 43
Chapter 4: Files and Folders: A Quick Course in Keeping Things Straight 53
Chapter 5: How You See It: Views and New Views 69
Chapter 6: Creating Your Own Forms 87

Part II: E-Mail and Contacts: Not Just Playing Post Office 99

Chapter 7: E-Mail: Basic Delivery 101
Chapter 8: E-Mail: Special Delivery 119
Chapter 9: Sorting Your Mail 131
Chapter 10: Your Little Black Book: Creating Contact Lists 155
Chapter 11: Personal Distribution Lists and Address Books 177
Chapter 12: Internet Mail Tricks 187

Part III: Taking Care of Business 195

Chapter 13: Days and Dates: Keeping Your Calendar 197
Chapter 14: A Sticky Subject: Using Notes 217
Chapter 15: Journaling 239
Chapter 16: Do It Yourself: Scheduling Your Own Tasks 251
Chapter 17: Outlook Express: Getting the Scoop on Newsgroups 273
Chapter 18: Mail Merge from Outlook to Microsoft Word 281
Chapter 19: The Net Effect: Sharing Information with Net Folders 293

Part IV: The Part of Tens 299

Chapter 20: Ten (Plus One) Office 97 Tricks for Creating Snappier E-Mail 301
Chapter 21: Ten Shortcuts Worth Taking 315
Chapter 22: Let's Go Surfin' Now: Ten Ways to Use Outlook with the Internet 321
Chapter 23: Ten Things You Can't Do with Outlook 325
Chapter 24: Ten Things You Can Do After You're Comfy 329
Chapter 25: Top Ten Accessories for Outlook 337

Index 341

Book Registration Information .... Back of Book

Cartoons at a Glance

By Rich Tennant

page 299

page 9

page 68

page 195

page 99

Fax: 978-546-7747 • E-mail: the5wave@tiac.net

Table of Contents

Introduction **1**

About This Book 2
Foolish Assumptions 2
How This Book Is Organized 3
    Part I: The Outlook Lookout 3
    Part II: E-Mail and Contacts: Not Just Playing Post Office 3
    Part III: Taking Care of Business 4
    Part IV: The Part of Tens 5
Conventions Used in This Book 5
    Dialog boxes 5
    Links 6
    Keyboard shortcuts 6
Icons Used in This Book 7
Getting Started 7

Part I: The Outlook Lookout **9**

Chapter 1: This Is Your Life with Outlook 11

An Out-of-Box Experience 12
    Reading e-mail 12
    Creating a contact 14
    Making an appointment 15
    Creating a task 16
    Taking a phone message 17
    Taking notes 18
    Returning a phone call 19
    Sending a file 21
The Bottom Line 23

Chapter 2: Inside Outlook: Mixing, Matching, and Managing Information 25

Outlook and Other Programs 26
Enter the PIM 27
There's No Place Like Home: Outlook's Main Screen 28
    Outlook modules 30
    Belly up to the Outlook Bar 31
        Adding items to the Outlook Bar 32
        Adding Outlook groups 33

Making the most of Outlook Today 34
The Information Viewer: Outlook's hotspot 35
Navigating the Folder List 37
A tale of two folders 37
Using the Folder List 38
Clicking Once: Outlook Toolbars 38
Viewing ToolTips 38
Using the New tool 39
Turning Parts of the Outlook Screen On and Off 40
Getting Help from the Office Assistant 41

Chapter 3: No Typing, Please! — Drag 'til You Drop 43

How to Drag 43
Creating E-Mail Messages 44
From a name in your Address Book 45
From an appointment 46
Sending a File by E-Mail 47
Creating Contact Records from E-Mail 50
Creating a Journal Entry for a Contact 51
Drag and Drop Dead: Deleting Stuff 52

**Chapter 4: Files and Folders: A Quick Course in Keeping
Things Straight 53**

Managing Your Files 54
Selecting files 56
Moving and copying files 56
Creating a new folder 56
Renaming folders 57
Renaming files 58
Using Views with Files and Folders 59
Sorting files in a folder 60
Icons view 60
Details view 61
By Author view 62
By File Type view 63
Document Timeline view 64
Programs view 66
Installing Outlook's File Management Tools 67
Final Facts on Filing 68

Chapter 5: How You See It: Views and New Views 69

Types of Views 69
Table view 70
Icons view 70
Timeline view 72
Card view 73
Day/Week/Month view 73

Playing with Columns in Table View 74
    Adding a column 75
    Moving a column 75
    Formatting a column 77
    Widening or shrinking a column 78
    Removing a column 78
Sorting 79
    From Table view 80
    From the Sort dialog box 80
Grouping 81
    Grouping views with drag-and-drop 81
    Using the Group By dialog box 82
    Viewing grouped items 84
    Viewing headings only 84
Creating Custom Table Views 85
A Bridge from the Views 85

Chapter 6: Creating Your Own Forms **87**
Adding a Standard Field to a Form 88
Adding a User-Defined Field to a Form 93
Using the Form You've Designed 95
Making a Custom Form a Folder's Default Form 96

**Part II: E-Mail and Contacts: Not Just Playing
Post Office** **99**

Chapter 7: E-Mail: Basic Delivery **101**
Front Ends and Back Ends 101
Creating Messages 102
    Setting the priority of a message 104
    Setting the sensitivity of a message 107
    Adding an Internet link to an e-mail message 108
Reading and Replying to E-Mail Messages 109
    Previewing message text 110
    Sending a reply 111
    Using a link to the Web from your e-mail 113
That's Not My Department: Forwarding Mail 113
Deleting Messages 115
Saving Interrupted Messages 116
Saving a Message as a File 116
Postscript 118

Chapter 8: E-Mail: Special Delivery **119**
Nagging by Flagging 120
    Adding a flag to an e-mail message 120
    Changing the date on a flag 121

Saving Copies of Your Messages 123
Automatically Adding Your Name to the Original
    Message When Replying 124
Setting Your Options 125
Sending Attachments 127
Creating Signatures for Your Messages 128

Chapter 9: Sorting Your Mail **131**

Creating a New Mail Folder 132
    Moving messages to another folder 133
    Using stationery 134
Viewing Your Messages 136
    Messages view 137
    AutoPreview view 138
    Flagged view 139
    Last Seven Days view 140
    Flagged for Next Seven Days view 140
    By Conversation Topic view 141
    By Sender view 142
    Unread Messages view 143
    Sent To view 144
    Message Timeline view 146
Using the Preview Pane 147
Using Rules 148
Filtering Junk E-Mail 150
Using Remote Mail 152

Chapter 10: Your Little Black Book: Creating Contact Lists **155**

Storing Names, Numbers, and Other Stuff 156
Viewing Contacts 164
    Sorting a view 165
    Rearranging views 166
    Using grouped views 168
Flagging Your Friends 170
    Adding a flag to a contact 170
    Hitting the Snooze button 172
Finding Contacts 173
Sending a Business Card 175

Chapter 11: Personal Distribution Lists and Address Books **177**

Figuring Out Whether You Have Corporate Outlook
    or Internet Outlook 177
About Address Books 178
Creating a Personal Distribution List 179
Using a Personal Distribution List 181
Editing a Personal Distribution List 183
Importing an Address Book from Schedule+ and Other Applications 184
Corporate Outlook: The Bottom Line 185

Chapter 12: Internet Mail Tricks 187

What's an ISP? 187
Online Services — Who's Who? 188
Picking a Provider 189
Setting Up Accounts 190
Setting Up Directory Services 192

Part III: Taking Care of Business 195

Chapter 13: Days and Dates: Keeping Your Calendar 197

The Date Navigator: Really Getting Around 198
Meetings Galore: Scheduling Appointments 200
   Not this time: Changing dates 205
   Not ever: Breaking dates 207
   We've got to keep seeing each other: Recurring dates ... 208
Getting a Good View of Your Calendar 212
Printing Your Appointments 215

Chapter 14: A Sticky Subject: Using Notes 217

Writing a Note 218
Finding a Note 220
Reading a Note 221
Deleting a Note 222
Changing the Size of a Note 223
Changing Your Colors 224
Viewing Your Notes 225
   Icons view 225
   Notes List view 226
   Last Seven Days view 227
   By Category view 228
   By Color 228
Assigning a Category to Your Notes 231
Printing Your Notes 233
   Printing a list of your notes 233
   Printing the contents of a note 234
Changing Your Default Options for New Notes 235
   Changing size and color 235
   Turning the date and time display on or off 236
Forwarding a Note 237
A Final Note 238

Chapter 15: Journaling 239

Don't Just Do Something — Stand There! 240
   Recording an Outlook item in the Journal manually ... 241
   Recording a document in the Journal 242

Viewing Journal Entries for a Contact 244
Finding a Journal Entry 244
Printing Your Journal 246
Viewing the Journal 247
    The Entry List 247
    By Type 247
    By Contact 248
    By Category 248
    Last Seven Days 249
    Phone Calls 249
It's All in the Journal 250

Chapter 16: Do It Yourself: Scheduling Your Own Tasks 251

Using the Outlook Tasks List 252
Entering New Tasks 252
    The quick-and-dirty way to enter a task 253
    The regular way to enter a task 254
    Adding an Internet link to a Task 258
Editing Your Tasks 259
    The quick-and-dirty way to change a task 259
    The regular way to change a task 259
    Copying a task 263
    Deleting a task 264
Managing Recurring Tasks 264
    Creating a regenerating task 267
    Skipping a recurring task once 268
Marking Tasks Complete 268
    Marking several tasks complete 269
    Picking a color for completed or overdue tasks 270
Viewing Your Tasks 271

Chapter 17: Outlook Express: Getting the Scoop on Newsgroups 273

Finding Newsgroups 274
Subscribing to Newsgroups 276
Reading Newsgroup Messages 276
Replying to a Newsgroup Message 277
Posting a New Message 278

Chapter 18: Mail Merge from Outlook to Microsoft Word 281

Creating Mailing Labels 281
Printing Envelopes 284
Creating a Form Letter from the Contact List 287
Merging Selected Records 289

Chapter 19: The Net Effect: Sharing Information with Net Folders **293**

Setting the Net 293
    Installing Net Folders 293
    Allowing another person to share your folders 295
Adding Shared Items to a Folder 298
Dealing with Shared Items in Net Folders 298

Part IV: The Part of Tens *299*

Chapter 20: Ten (Plus One) Office 97 Tricks for Creating Snappier E-Mail **301**

Tricks That Work in Word 302
    Animated text 302
    Table tools 303
    Office Art 304
    Hyperlinks 305
    Document Map 306
    Versions 306
    Browsing 308
    Check grammar as you type 309
Tricks You Can Do in Excel 310
    Apply conditional formatting 310
    Merge Excel cells 312
    Angle Excel text 312
Now for This Message 314

Chapter 21: Ten Shortcuts Worth Taking **315**

Using the New Item Tool 315
Sending a File to an E-Mail Recipient 316
Sending a File from an Office 97 Application 317
Clicking Open the Folder List 317
Keeping the Folder List Open 318
Undo-ing Your Mistakes 318
Using the Go To Date Command 318
Adding Items to List Views 318
Keeping a Note Open 318
Navigating with Browser Buttons 319

Chapter 22: Let's Go Surfin' Now: Ten Ways to Use Outlook with the Internet **321**

Using the Favorites Folder 321
Storing a Contact's Web Pages 322
Sending Internet E-Mail 322

Receiving Internet E-Mail 322
Including Internet Hot Links in E-Mail Messages 322
Including Internet Hot Links in Any Outlook Item 323
Saving Internet E-Mail Addresses in Your Address Book 323
Dragging Scraps of Text from a Web Page 323
Downloading Outlook Stationery from the Internet 324
Getting Help on the Web 324

Chapter 23: Ten Things You Can't Do with Outlook 325

The Top Ten List 325
Using Outlook categories in a Word 97 Mail Merge 326
Running Outlook 98 without installing Internet Explorer 4.0 326
Backing up your Outlook files to a floppy disk 326
Making Outlook start other programs 327
Displaying parts of different modules in the same view 327
Saving the Folder List in a custom view 327
Embedding pictures in notes 327
Automatically recording all contact stuff in the Journal 327
Calculating expenses with Journal Phone Call entries 328
Cross-referencing items to jump to different modules 328
Ten More Things Outlook Can't Do for You 328

Chapter 24: Ten Things You Can Do After You're Comfy 329

Adding a Group to the Outlook Bar 329
Renaming a Group in the Outlook Bar 330
Deleting a Group from the Outlook Bar 330
Renaming an Icon in the Outlook Bar 331
Using Outlook Fields to Create Special Mailings 331
Selecting Dates as a Group 332
Turning On the Advanced Toolbar 332
Customizing the Toolbar 333
Creating Your Own Type of Outlook Field 334
Setting Up Fax Service 335

Chapter 25: Top Ten Accessories for Outlook 337

PalmPilot 337
Microsoft Office 97 338
Desktop to Go 338
Winfax Pro 338
A Business Card Scanner 338
Laplink 339
A Large, Removable Disk Drive 339
A Tape Backup 339
Microsoft Exchange 339
Keyview 340

Index *341*

Book Registration Information .... *Back of Book*

Introduction

· ·

*D*eep space adventurers have control panels on their spaceships, explorers in the Wild West had their faithful guides, and detectives have their little black books. Why? Because every adventurer knows how important it is to have good information. Knowing about the people with whom you're dealing, the things you need to do, and when you have to do those things can make the difference between triumph and failure.

Okay, maybe your daily adventures aren't exactly life-and-death struggles, but having a tool to help you keep a handle on whom and what you need to take care of from day to day is really nice. Even if your daily challenges are limited to dealing with a phone and a personal computer, having one place to look for all your daily details is convenient and timesaving.

Microsoft Outlook was designed to make organizing your daily information easy — almost automatic. You already have sophisticated programs for word processing and number crunching, but Outlook pulls together everything you need to know about your daily tasks, appointments, e-mail messages, and other details. More important, Outlook lets you use the same methods to deal with many different kinds of information, so you only have to learn one program in order to deal with the many kinds of details that fill your life, such as

  ✔ Finding a customer's phone number.

  ✔ Remembering that important meeting.

  ✔ Planning your tasks for the day and checking them off after you're done.

  ✔ Recording all the work you do so that you can find what you did and when you did it.

Outlook is a Personal Information Manager (Microsoft calls it a Desktop Information Manager) that can act as your assistant in dealing with the flurry of small but important details that stand between you and the work you do. You can just as easily keep track of personal information that isn't business-related and keep both business and personal information in the same convenient location.

About This Book

As you read this book and work with Outlook, you'll discover how useful Outlook is, as well as new ways to make it more useful for the things you do most. If you fit any of the following categories, this book is for you:

- ✔ You're planning to purchase Outlook and want to know what you can do with Outlook and how to do it.
- ✔ You've already purchased Outlook and want to get up to speed quickly.
- ✔ You want an easier, more efficient tool for managing tasks, schedules, e-mail, and other details in your working life.

Even if you don't fall into one of these groups, this book gives you simple, clear explanations of how Outlook can work for you. It's hard to imagine any computer user who wouldn't benefit from the features that Outlook offers.

If all you want is a quick guided tour of Outlook, you can skim this book — it covers everything that you need to start with. Getting a handle on most of the major features of Outlook is fairly easy — that's how the program is designed. You can also keep the book handy as a reference for the tricks that you may not need every day.

The first part of this book gives you enough information to make sense of the whole program. Because Outlook is intended to be simple and consistent throughout, when you've got the big picture, the details are fairly simple (usually).

Don't be fooled by Outlook's friendliness, though — you'll find a great deal of power in it if you want to dig deeply enough. Outlook links up with your Microsoft Office applications, and it's fully programmable by anyone who wants to tackle a little Visual Basic script writing (I don't get into that in this book). You may not want to do the programming yourself, but finding people who can do that for you isn't hard; just ask around.

Foolish Assumptions

I'm assuming that you know how to turn on your computer and how to use a mouse and keyboard. In case you need a brushup on Windows 95 or Windows NT 4.0 or later, I throw in reminders as I go along. If Windows 95 and Microsoft Office are strange to you, picking up Andy Rathbone's *Windows 95 For Dummies,* 2nd Edition, or Wally Wang's *Microsoft Office 97 For Windows For Dummies,* both from IDG Books Worldwide, Inc., will be a big help.

If all you have is a copy of this book and a computer running Outlook, you'll certainly be able to do basic, useful things right away, as well as a few fun ones. And after some time, you'll be able to do many fun and useful things.

How This Book Is Organized

To make it easier to find out how to do what you want to do, this book is divided into parts. Each part covers a different aspect of using Outlook. Because you can use similar methods to do many different jobs with Outlook, the first parts of the book focus on how to use Outlook. The later parts concentrate on what you can use Outlook to do.

Part I: The Outlook Lookout

I learn best by doing, so the first chapter is a fanciful, but not entirely fictional, story about the things you can do with Outlook on a typical day. You find out how easy it is to use Outlook for routine tasks like handling messages, phone calls, and appointments. You can get quite a lot of mileage out of Outlook even if you only do the things our fictional detective does in the first chapter.

Because Outlook allows you to use similar methods to do many things, I go on to show you the things that stay pretty much the same throughout the program: how to create new items from old ones by using drag-and-drop, ways to view items that make your information easy to understand at a glance, and the features Outlook offers to make it easier to move, copy, and organize your files.

Part II: E-Mail and Contacts: Not Just Playing Post Office

E-mail is now the most popular function of computers. Tens of millions of people are hooked up to the Internet, an office network, or to one of the popular online services, such as the Microsoft Network or CompuServe.

The problem is that e-mail can still be a little too complicated. As I show you in Part II, however, Outlook makes e-mail easier. Computers are notoriously finicky about the exact spelling of addresses, correctly hooking up to the actual mail service, and making sure that the text and formatting of the message fit the software you're using. Outlook keeps track of the details involved in getting your message to its destination.

Outlook also allows you to receive e-mail from a variety of sources and manage the messages in one place. You can slice and dice your list of incoming and outgoing e-mail messages to help you keep track of what you send, to whom you send it, and the day and time you send it. Some folks even use their e-mail as primitive to-do lists; Outlook allows you to flag each message to make it easier to use your collection of e-mail messages any way you want.

Part III: Taking Care of Business

Outlook takes advantage of its special relationship with your computer and your office applications (Microsoft Outlook with Microsoft Office, Microsoft Internet Explorer, and Microsoft Windows — notice a pattern emerging here?) to tie your office tasks together more cleanly than other such programs and make it easier for you to deal with all the stuff that you have to do. The chapters in Part III show you how to get the job done with Outlook.

Beyond planning and scheduling, you probably spend a great deal of your working time with other people, and you need to coordinate your schedule with theirs (unless you make your living doing something strange and antisocial, such as digging graves or writing computer books). Outlook allows you to share schedule and task information with other people (if you're on the same network) and synchronize with them. You can also assign tasks to other people if you don't want to do them yourself (now *there's* a time-saver). Be careful, though; other people can assign those tasks right back to you.

If you've got yellow sticky notes covering your monitor, refrigerator, desktop, or bathroom door, you'll get a great deal of mileage out of Outlook's Notes feature. Notes are little yellow (or blue, or green) squares that look just like those handy paper sticky notes that you stick everywhere as reminders and then lose. About the only thing that you can't do is set your coffee cup on one and mess up what you wrote.

Sometimes, the "find-the-sticky-note" game takes a dark turn — you don't remember *what* you jotted down, you don't remember *where* you put the note, but you do remember *when* you wrote it. That's when Outlook's automatic Journal feature comes in handy. The Journal keeps track of every document that you create, edit, or print. It remembers when you sent e-mail to anyone and when you scheduled that important appointment. You can also make a Journal entry to remember any task you scheduled or any conversation you had with anyone. If it sounds too Big Brother-ish to have a computer recording everything you do, I'll tell you how to turn the Journal off.

Part IV: The Part of Tens

Why ten? Why not! If you must have a reason, ten is the highest number you can count to without taking off your shoes. A program as broad as Outlook leaves a great deal of flotsam and jetsam that doesn't quite fit into any category, so I sum up the best of that material in groups of ten.

Conventions Used in This Book

Outlook has many unique features, but it also has lots in common with other Windows programs — dialog boxes, pull-down menus, toolbars, and so on. To be productive with Outlook, you need to understand how these features work, and you need to recognize the conventions I use for describing these features throughout this book.

Dialog boxes

Even if you're not new to Windows, you deal with dialog boxes more in Outlook than you do in many other Microsoft Office programs because so many items in Outlook are created with dialog boxes, which may also be called forms. E-mail message forms, appointments, name and address forms, and plenty of other common functions in Outlook use dialog boxes to ask you what you want to do. The essential parts of a dialog box are

- **Title bar.** The title bar tells you the name of the dialog box.

- **Text boxes.** Text boxes are blank spaces where you type information. When you click a text box, you see a blinking I-beam pointer, which means that you can type text there.

- **Control buttons.** In the upper-right corner of a dialog box, you find three control buttons. The *close button* looks like an X and makes the dialog box disappear. The *size button* toggles between maximizing the dialog box (making it take up the entire screen) and resizing it (making it take up less than the entire screen). The *minimize button* makes the dialog box seem to go away but really just hides it in the taskbar at the bottom of your screen until you click the taskbar to make the dialog box come back.

- **Tabs.** Tabs look like little file-folder tabs. If you click one, you see a new page of the dialog box. Tabs are just like the divider tabs in a ring binder; click one to change sections.

The easiest way to move around a dialog box is to click the part that you want to use. If you're a real whiz on the keyboard, you may prefer to press the Tab key to move around the dialog box; this method is much faster if you're a touch typist. Otherwise, you're fine just mousing around.

Links

Links are special pictures or pieces of text that you can click to change what you see on the screen. If you're used to surfing the Internet, you're used to clicking blue underlined text to switch from one Web page to another. Outlook has some links that work just like links on the Internet. When you see underlined text, the text is most likely a link, so you can click the text if you want to see where it leads.

Keyboard shortcuts

Normally, you can choose any Windows command in at least three ways (and sometimes more). You can

- ✔ Choose a menu command or click a toolbar button.
- ✔ Press a keyboard combination, such as Ctrl+B, which means holding down the Ctrl key and pressing the letter B. (You use this command to make text bold.)
- ✔ Press the F10 key or the spacebar to pull down a menu, press an arrow key to choose a command, and press Enter (way too much trouble, but possible for those who love a challenge).

You often tell Outlook what to do by choosing from menus at the top of the screen. Each menu command has one letter underlined (such as File, Edit, Help), which means that you can hold the Alt key while pressing the underlined letter to open the menu. Press Alt+F to open the File menu, Alt+E to see the Edit menu, or Alt+H to see the Help menu.

I normally simplify menu commands by saying something like "Choose Yeah⇨Sure," which means "Choose the Yeah menu; then choose the Sure command."

Icons Used in This Book

Sometimes the fastest way to go through a book is to look at the pictures —
in this case, icons that draw your attention to specific types of information
that's useful to know. Here are the icons I use in this book:

 The Remember icon points out helpful information. (Everything in this book
is helpful, but this stuff is even *more* helpful.)

 A hint or trick for saving time and effort, or something that makes Outlook
easier to understand.

 The Warning icon points to something that you may want to be careful about
in order to prevent problems.

 The Technical Stuff icon marks background information that you can skip,
although it may make good conversation at a really dull party.

 The Time Saver icon points out a trick that can save you time.

 The Network icon points out information that applies primarily to people
using Outlook on a computer network at the office.

 The Internet icon points out a feature of Outlook that helps connect you to
the Internet or use the Internet more effectively.

Getting Started

A wise person once said, "The best way to start is by starting." Okay, that's
not all that wise, but why quibble? Plunge in!

Part I
The Outlook Lookout

The 5th Wave   By Rich Tennant

"THE ENTIRE SYSTEM IS DOWN. THE COMPUTER PEOPLE BLAME THE MODEM PEOPLE WHO BLAME THE PHONE PEOPLE WHO BLAME IT ON OUR MOON BEING IN THE FIFTH HOUSE WITH VENUS ASCENDING."

In this part . . .

Outlook is an all-in-one information management system that lets you organize and manage your appointments, activities, e-mail, and office life with a few clicks of the mouse. In this part, I give you a basic vision of how Outlook works to improve the way you manage your days.

Chapter 1

This Is Your Life with Outlook

In This Chapter

▶ Enjoying an out-of-box experience

▶ Reading e-mail

▶ Creating a contact from a message

▶ Creating an appointment from a contact

▶ Creating a task from an appointment

▶ Creating a phone message from a contact

▶ Taking notes

▶ Using AutoDialing

▶ E-mailing a file

*O*utlook is an information manager, which means that Outlook doesn't just help you deal with your computer, it also helps you deal with people. I'm not just talking about documents or databases here. Dealing with other people and the things you do in connection with other people is much more important than what kind of documents you produce.

I leave Outlook running on my computer constantly. Why? Because I'm never sure when an idea will hit me or when I'll remember a new task I have to complete. I find it handy just to have Outlook going so that I can deal with whatever comes up at the spur of the moment.

You can use the same methods to do many different things in Outlook — click an icon to do something, view something, or complete something. Drag an item from one Outlook module to the icon for another module to create an item that represents something else you have to do. (I explain things such as icons and modules as I go along.)

The pictures that I show you in this book and the instructions that I give you assume that you're using Outlook the way it comes out of the box from Microsoft with all the standard options installed. If you don't like the way the program looks or what things are named when you install Outlook, you can change nearly everything. If you change many things, however, some of the instructions and examples that I give you won't make sense because the parts of the program I talk about may have names that you gave them, rather than the ones that Microsoft originally assigned. The Microsoft people generally did a good job of making Outlook easy to use. I suggest leaving the general arrangement alone until you're comfortable with Outlook.

An Out-of-Box Experience

Warning — the story that you are about to read could be true, with a few small changes. Just change the names to those of the people you need to meet, call, and work with. The actual work you do may differ, but all the things that Outlook does in the story are true.

The story starts in the offices of your successful business, Dot Company. You sell dots. You have a Web site (www.dotcom.com). You're a dot dealer. Everybody knows that you've got dots (megadots, baby!). It's your job to keep those dots moving and to make sure that they get to their destinations by 10 a.m. on the dot.

Reading e-mail

You start your computer and double-click the Outlook icon on the desktop. A message is waiting for you. Before you open it, you know that this message means the start of another busy day. The title of the message tells you that it's from Stan Spotman, the dotmaster of Megacorp. That outfit needs lots of dots. Something about the message tells you that Stan's got trouble and needs your help fast. It's not just your keen instincts that give you the clue — you can see the first three lines of the message. The message is new, so it's in AutoPreview (see Figure 1-1).

Here's how to see the entire message:

1. Click Inbox in the Outlook Bar.

You instinctively click the Inbox icon. You don't need this step if you can already see the messages, but it doesn't hurt.

Inbox icon

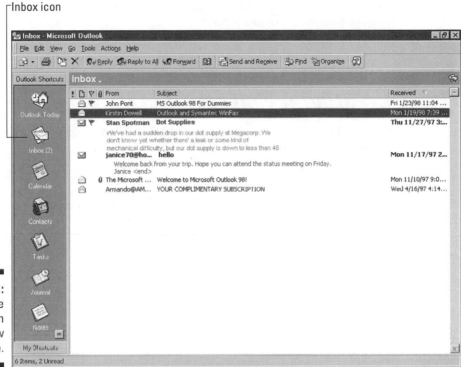

Figure 1-1:
A message
in
AutoProview
mode.

2. Double-click the title of the message.

Now you can see the entire message, which reads as follows:

We've had a sudden drop in our dot supply at Megacorp.
We don't know yet whether there's a leak or some kind of
mechanical difficulty, but our dot supply is down to less
than 48-hours worth. We're willing to pay up to 5 cents
per dot for top-quality dots that last more than 48 hours.
We've contacted you and Dot's Dots for immediate supplies.

Contact me ASAP!
Stan Spotman
Megacorp, Inc.
555 Grand Avenue
Chicago, IL 60632
312 555-9730

3. Press Esc.

Pay — the magic word! What is the massive but miserly Megacorp ready to shell out for your premium dots?

You close the message and swing into action. There's no time to lose.

Creating a contact

You need to keep Stan's vital statistics handy for messages, phone calls, deliveries, and (most important) the bill.

Here's how you save stats on Stan:

1. **Hold down the mouse button and drag the mail message to the Contacts icon.**

   The Contact form opens with Stan's name and e-mail address already filled in. You think back to the old days, when you had to waste time entering e-mail addresses again and again. You always figured that computers should know how to do that; that's what they're for. The text of Stan's e-mail message is in the box at the bottom of the Contact form (see Figure 1-2).

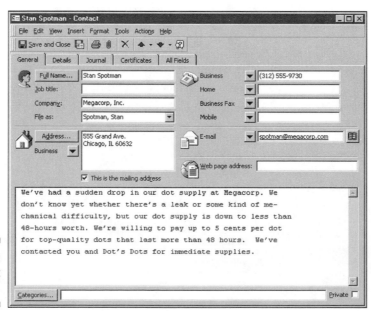

Figure 1-2: The Contact form.

To save time, swipe your mouse over the part of the message where Stan put his phone number and drag it up to the Business Phone block of the Contact form. Then do the same with his mailing address. You've got the goods on Stan.

2. **Click the Save and Close button (or press Alt+S).**

You click the Contacts icon again to see whether Stan's stats wound up in the Contact list. You know Outlook has never let you down, but you like to be sure.

Making an appointment

Your finely tuned business instincts tell you that you need to meet a client in person when he's in a really tough spot. Also, something fishy about this sudden dot loss makes you want to see Stan face to face. You decide to invite Stan to lunch tomorrow.

Here's how you enter an appointment in your calendar:

1. **Click the Contacts icon.**

You see Stan's record in the Contact list.

2. **Drag the icon next to the name on the Contact list to the Calendar icon.**

The Meeting form appears (see Figure 1-3). Stan's e-mail address is already in that form, with an underline — Outlook's way of telling you that it will handle the e-mail, leaving you to handle Stan.

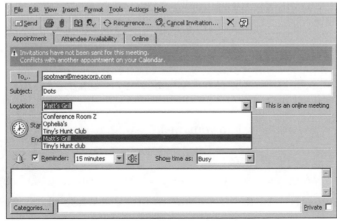

Figure 1-3:
The New
Meeting
form.

3. **Type a subject in the Subject box.**

   Your subject — **Dots** — gets right to the point.

4. **Open the Location menu and choose one of your favorite haunts as a meeting location.**

   You can type any place you want, but for people in the dot game, Matt's Grill is the spot. You go there often, so Outlook automatically stores it in your location list.

5. **Click the Start Date box and type** Tomorrow.

   What's tomorrow's date? That's not your concern; Outlook takes care of it.

6. **Click the Start Time box and type** Noon.

   You know a lot, but whether noon is 12 a.m. or 12 p.m. is still confusing. Leave the problem to Outlook — you've got better things to do.

7. **Click the Reminder box and choose 30 minutes in the adjacent box.**

   You like to have Outlook remind you to leave early enough to get your regular seat at Matt's Grill.

8. **Type a message in the text box at the bottom of the form.**

   Your message could say something like "Let's have lunch tomorrow. Matt's at noon? Call to confirm." You know that Stan's a regular at Matt's Grill, so lunch won't be a problem.

9. **Click the Send button.**

Saving steps is the name of the game, and you just saved three: You simultaneously suggested a meeting with Stan, entered the meeting in your calendar, and set a reminder for yourself.

Creating a task

Before you make a deal with Stan, you have to check the dot market. If you're meeting him at noon, you should check the market in the morning.

Here's how you add a task to your Tasks list:

1. **Click the Calendar icon.**

   The appointment that you entered for Stan is already in your calendar.

2. **Drag the icon for the appointment that you made to the Tasks icon.**

   The new task borrows the subject and the date from your Dots appointment.

3. **Change the subject to** Check dot market.

This message is just for you — now you have a task to do!

4. **Click the Reminder check box.**

The reminder is already set for 8 a.m. Because you don't get to the office until 9, a reminder message will pop up at 8 a.m. and remain on your screen until you postpone or dismiss the message. You could change the reminder to later if you want, but it's best to get to your top task first thing.

5. **Click Save and Close.**

The Task form closes and your task is entered on the Tasks list.

Taking a phone message

No sooner do you send your message to Stan than the phone rings. Stan sounds worried. "I have to do this dot deal today," he stammers. "Dot's Dots is out of dots; you're my only shot for dots."

"For only a nickel a dot?" you shoot back, knowing that he'll get your point.

"Okay," he says. "Eight cents."

Without a pause, you respond, "I'll have to check my sources." You know that you've got him on the spot.

"Ten cents. Period," he replies.

You have some fast work to do. You tell Stan you'll get back to him.

First, you need to get a record of this conversation in the Journal in case Stan "forgets" what he offered.

Here's how you create a Journal entry to keep a record of a phone conversation:

1. **Click the Contacts icon.**

Stan's record is there on-screen.

2. **Drag the contact record to the Journal icon.**

The Journal form opens with Stan's name and the current time filled in. In the lower part of the form is an icon which is a shortcut to Stan's contact record, in case you need to refer to it. Below that icon is a blinking bar that indicates where text will appear when you start typing (see Figure 1-4).

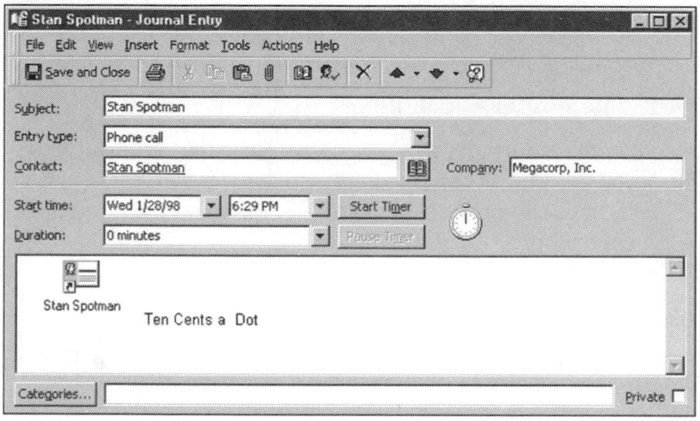

Figure 1-4:
Journal
entry for
recording a
phone call.

> **3. Type** Ten Cents a Dot.
>
> **4. Click the Save and Close button.**

Now you have a record of exactly when Stan called and what you need to remember about the call.

Taking notes

The fact that your competitor, Dot's Dots, is totally out of stock is curious. You don't have much time to check out the situation, but you want to make a note of it for later reference.

Here's how you can take a quick note:

> **1. Click the New tool at the left end of the toolbar and then choose Note from the New items menu that appears.**
>
> A yellow square pops up on-screen; it looks like a yellow paper stick-on note (see Figure 1-5).

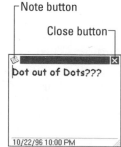

Figure 1-5:
A Note.

2. **Type the note that you want to remember.**

   In this case, type **Dot out of Dots???**. That note will be enough to jog your memory later. The note automatically includes the date and time when you wrote it, just for your records.

3. **Click the Close button in the upper-right corner of the note (or press Alt+F4).**

This note is just for your own use; you won't be reminded. Sometime later, though, you may want to search for the phrase *out of dots,* and you'll have a note of exactly when it happened.

Returning a phone call

You've checked your own dot supply, and you've decided to do the dime-a-dot deal with Stan. You don't need to look up his number to call him back because your modem is set up to dial for you.

Here's how you use the AutoDialer to make a call:

1. **Click the Contacts icon.**

   Stan's record is on screen (see Figure 1-6).

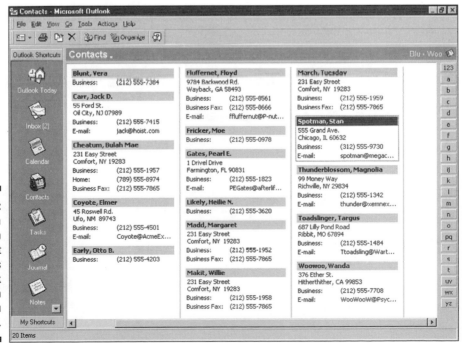

Figure 1-6: Clicking a name in the Contact list tells Outlook which person you want to call.

2. Click Stan's name in the Contacts screen.

Stan's record is highlighted to show that he's the one you want to call. You see Stan's name and address in a little box that looks like an address card, because you're using the Address Card view of the Contact list. (See Chapter 10 for more information about the Contact list.)

3. Choose Actions⇨Call Contact and choose the contact's phone number from the menu.

The New Call dialog box pops up with Stan's name and phone number already filled in (see Figure 1-7).

Figure 1-7:
The New Call dialog box shows you the name of the person you're dialing.

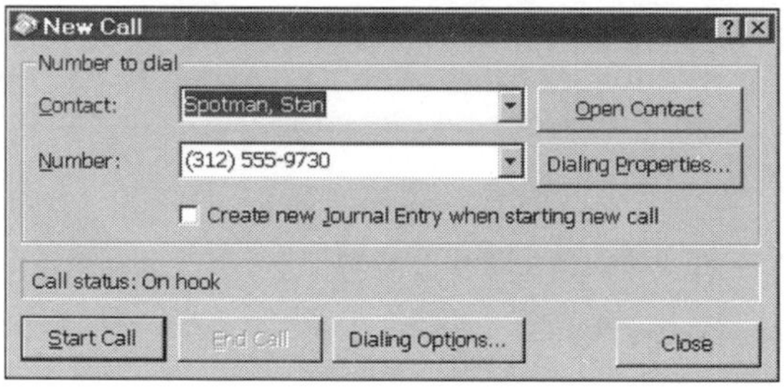

4. Pick up the phone and click the Start Call button in the New Call dialog box.

The Call Status dialog box opens (see Figure 1-8).

Figure 1-8:
The Call Status dialog box tells you whether your call is going through.

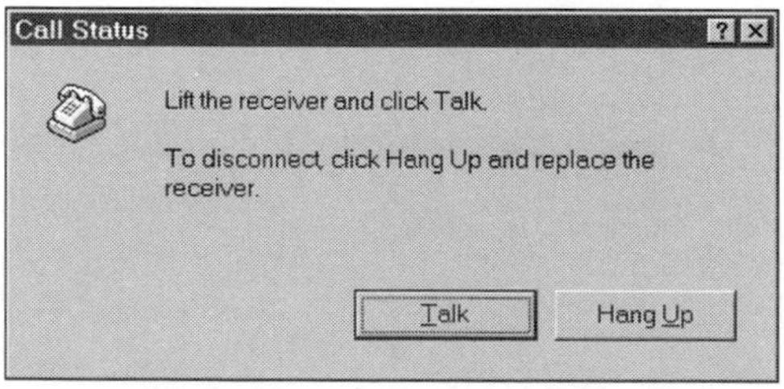

5. **Click Talk to begin talking.**

   You reach Stan and tell him that dimes for dots is a done deal. He recalls offering eight cents. You refresh his memory and tell him that you're sending a contract by e-mail. He agrees, grudgingly.

6. **Click the Hang Up button.**

   You're back in the New Call dialog box.

7. **Click the Close button in the New Call dialog box.**

You're done with the call, but you're not done with Stan just yet.

Sending a file

The file for your standard contract for dots is stored in your My Documents folder; it's called DotCom Standard Contract. You can mail Stan this contract file without using the Post Office — just your computer.

Here's how you send a file by e-mail:

1. **Click the words *Other Shortcuts* in the lowest gray bar in the Outlook Bar.**

   The My Computer icon appears.

2. **Click the My Computer icon.**

   A list of your disk drives appears (see Figure 1-9).

3. **Double-click the (C:) icon.**

   A list of the folders on your C drive appears.

4. **Double-click the My Documents folder icon.**

   A list of the files in your My Documents folder appears; DotCom Standard Contract is among them.

5. **Click the word *Outlook* in the highest gray bar in the Outlook Bar.**

   The list of Outlook icons appears — Inbox, Contacts, Calendar, and so on — but the main part of the screen still shows the files in your My Documents folder.

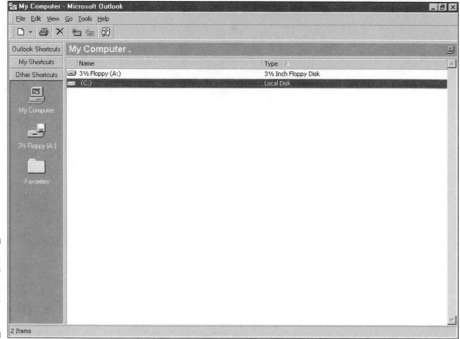

6. Click the name of a file and drag it to the Inbox icon.

In this case, you drag DotCom Standard Contract to the Inbox icon. The Message form appears, with an icon in the bottom box titled DotCom Standard Contract. That icon represents the file that you're sending to Stan (the contract). The title of the message is the same as the name of the file (DotCom Standard Contract).

7. Click the To box and type the name of the person to whom you're sending the file.

Because you've already entered Stan in your Contact list, all you have to do is type **Stan Spotman**. Outlook figures out what to do about sending the message.

8. Click Send.

Your contract is on the way to Stan, and you're ready to return to business as usual.

The Bottom Line

Your daily working life may not run like a detective story, but a well-organized desktop information manager such as Outlook can help you out. If you use Outlook only for the few things I mention in this chapter, you'll save time. But Outlook has more — lots more.

Later in the book, I show you other ways to use Outlook to save steps and combine tasks automatically. Some tasks, such as keeping track of your files, make more sense when you handle them through Outlook than if you use the Windows Explorer that comes with Windows 95. You can also use the drag-and-drop method of creating new Outlook items from old items so that you don't have to keep retyping the same information over and over. I get into more ways to save time and effort with drag-and-drop techniques in Chapter 3.

You can install Outlook in a variety of ways that can make a difference in how you do things. I'm assuming that, if you're on a corporate network, a computer staff deals with setup and configuration. Corporate users may have different names for the folders and icons from those that I describe depending on how their computer departments are set up. I use the names that Office 98 gives to commonly used files and folders in which most documents are stored, such as the My Documents folder. Where names may differ wildly, I try to make a note of that fact so that you know.

Chapter 2

Inside Outlook: Mixing, Matching, and Managing Information

. . . .

In This Chapter

▶ Examining the many faces of Outlook

▶ Choosing menus: One from column A and one from column B

▶ Using the tools of the trade

▶ Taking the shortcut: Speedier keystrokes

▶ Getting the big picture from the Information Viewer

▶ Fine-tuning with the Folder List

. . . .

Computer companies love new stuff. Every so often, they beef up their products with new names and new features and release them just before I've figured out how to use the old products. It's kind of confusing, but I can't deny that many of these newfangled features make my life easier after I get a handle on them.

In the old days B.C. (Before Computers), every task in an office required a different machine. You'd type letters on a typewriter, calculate on an adding machine, file names and addresses in a card file, and keep your appointments in a datebook. It would be very difficult to add up your monthly sales on the typewriter and even harder to type a letter on the calculator.

When computers started creeping in, each of those functions was taken over, one by one, by the computer. Each machine was replaced by a different program. First, the word-processing program eliminated the typewriter; next, the spreadsheet replaced the calculator. After a brief flirtation with the giant record-keeping database, the frequent job of keeping track of names, addresses, and dates slowly (but not completely) gave way to a program called the Personal Information Manager (PIM). Microsoft claims to take the information manager concept one step further with Outlook.

The many flavors of Outlook

You can tell that the folks at Microsoft are enthusiastic about Outlook because they've given the name Outlook to at least seven different programs, each of which differs very slightly from the others. Three of those programs come in the box with Outlook 98:

✔ **Outlook 98 Corporate version:** Most similar to Outlook 97 and best suited to people using corporate computer networks, especially those who use Microsoft Exchange Server on those networks.

✔ **Outlook 98 Internet Mail Only version:** Looks quite a bit like the Corporate version but it's best suited for home or small office users of Outlook who get their e-mail from an online service, like CompuServe, or an Internet Service Provider, such as AT&T WorldNet.

✔ **Outlook Express:** A small program that lets you exchange e-mail and read and post messages to Internet newsgroups.

You can use Outlook Express at the same time as you use either version of Outlook 98, but you must choose between the Outlook 98 Corporate version and the Internet Mail Only version. If you're setting up Outlook yourself, the Internet Mail Only version is probably your best bet. If you work in a company with a corporate network, your systems administrators will probably take charge of setting up Outlook 98 Corporate version for you, so you won't have to mess with installing it. The Corporate version and the Internet Mail Only version work pretty much the same way and look alike, so if you know how to use one, you know how to use both.

In case you're curious, the other versions of Outlook include a Mac version, a Windows 3.1 version, and a version called Outlook Web View, all of which are designed for use on a corporate network. The seventh version of Outlook, by my count, is Pocket Outlook, which comes with those pocket-sized computers that run Windows CE.

Outlook and Other Programs

Outlook was first released as part of Microsoft Office 97. Office 97 is an Office *suite,* which means it's a collection of programs that includes everything you need to complete most office tasks. Ideally, the programs in a suite work together and let you create documents that you couldn't create as easily with any of the individual programs. For example, you can copy a chart from a spreadsheet and paste it into a sales letter you're creating in your word processor. You can also keep a list of mailing addresses in a spreadsheet or database and use the list as a mailing list for form letters (see Chapter 18).

Microsoft Office 97 includes five programs that cost less to buy together than you would pay to buy them separately. The concept is a little like buying an encyclopedia; it's cheaper to buy the entire set than it is to buy one book at a time. Besides, who wants just one volume of an encyclopedia (unless you're only interested in aardvarks)?

If you own Office 97 (or if Office 97 is the program you use at work), Outlook was the Big New Thing that was added since Microsoft's earlier model, Office 95. What happened to Office 96? Good question. For people who love numbers so much, these computer geeks sure can't count.

Now Outlook turns up in connection with several other Microsoft products. Microsoft Exchange Server is the backbone of the e-mail system in many corporations, and Outlook is often the program that employees of those corporations use to read their company e-mail. Outlook's junior version, Outlook Express, is included free when you install Internet Explorer 4.0, and will also be included as a part of Windows 98 and all future versions of Windows. Outlook 98 is also linked strongly to Internet Explorer 4.0, although technically they're separate programs. You don't need to worry about all this, though. You can start up Outlook and use it the same way no matter which other programs it's bundled with.

Enter the PIM

When it comes to the basic work of managing names, addresses, appointments, and e-mail, the word-processing and spreadsheet programs just don't get it. If you're planning a meeting, you need to know whom you're meeting, what the other person's phone number is, and when you can find time to meet.

Several small software companies recognized the problem of managing addresses and appointments long ago and offered Personal Information Managers (PIMs) to fill in the gap. PIMs such as Lotus Organizer, SideKick, and Act! specialized in names, addresses, dates, and tasks, leaving the word processing and number crunching to brawnier business applications such as Microsoft Word and Excel.

The problem with PIMs before Outlook has been that they must communicate with the word processors of the world, but they often can't. If you have a person's name and address stored in a PIM like SideKick, and you want to write a letter to that person in Microsoft Word, you have to copy and paste the address from the PIM into your letter, assuming both programs allow you to do that. Even if they do allow that, however, the address is likely to be sliced up in the PIM in a way that doesn't work in Word. So the PIM that was supposed to make your life easier, in fact, doubled your workload.

In designing Outlook, Microsoft took advantage of the fact that many people use Microsoft products for most of the work that they do. The company created a PIM that speaks a common language with Microsoft Word, Excel, and the rest of the Office 97 suite. Microsoft also studied what kind of information people use most often and tried to make sure that Outlook can handle most of it. The company also added the capability to move, copy, rename, and manage your files, using the same simple drag-and-drop techniques that you use for managing e-mail, tasks, appointments, and the like. The program also has enough customizability (what a tongue-twister — it just means you can set it up however you need, after you know what you're doing) that Microsoft doesn't even call Outlook a PIM but rather a Desktop Information Manager. Yeah, that's right — it's a DIM. Microsoft doesn't always come up with the swiftest names for things.

Above all, Outlook is easy to understand and hard to mess up. If you've used any version of Windows, you can just look at the screen and click a few icons to see what Outlook does. You won't break anything. If you get lost, going back to where you came from is easy. Even if you have no experience with Windows, Outlook is fairly straightforward to use.

There's No Place Like Home: Outlook's Main Screen

Outlook's appearance is very different from the other Microsoft Office applications. Instead of confronting you with a blank screen and a few menus and toolbars, Outlook begins by offering you large icons with simple names and a screen with information that's easy to use and understand. If you've spent much time surfing the World Wide Web, you'll find Outlook's layout pretty similar to many pages on the Web. Just select what you want to see by clicking an icon on the left side of the screen, and the information you selected appears on the right side of the screen.

PIMs of the past

Microsoft Office 95 provides a pair of programs for personal-information management: Schedule+ and Exchange. Schedule+ is designed to store names, addresses, tasks, and calendar items while Exchange can send and receive e-mail. Although both programs are fairly efficient at their appointed jobs, they weren't designed to be easy to use. They acknowledge each other and even exchange some information if you push them into it. But the two programs were something of an afterthought for Microsoft; the company never really took PIMs seriously until Outlook.

Other manufacturers of PIMs talk about making everything work with your word processor, but you still have to start the PIM and the word processor separately and then beat them both over the head to get them to talk to each other politely. Even then, the things that you enter into the PIM aren't always easy to use when you're doing something simple, like writing a letter.

With Outlook, you can access any of Microsoft's other Office 97 programs with the click of a mouse, making information management much more manageable.

Feeling at home when you work is nice. (Sometimes when I'm at work, I'd rather be at home, but that's something else entirely.) Outlook makes a home for all your different types of information: names, addresses, schedules, to-do lists, reminders, and even a list of all the files on your computer. You can customize the main screen as easily as you rearrange your home furnishings — although, to make it easier to find your way around at first, I recommend that you wait until you feel entirely at home with Outlook before you start rearranging the screen.

The Outlook main screen has all the usual parts of a Windows screen (see the Introduction if you're not used to the Windows screen), with a few important additions. At the left side of the screen, you see the Outlook Bar. Next to the Outlook Bar are the parts of the screen that take up most of the space: the Information Viewer and the Folder List (see Figure 2-1).

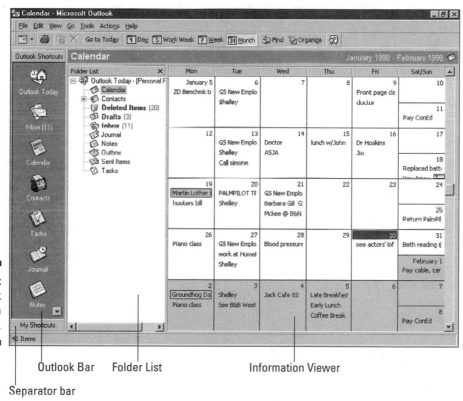

Figure 2-1:
The Outlook
main
screen.

Outlook Bar   Folder List   Information Viewer

Separator bar

Outlook modules

All the work you do in Outlook is organized into modules, or sections. Each module performs a specific job for you: the Calendar stores and manages your schedule, the Tasks module stores and manages your to-do list, and so on. Outlook is always showing you one of its modules in the main screen or Information Viewer. Whenever you're running Outlook, you're always using a module even if the module contains no information — the same way your television can be tuned to a channel, even if nothing is showing on that channel. The name of the module you're currently using is displayed in large type at the top of the Information Viewer part of the screen, so you can easily tell which module is showing.

Each module has an *icon* (picture) in the Outlook Bar portion of the screen. Clicking the module's icon is a shortcut that takes you to a different module of Outlook. The Inbox collects your incoming e-mail. The Contacts module stores names and addresses for you. The Tasks module keeps track of all the work that you do. The Journal records all your activities. And the Notes module allows you to keep track of random tidbits of information that don't quite fit anywhere else.

To change Outlook modules, do either of the following things:

✔ Click Go in the menu bar to display the menu shown in Figure 2-2 and then choose the module you want.

✔ For faster action, simply click the module's icon in the Outlook Bar.

Figure 2-2:
Click Go to
get a new
module.

If you're using Outlook on your company network, your network's system administrator may have created a different set of icons for you to work with. You may have a few more or a few less than you see in this book, but the icons should work the same way.

After you're comfortable with Outlook, you may want to customize it to suit your taste. For example, you may want to add an icon for your floppy drive to make it easier to move or copy files onto a floppy disk. In Chapter 6, where I show you how to create custom forms, you see how to create a new Outlook folder, which acts like a separate module. In Chapter 24, you can see how to add or remove tools and menu items. You can customize Outlook 98 beyond recognition, if you want. What the heck — have it your way!

Beware, however; your local computer guru may get cranky if you keep deleting an icon installed expressly for you to use on your company's system.

Belly up to the Outlook Bar

Although you don't get purple drinks with umbrellas at the Outlook Bar, it's still where the action is in Outlook. When you use Outlook, you see a column on the left side of the screen containing some icons (pictures) with names such as Calendar, Contacts, Tasks, Journal, and Notes — the basic Outlook modules. I explain these modules later, but the names alone already tell you the story.

Just click an icon, any icon, and you'll see what it sets in motion. Clicking the icon changes the stuff on the main screen to fit what the icon describes. Click the Calendar icon, and a Calendar screen shows up. Click Contacts, and you get a screen for names and addresses. The process is like changing the channels on the TV set. If you switch to a channel that you don't want, switch to another — no problem.

Although having the items that you use most often in the Outlook Bar is handy, finding them can be hard if you add too many things to that little bar. That's why the Outlook Bar is divided into groups. Each group is like a drawer in your file cabinet. You put different types of things in different file drawers so that you know right where to look when you want to find something. If you threw everything in one big box, finding anything would be harder. Outlook groups work the same way.

At the top and bottom of the Outlook Bar, you see little gray *separator bars* with names such as Outlook Shortcuts, My Shortcuts, and Other Shortcuts. Click each of these separator bars, and you see the column slide up or down to reveal a different group of icons representing different things you can do with Outlook. The technical term for one of these groups is . . . *group*. (That's easy.) Again, if you don't like the group that you chose, choose a different one.

Table 2-1 lists the icons you can expect to see in each group when you use Outlook.

Table 2-1	The Groups in the Outlook Bar
Group	*Icons*
Outlook Shortcuts	Outlook Today
	Inbox
	Calendar
	Contacts
	Tasks
	Journal
	Notes
	Deleted Items
My Shortcuts	Drafts
	Outbox
	Sent Items
Other Shortcuts	My Computer
	Favorites

To change Outlook groups, click the separator bar that has the name of the group you want, such as Outlook Shortcuts, My Shortcuts, or Other Shortcuts. You see the little bars slide up or down to reveal the group that you select. If nothing happens, the group that you selected was already selected.

Adding items to the Outlook Bar

The Outlook Bar comes set up with the icons that Microsoft thinks you'll use most often. You can add or remove icons if you don't like the ones that Microsoft gave you. You can also add or remove the separator bars that separate groups in the Outlook Bar, which I discuss in the next section about Outlook groups.

You can add nearly anything to the Outlook Bar — folders, documents, network drives, and even icons that launch other programs.

To add an item to the Outlook Bar, follow these steps:

1. **Choose File⇨New⇨Outlook Bar Shortcut from the menu bar.**

   The Add to Outlook Bar dialog box appears. Your list of folders is displayed in the box at the bottom of the Add to Outlook Bar dialog box.

2. Click the folder or drive that you want to add to the Outlook Bar.

The name of the folder or drive you clicked is highlighted.

3. Click OK.

You see a new icon for the folder or drive you selected in the Outlook Bar. That icon comes in handy when you want to copy files between folders or drives that you use frequently. I get into that in Chapter 4 when I talk about file management.

The Look In text box lets you choose between the two different types of folders that you can add to the Outlook Bar: Outlook folders that only contain Outlook items, or Windows file system folders that contain all the other types of files you create in Windows as well as disk drives. For more about the two types of folders you can use in Outlook, see "Navigating the Folder List" later in this chapter. You need to install Integrated File Management tools before you can install an icon for a floppy drive or for any folder from the Windows file system. Chapter 4 talks about that, too.

Adding Outlook groups

Wouldn't it be nice if you could divide your filing cabinet into an unlimited number of file drawers? You can create as many Outlook groups as you want and name them whatever will make it easier for you to find things — on your computer, at least. Finding that one lost sock in your dresser drawer is still a problem.

To add a group to the Outlook Bar, follow these steps:

1. Right-click any group name in the Outlook Bar.

A menu appears with choices that pertain to items in the Outlook Bar.

2. Choose Add New Group.

A new group divider, called New Group, appears at the bottom of the Outlook Bar, highlighted in blue.

3. Type the name that you want to use for your new group (something like Special Group**).**

4. Press Enter.

No matter what you do, the new group winds up at the bottom of the list. Sorry about that.

You can also change the name of any icon or group. You could rename the three original groups Larry, Curly, and Moe, for example, after the Three Stooges. Renaming the sections that way might make Outlook more fun but harder to explain.

You can do most of your work in one Outlook group; that's okay. The main reason for having groups is to be able to keep all your icons visible on-screen. You can just as easily have a list of icons scrolling way below the screen; the icons will just be harder to use. You can also add icons for folders that pertain to different functions you perform or areas of interest. For example, you may have a group of icons that relate to sales matters, others for production, and others for human resources.

The name of the group that's open appears in the separator bar at the top of the icons. If you click the name of the group that's already open, nothing happens. Don't worry — that's normal. You have to click a different group to see a change.

Making the most of Outlook Today

Outlook is designed to pull all your personal information into one handy package. The Outlook Today page pulls all the Outlook data that you're likely to need to see at any moment onto a single screen. All you really need to do is click the Outlook Today icon in the Outlook Bar. If you can't see the Outlook Today icon, just choose Go⇨Outlook Today from the menu bar (see Figure 2-3).

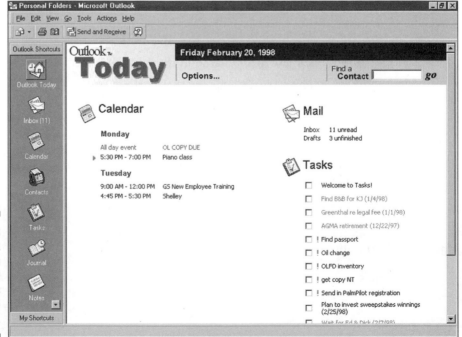

Figure 2-3:
Outlook Today pulls together all the items you need right now.

The Outlook Today page is like a page on the World Wide Web. Most of the text on the page is made of something called *hypertext,* which means that if you click the text, the screen changes to show you the full text of the Outlook module or item it refers to. For example, if you click the word *Mail* in the Outlook Today page, the screen switches to a view of your Inbox and displays all the messages that are waiting for you.

I like to print Outlook Today each day to help remind me of what I need to do. That's the best way I know of to see a single summary of my most current appointments, tasks, and messages. If you want to print your Outlook Today page, click the Outlook Today icon in the Outlook Bar and then choose File➪Print from the menu bar.

The Information Viewer: Outlook's hotspot

The Information Viewer is where most of the action happens in Outlook. If the Outlook Bar is like the channel selector on your TV set, the Information Viewer is like the TV screen. When you're reading e-mail, you look in the Information Viewer to read your messages; if you're adding or searching for contacts, you see contact names here. The Information Viewer is also where you can do all sorts of fancy sorting tricks that each module in Outlook lets you perform. (I talk about sorting Contacts, Tasks, and so forth in the chapters that apply to those modules.)

Because you can store more information in Outlook than you want to see at any one time, the Information Viewer shows you only a slice of the information available. The Calendar, for example, can store dates as far back as 1600 and as far ahead as 4500. (Got any plans on Saturday night 2,500 years from now?) That's a lot of time, but Outlook breaks it down and shows it to you in manageable slices in the Information Viewer. The smallest Calendar slice you can look at is one day, and the largest slice is a month.

The Information Viewer organizes the items it shows you into units called views. You can use the views that are included with Outlook when you install it, or you can create your own views and save them. I go into more details about views in Chapter 5.

You can navigate between the slices of information that Outlook shows you by clicking different parts of the Information Viewer. Some people use the word *browsing* for the process of moving around the Information Viewer — it's a little like thumbing through the pages of your pocket datebook (that is, if you have a million-page datebook).

To see an example of how to use the Information Viewer, look at the Calendar module in Figure 2-4.

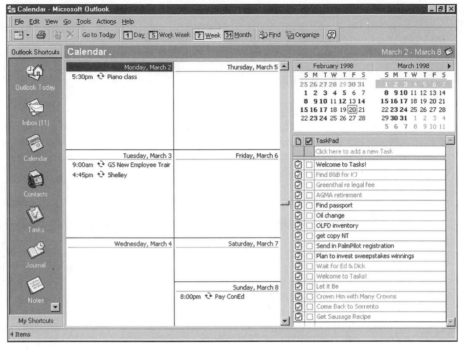

Figure 2-4:
A calendar in the Information Viewer.

To browse the Calendar data in the Information Viewer, follow these steps:

1. Choose G̲o⇨C̲alendar.

   The Calendar appears.

2. Choose V̲iew⇨Current V̲iew⇨Day/Week/Month.

   The information in the Calendar appears in a form that looks like a conventional calendar.

3. Choose V̲iew⇨W̲eek.

   The weekly view of the Calendar appears, showing a small calendar in the upper-right corner of the Information Viewer and a larger calendar on the left half of the screen.

Try these tricks to see how the Information Viewer behaves:

✔ Click a date in the small calendar in the upper-right corner. Notice that the large calendar changes to a one-day view.

✔ Click the *W* for *Wednesday* at the top of one of the small calendars. Notice that the large calendar changes to a monthly view.

You can change the appearance of the Information Viewer an infinite number of ways to make the work that you do in Outlook make sense to you. For example, you may only need to see appointments for a single day or items that you've assigned a certain category. Views can help you get a quick look at exactly the slice of information you need.

Navigating the Folder List

If you want to navigate Outlook in a more detailed way than you can with the Outlook Bar, you can use the Folder List. If you think of the Outlook Bar as being like your car's radio buttons, which you use to pick your favorite stations, then the Folder List is like the fine-tuning button, which you use to tune in any of the stations between your favorite ones. The Folder List simply shows you your folders — your Windows folders or your Outlook folders — which are where your files and Outlook items are stored.

A tale of two folders

Folders can seem more confusing than they need to be because, once again, Microsoft gave two different things the same name. Just as two kinds of Explorer (Windows and Internet) exist and more than two kinds of Outlook and more than two kinds of Windows (3.1, 95, CE, and NT), you may run across two different kinds of folders when you use Outlook, and each behaves differently.

You may be used to folders in Windows 95, which are the things you look in to organize files. You can copy, move, and delete files to and from folders on your disk drive. When you're using Outlook for file management, as I describe in Chapter 4, those are the kinds of folders you're dealing with. The part of Outlook that allows you to look at regular Windows files is optional in Outlook 98. If that option hasn't been installed in your copy of Outlook, you don't have to worry about using different types of folders in Outlook, because you only get to use one type.

Outlook has its own kind of folders for storing items that you create in the various Outlook modules: calendar items, contact names, tasks, and so on. Each module has its own folder that you can see in the Folder List.

If you're looking at an Outlook module such as the Inbox, for example, and you turn on the Folder List by choosing View➪Folder List, you see a list of folders that represent the other standard Outlook modules, like the Tasks List, Contacts, Calendar, and so on.

Using the Folder List

The only times you must use the Folder List are when you want to add a new icon to the Outlook Bar or create a new folder for a separate type of item (such as a special Contact list or a folder for filing e-mail). Using the Folder List is also a faster way to move, copy, or delete files when using Outlook.

You may quite possibly never use the Folder List at all. The Outlook Bar includes the folder choices that most people use most of the time. You may never need to get a different one. Fortunately, you can leave the Folder List turned off except when you really want it, if at all. I've run across people who leave the folder list on all the time and turn off the Outlook Bar to save space. It's a matter of taste, so take your pick.

Clicking Once: Outlook Toolbars

Tools are those little boxes with pictures in them that are all lined up in a row just below the menu bar. Together, they're called a *toolbar,* and they're even more popular than menus when it comes to running Windows programs. Outlook 98 has two toolbars to choose from: the Standard toolbar and the Advanced toolbar. If you don't do anything special, the Standard toolbar is the one you see, and it will probably do everything you need. If you want to get fancy and open the Advanced toolbar or customize either toolbar, see Chapter 24. Toolbars are great time-savers; one little click on a little picture, and voilà — your wish is granted and you're off to lunch.

Viewing ToolTips

Like menus, tools in Office 97 programs get a little drop shadow when you hover the mouse pointer over them. The shadow tells you that if you click there, the tool will do what it's there to do: paste, save, launch missiles, whatever.

Another slick thing about tools is that when you rest the mouse pointer on them for a second or so, a little tag pops up to tell you what the tool's name is (see Figure 2-5). Tags of this sort, called *ToolTips,* are very handy for deciphering the hieroglyphics on those tool buttons.

To view a ToolTip, follow these steps:

1. **Place the mouse pointer on the word File in the menu bar.**

2. **Slide the mouse pointer straight down until it rests on the icon just below the word File.**

   After about half a second, you see a little yellow tab that says "New Office Document" or "New *Something-or-Other.*" (The text changes, depending on what section of Outlook you're in.)

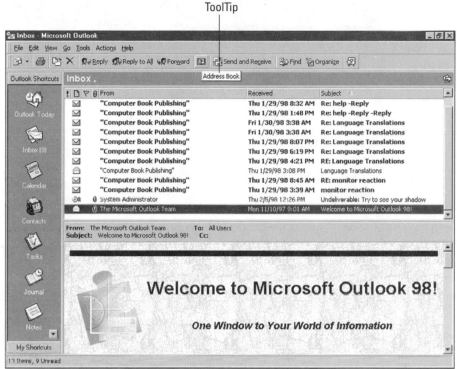

Figure 2-5:
A ToolTip tells you the name of the tool you're using.

Some tools have a little down-pointing triangle to their right. This triangle means that the tool has a pull-down menu. The very first tool at the left end of any Outlook toolbar is the New tool. Click the triangle to pull down its menu, and you see all the new things that you can create — a new appointment, a new e-mail message, or even a new Office document.

Using the New tool

You can use the New tool, which is available in any module of Outlook, to create an item in any other module. Perhaps you're entering the name and address of a new customer who is also mentioned in an interesting article in today's paper, and you want to remember the article, but it doesn't belong in the customer's address record. While you're still in the Contacts module (see Figure 2-6), you can pull down the New button's menu and create a quick note, which gets filed in the Note section. Using the New tool to create a new note when you're looking at the Contacts screen can get confusing. At first, you may think that the note isn't entered, but it is. Outlook just files it in the Notes module, where it belongs.

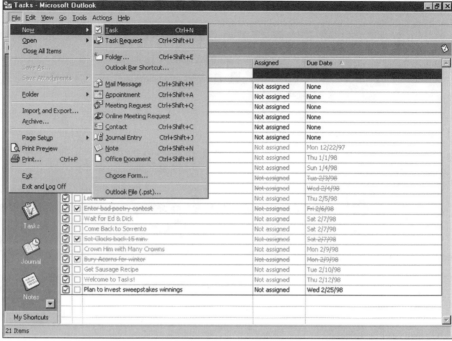

Figure 2-6:
With the
New tool,
you can
create a
note,
request a
meeting, or
perform a
variety of
new tasks
without
switching to
another
Outlook
module.

Turning Parts of the Outlook Screen On and Off

You can work with any part of the Outlook screen in any view, or you can turn parts of the screen off. The buttons near the bottom of the View menu allow you to change what you see. Sometimes, for example, you want to look at your Calendar in the largest possible view so you can see a whole month and all its appointments clearly. In that case, you could switch to the Calendar module, and then turn off the Outlook Bar, the Folder List, and even possibly the toolbar in order to make room for the Calendar. You also may need to turn on the Folder List when you're moving or copying files, but turn it off when you're scheduling tasks.

For example, to view the Folder List:

✔ Choose View➪Folder List.

✔ Alternatively, if you see a triangle below the title of the Information Viewer, click the title (such as Calendar), and the Folder List appears.

The View menu has icons for both the Outlook Bar and the Folder List; these icons allow you to turn those elements on or off. So if you want to run Outlook with just the Outlook Bar open, or just the Folder List, or both, or neither, it's up to you. I think that leaving the Outlook Bar open is the easiest way to go.

Getting Help from the Office Assistant

Even though Outlook is as user-friendly a program as you could hope to find, at times you may want to take advantage of the efficient Windows 95 online help system when you're temporarily stumped (of course, you can turn to this book for help, but sometimes online help is faster).

The Windows Help system was always helpful, but now it's downright sociable. A little animated character pops up in a box and cavorts around when you ask for help; it even does little tricks when you do things like save a file or search for text. Try it!

You can change the type of character you use as your Office Assistant: You can use the Clipit character that Office begins with, or the Einstein-like Genius character, or my favorite, the Power Pup (see Figure 2-7). All you have to do is right-click the Office Assistant character, choose a new character, and click OK. Microsoft Office includes a larger selection of Office Assistant characters than Outlook alone, so if you're an Office user, you're in luck.

Figure 2-7:
The Genius
and the
Power Pup
assistants.

The new Office Assistant character is included because research showed that people treat their computers as though they are other people. No kidding. Most people report more negative things about a computer to a second computer than they will to the computer that they're saying the bad things about; it's like they're trying not to hurt the computer's feelings.

You don't have to worry about hurting the Office Assistant's feelings. Just press the F1 key any time; your Office Assistant pops up and invites you to ask a question (see Figure 2-8). Just type your question in plain English, and the Assistant scratches its head and returns with a list of help topics that are likely to answer your question. If you want to delete a message, for example, just press F1 and type **delete a message**. The list of choices includes everything that has to do with deleting messages.

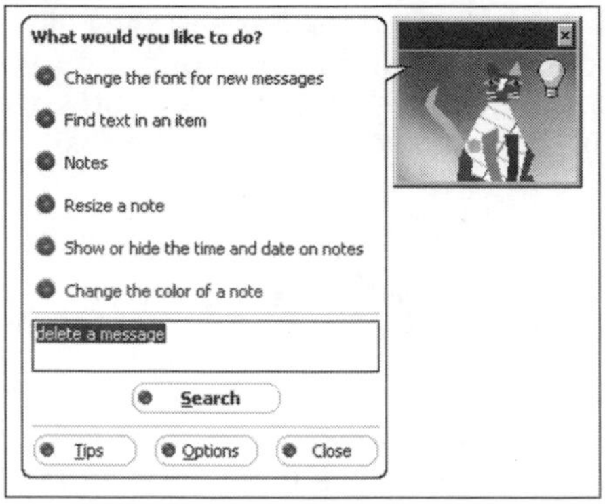

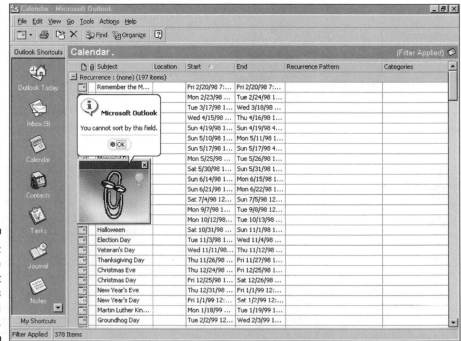

Figure 2-8:
You can tell the Office Assistant what you need in plain English.

If you keep the Office Assistant open, some of the questions that you usually answer through dialog boxes are asked by the Assistant (see Figure 2-9). Click the response that you want, just as you would in a regular dialog box.

The Office Assistant will get smarter with time; it's supposed to notice the things you do wrong repeatedly and chime in with suggestions about how to do them better. Microsoft calls this system the Social Interface; some people call it nagging. **_Remember:_** The Office Assistant only means to be helpful (just like your mother-in-law).

Figure 2-9:
The Office Assistant sometimes acts like a dialog box.

Chapter 3

No Typing, Please! — Drag 'til You Drop

In This Chapter

▶ Doing the drag-and-drop

▶ Creating and sending e-mail messages

▶ Creating Contact records

▶ Creating Journal entries

▶ Information — Deleting

*T*yping — ugh! Who needs it? It's amazing to think that we still use a nineteenth-century device — the typewriter keyboard — to control our computers on the cusp of the twenty-first century. We appear to be stuck with the QWERTY keyboard for a while longer, but we can give our carpal tunnels a rest now and then by using the mouse, trackball, or glidepoint to drag and drop rather than hunt and peck.

How to Drag

When I say drag, I'm not referring to Monty Python's men in women's clothing. I mean the process of zipping items from one place to another with quick, easy mouse moves rather than slow, laborious menu choices. Throughout the rest of this book, I tell you how to do nearly everything in Outlook by the menu method only because it's the clearest way to explain how to do most things reliably. But if you want to work quickly in Outlook, drag-and-drop is the ticket to simple and speedy completion of your tasks.

Before you can drag an item, you have to *select* it — that simply means to click the item once:

- ✔ *Dragging* means clicking your mouse on something and moving the mouse to another location while holding the mouse button down at the same time.
- ✔ *Dropping* means letting go of the mouse button.

When you drag an item, you see an icon hanging from the tail of the mouse pointer as you move the pointer across the screen. The icon makes the pointer look like it's carrying baggage, and to some degree that's true; dragging your mouse between Outlook modules "carries" information from one type of item to another.

When you drag and drop items between different Outlook modules, you can keep creating new types of items from the old information, depending on what you drag and where you drop it.

Everything that you can do by using the drag-and-drop method, you can also do through menu choices or keystroke shortcuts, but you lose the advantage of having the information from one item flow into the new item, so you have to retype information. I'm too lazy for that, so I just drag and drop.

Because I'm using this chapter to extol the benefits of drag-and-drop, I describe every action in terms of a drag-and-drop movement rather than through menu choices or keyboard shortcuts. Throughout the rest of the book, I describe how to do things in terms of menu choices because the menus never change, whereas you can change the names of the icons in the Outlook Bar if you customize them. So when you read other parts of the book, don't think that I'm discouraging you from trying drag-and-drop; I'm just trying to offer you the clearest explanation I can. (Whew! I'm glad that's off my chest.)

Creating E-Mail Messages

Anything that you drag to the Inbox becomes an outgoing e-mail message. If the thing that you drag to the Inbox contains an e-mail address, such as a contact, Outlook automatically creates the message with that person's e-mail address filled in.

If the item that you drag to the Inbox contains a subject, such as a task, Outlook automatically creates the message with that subject filled in.

From a name in your Address Book

Addressing messages is one of the most useful drag-and-drop techniques in Outlook. E-mail addresses can be cumbersome and difficult to remember, and if your spelling of an e-mail address is off by even one letter, your message won't go through. It's best to just keep the e-mail addresses of the people to whom you sent messages in your Contact list and use those addresses to create new messages.

To create an e-mail message from your Contact list:

1. Click the Contacts icon.

The Contact list appears (see Figure 3-1). You can use any view, but Address Cards view is easiest, because you can click the first letter of the person's name to see that person's card. For more about viewing your Contact list, see Chapter 10.

2. Drag a name from your Contact list to the Inbox icon.

The Message form appears, with the address of the contact filled in.

3. Type a subject for your message.

Keep it simple; a few words will do.

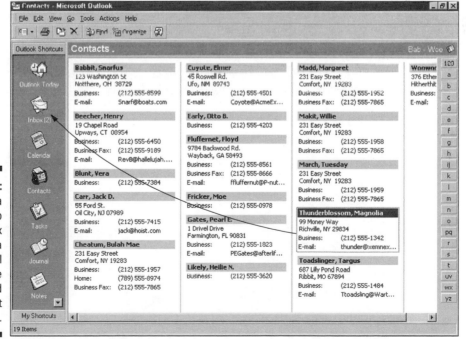

Figure 3-1:
Dragging a contact to your Inbox creates a new e-mail message addressed to that person.

4. **Click in the text box and type your message.**

You can also format text with bold type, italics, and other effects by clicking the appropriate buttons on the toolbar.

5. **Click Send.**

The display returns to the Contact list, and your message is sent.

From an appointment

After you enter the particulars about an appointment, you may want to send that information to someone else, to tell that person what the appointment is about, where it occurs, and when it occurs.

To send an e-mail message with information about an appointment:

1. **Click the Calendar icon.**

The Calendar appears.

2. **Drag the appointment you're interested in from the Calendar to the Inbox icon (see Figure 3-2).**

The Message form appears.

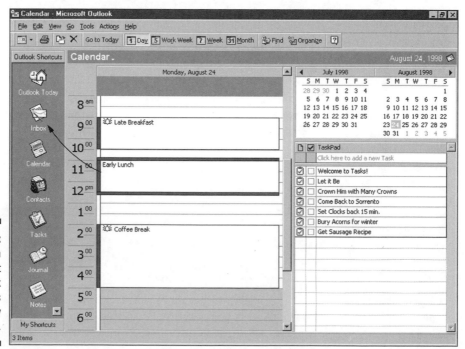

Figure 3-2:
Dragging an appointment to the Inbox creates a new message.

3. **In the To text box, type the name of the person to whom you want to send a copy of the appointment.**

   Alternatively, you can click the To button and choose the person's name from the Address Book. If you use the Address Book, you have to click To again and then click OK.

4. **Click the Send button.**

   Your recipient gets an e-mail message with details about the meeting. You can add additional comments in the text box.

If you plan to invite other people in your organization to a meeting, and you want to check their schedules to plan the meeting, you can also use the Meeting Planner tab of the Appointment form. For this method to work, the people whom you plan to invite to the meeting must be sharing their schedules through Microsoft Exchange Server.

Sending a File by E-Mail

Sometimes, you don't need to type a message; you just want to send a file by e-mail — that Excel spreadsheet with sales figures, for example, or your new book proposal in Word.

When you send someone a file (or when someone sends you a file), the file travels as a part of the message called an *attachment*. When you attach a file to your e-mail message, the recipient gets a copy of the file, and you still have one, too. The process is like sending a fax, except that no paper is involved, and it's better than a fax because the person who gets the file can make changes in the file.

Dragging a file to the Inbox is a tiny bit more complicated than dragging contacts or appointments because you locate files using the My Computer icon, which is in a different section of the Outlook Bar from the Inbox. Also, some people remove the My Computer section when they install Outlook, so that icon may not be available. But when everything's installed and you're accustomed to the different groups in the Outlook Bar, it's a breeze to drag and drop files anywhere you want them.

To send a file using e-mail:

1. **Click the words *Other Shortcuts* in the Outlook Bar.**

   The My Computer folder appears.

2. **Click the My Computer icon in the Outlook Bar.**

   The list of your computer's disk drives appears.

3. **Double-click the icon for the C: drive (or whatever drive contains the file you want to send).**

   The list of folders on your disk drive appears.

4. **Click the My Documents icon (or the icon for whatever folder contains the file you want to send).**

   The list of files in the folder you selected appears.

5. **Click the name of the file that you want to send.**

   The file darkens, indicating that it has been selected (see Figure 3-3).

6. **Click the Outlook Shortcuts group divider in the Outlook Bar.**

   The Inbox icon appears, along with all the usual Outlook icons.

7. **Drag the file that you selected to the Inbox icon.**

   The New Message form appears, with an icon in the message space (see Figure 3-4).

8. **In the To text box, type the name of the person to whom you want to send a copy of the file.**

   Alternatively, you can click the To button and choose the person's name from the Address Book. If you use the Address Book, you have to click To again and then click OK.

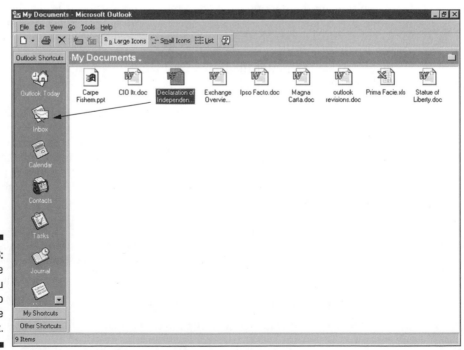

Figure 3-3:
Select the file that you want to drag to the Inbox.

Figure 3-4:
Your file
attachment
message is
all set to be
sent. You
can add
a text
message if
you want,
or send a
copy to
your boss.

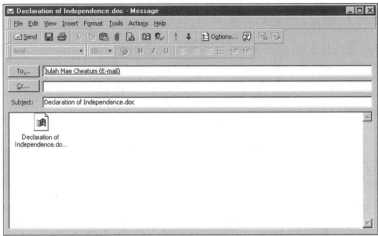

9. Click the Send button.

Your file is on its way.

Isn't that easy? There's actually an even easier way: When you're working on a file in Word, Excel, or PowerPoint, choose File➪Send To➪Mail Recipient, and then perform Steps 8 and 9 of the preceding list.

Look out for heavy files!

When it comes to sending e-mail, all files are created equal, but some are much bigger than others. You can e-mail all files, big and small, but the big ones can take a long time to send and receive. If you and the person to whom you're sending a file are on the same network, the size of the file isn't such a big problem. If you're sending the file to someone who gets e-mail from an online service over a regular telephone line, however, it's a good idea to check with that person to see whether he or she is willing to accept a file that could take 10 to 15 minutes, or more, to download. Not all online services let your recipient know the size of the files he or she is getting.

Think about that when you send a file. If the size of the file that you're sending is measured in megabytes, it could take some time for the person to whom you're sending the file to receive it. Some people think that you broke their machines because the file took so long to receive. You can't break someone's machine by sending a file, but there are people to whom you don't want to give that impression. You can use compression programs like PKZIP or WinZip to reduce the size of your files before you send them, but it's still possible to create files that take a long time to send through a phone line even when you compress them.

Creating Contact Records from E-Mail

You can drag an item from any other Outlook module to the Contacts icon, but the only item that makes sense to drag is an e-mail message, so as to create a Contact record that includes the e-mail address. You not only save work by dragging a message to the Contacts icon, but also eliminate the risk of misspelling the e-mail address.

To create a new Contact record:

1. **Click the Inbox icon.**

   A list of your current incoming e-mail messages appears. Select the message for which you want to make a Contact record (see Figure 3-5).

2. **Drag the selected message to the Contacts icon.**

   The New Contact form opens, with the name and e-mail address of the person who sent the message filled in.

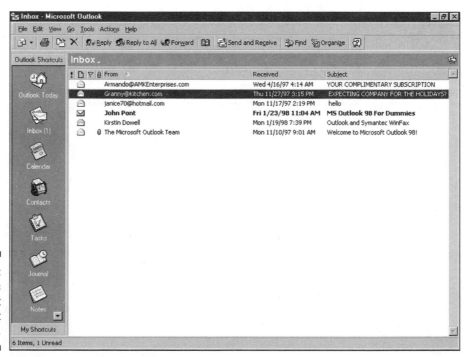

Figure 3-5:
Granny is about to get a Contact record.

3. If you want to include more information than the e-mail address of the contact, enter that information in the appropriate box on the Contact form.

You can change existing information or add information — the company for whom the person works, the postal mail address, other phone numbers, and so on.

If the body of the e-mail message contains information that you want to use as contact information, select that information and drag it to the appropriate box of the New Contact form.

4. Click the Save and Close button.

You now have the e-mail address and any other information for the new contact stored for future reference.

Another quick way to capture an e-mail address from an incoming message is to right-click the name of the sender in the From line of the incoming message block. The From line is not a normal text box, so you may not think that right-clicking it would do anything, but it does. A shortcut menu appears. Click Add to Contacts to open the New Contact dialog box. Then follow the last two steps of the preceding list.

Creating a Journal Entry for a Contact

The most useful thing to drag to the Journal icon is a contact listing, which automatically opens a Journal entry in the name of that contact. You can make a note of a phone call or letter you've received from that person, or you can make a note of a conversation you had with that person.

To open a Journal entry:

1. Click the Contacts icon.

The Contact list appears.

2. Drag a name from your address list to the Journal icon.

A Journal Entry form appears, with the contact record that you dragged as an attachment.

3. From the Entry type menu, choose the type of event that you're recording.

Phone call is the default choice, because it's most useful (see Figure 3-6). You may also want to use letter, fax, or conversation. The e-mail and other contact information is nice, but most of that information is entered in the Journal automatically, so making Journal entries for e-mail and other new contact information is not entirely necessary.

4. Click Save and Close.

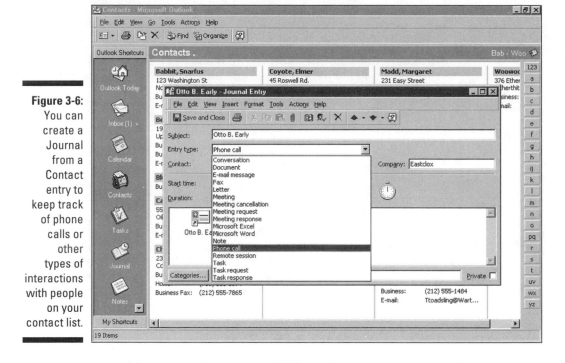

Figure 3-6:
You can
create a
Journal
from a
Contact
entry to
keep track
of phone
calls or
other
types of
interactions
with people
on your
contact list.

The benefit of creating Journal entries for the phone calls you receive is that you can check your contact entries later and see a record of all the phone calls and other messages you've exchanged.

Drag and Drop Dead: Deleting Stuff

If in doubt, throw it out. You know the drill.

Here's how to delete an item using drag-and-drop:

1. **Click the Notes icon in the Outlook Bar.**

   Your list of notes appears. You can click any icon that has items you want to delete (I'm just using notes as an example).

2. **Drag a note to the Deleted Items icon in the Outlook Bar.**

   Kiss it good-bye — it's gone.

If you change your mind after deleting something, just click the Deleted Items folder. The folder opens and a list of everything that you've deleted is there. It's like being a hit man in the afterlife — you get another chance to see everyone you've disposed of. Except in this case you can bring items back to life. Just drag them back to where they came from. Even Don Corleone couldn't do that.

Chapter 4

Files and Folders: A Quick Course in Keeping Things Straight

● ●

In This Chapter

▶ Seeing your basic drives and other stuff

▶ Moving, copying, and renaming files and folders

▶ Viewing and sorting files and folders

▶ Installing Outlook's Integrated File Management tools

● ●

*F*iles and folders frequently flummox folks who use Windows. Fortunately, Outlook has a good set of tools for managing files and folders, so the issue of file management should be easier to understand if you're using Outlook. But you still need to understand basic file management to take advantage of the improved tools in Outlook.

Although the file management tools are one of my favorite parts of Outlook, Microsoft decided to make that part of Outlook optional in Outlook 98. If the person who installed your copy of Outlook didn't choose to install the Integrated File Management tools, you won't see the stuff I discuss in this chapter. (Look for all these tools under the My Computer icon in the Other Shortcuts section of the Outlook Bar.) If you don't have these tools but you want them, refer to "Installing Outlook's File Management Tools" later in this chapter.

I assume that you're familiar with using files and folders in Windows so that I can focus on showing you Outlook's file management features. For an excellent explanation of how to deal with files, see *DOS For Dummies,* Windows 95 Edition, by Dan Gookin (IDG Books Worldwide, Inc.), which describes the concepts in full detail.

If your experience goes way back to 1993, when people used Windows 3.1 (heaven help 'em!), these critters were called files and directories. When Windows 95 came out, Microsoft started using the word *folders* rather than directories, but folders and directories are exactly the same thing.

Whatever you call them, files and folders still reside on floppy disks, hard drives, and network drives. Floppy disks and hard drives have letter names (A, B, C, and so on), while files and folders are named in plain English.

If your computer is connected to a network, you also have hard drives that belong to the network. These drives are not on your computer; they're somewhere else in the building. But on your computer they show up in Outlook or Windows Explorer as if they were on your own machine. The network makes the hard drives on the network look just like the one inside your machine when you're looking for files, and that's fine. You can treat files on the network just as though they are files on your computer.

Networks also allow you to share files with other people. A network is a little like a library; you can use a file when you need it and then put it back. Later, someone else may come along and use the file; then that person puts the file back so that yet another person can use it. Your network administrator can configure the system to prevent other people from changing your files or to prevent you from changing other people's files.

Managing Your Files

File management is a fancy term for looking at your files and folders and arranging what you have the way you want it. The first step toward managing your files is seeing them.

To see a listing of your files, follow these steps:

1. **Click the My Computer icon in the Outlook Bar.**

   There it is — you see a list of your drives, in all their glory (see Figure 4-1). Why would you want to see a list of your drives? To see a list of your folders, of course.

2. **Double-click the icon for the C drive.**

   A list of the folders on your C drive appears. Doesn't that make your day?

3. **To view a list of the files in your folders, double-click the icon for the folder whose contents you want to see (such as the My Documents folder).**

   You see a listing of all the files in the My Documents folder (see Figure 4-2). If you have subfolders within the My Documents folder, you can see the names of the files in any of those folders by double-clicking the icon for a folder whose contents you want to see.

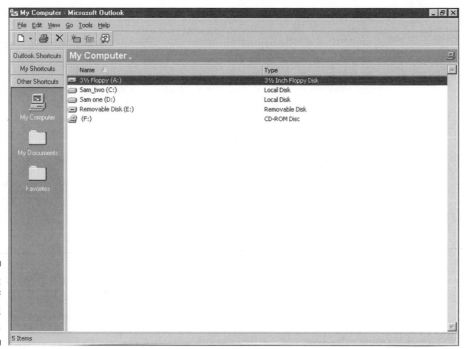

Figure 4-1:
A list of
your disk
drives.

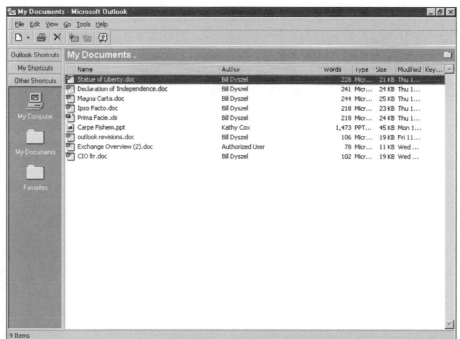

Figure 4-2:
Now that's
a list of
files!

I assume that you have a folder called My Documents, because Office 97 creates a folder like that during installation. My Documents is the folder where Office 97 programs like to save the documents that you create, unless you tell the programs to save the documents somewhere else. If you don't have a My Documents folder, double-click another folder — whichever folder you want. You get the idea; double-clicking the icon for a folder makes Outlook show you a list of the files in the folder.

Selecting files

After you open a folder to see the list of files in it, you need to select a file or files in order to move, copy, or delete a file or group of files. Here's what you do:

- ✔ To select a single file, click its name.
- ✔ To select several files that are next to one another, click the first one, hold down the Shift key, and click the last one. The first and last files are selected, along with all the files in between.
- ✔ To select several files that are not next to one another, click one and then hold down the Ctrl key while clicking the others.

Moving and copying files

To move a file from one folder to another, follow these steps:

1. **Click the file that you want to move.**

   The selected file is highlighted.

2. **Drag the file to the folder where you want to move it.**

If the folder to which you drag the file is on the same drive (such as the C drive) as the folder where the file was originally located, the file is moved. If you drag the file to a different drive, the file is copied.

Creating a new folder

Sometimes you just need a new place to put things. You may need to create a new folder for a new group of files from a client or to keep the documents concerning a certain project together to make them easier to find.

Here's how you create a new folder:

1. **Click the My Computer icon in the Outlook Bar.**

   Your list of drives appears.

2. **Double-click the icon for the drive where you want to create a new folder (such as the C drive).**

   The list of folders on the drive you selected appears.

3. **Choose File⇨New⇨Folder (or press Ctrl+Shift+E).**

   The Create New Folder dialog box appears.

4. **Type the name you want to give to your new folder.**

   The name appears in the dialog box.

5. **Click OK.**

   Your new folder appears in your list of folders. If you want to create a new folder inside an existing folder, double-click the icon next to the existing folder before choosing File⇨New⇨Folder.

Renaming folders

Marilyn Monroe and John Wayne changed their names from Norma Jean and Marion (guess who was Marion). That just goes to show you that sometimes a darn good reason exists for changing a name. You can change the name of any folder to anything you want.

You shouldn't rename some folders — two in particular. Renaming your My Documents folder may make it difficult to find your documents when you're using other Office programs, because these programs normally look in the My Documents folder for the documents they created. You can configure the programs to find the folder by its new name if you rename it, but leaving it alone is easier. Renaming your Windows folder can cause big problems; your programs may not run and your computer may not start without some serious glaring and grumbling from your computer guru. You're better off leaving those two folders with their original names.

To rename a folder:

1. **Right-click the name of the folder that you want to rename.**

   A menu appears.

2. **Choose Rename.**

   The Rename dialog box appears with the old folder name highlighted.

3. Type the new name of the folder.

The new folder name replaces the old name in the dialog box.

4. Click OK.

You can't rename a folder when it's open. If you can see the names of the files in a folder, the folder is open, and you can't rename that folder. You can choose Go⇨Up One Level, select the folder, and try again.

Renaming files

Renaming files is nearly identical to renaming folders, except that a filename has a three-letter *extension* — that is, a three-character suffix such as .DOC or .XLS or .EXE. Windows uses the filename's extension to identify which program should run when you double-click a file to open it. If you try to rename a file that ends in .EXE, Windows warns you that it's a program file and suggests that you think twice before renaming it. As long as you keep the last three letters the same as they started, you should have no problem.

To rename a file:

1. Right-click the name of the file that you want to rename.

A menu appears, with commands including Open, Delete, and Rename.

2. Choose Rename from the menu.

The Rename dialog box appears (see Figure 4-3).

Figure 4-3:
The Rename dialog box lets you change the name of any file.

3. Type the new name of the file.

The new filename replaces the old name in the dialog box.

4. Click OK.

When you first open the Rename dialog box, the old name of the file is displayed and highlighted. As soon as you start typing, the old name disappears; whatever you type as the new name replaces it.

What's in a name: File extensions

Windows 95 normally hides the last three letters of a file's name, known as the file extension. The extension starts with a period and indicates which program created a file. Well, not always; that's the problem. Although the file extension is a leftover from the days of DOS that we'd all rather forget, Windows 95 uses the file extension when it tries to figure out what kind of program created a certain file. The file extension is how Windows 95 knows which program to run when you double-click the name of a file. Windows 95 knows that it should open Word and not Excel when you click a Word file, for example, because Word files have names that end in .DOC.

When you rename a file, it's possible to change the file extension, which makes Windows very confused. Windows may not know what to do with a file that doesn't have exactly the right extension. The situation is pretty silly. It's as though you picked up a clear Coke bottle with dishwater in it but didn't know that it was dishwater because the label said Coke. You'd know better than to drink it, but Windows 95 wouldn't.

If your machine is showing you the file extensions, be careful not to change the extensions when you're changing filenames. You can tell that file extensions are showing if the names of all the files created by Microsoft Word end in .DOC, for example, and all the Excel filenames end in .XLS. Changing the extensions of your filenames can make Windows 95 so confused that it will refuse to view or open certain documents unless they're properly named.

Using Views with Files and Folders

A way to see what files you have and where you have them has always been available to you. For example, the Windows Explorer is the file management tool that comes with Windows 95. Making sense of your collection of documents gets more complicated after you collect a few hundred files. Sometimes you need to know more than you can get from the simple list of your files that Explorer shows you. Outlook can show you more information about each file, including things like the author, the page count, or the time and date that a file was most recently printed.

Outlook allows you to arrange and sort information about your files in many slick ways. I show you the most useful approaches to viewing your lists of files in this chapter.

Sorting files in a folder

Every view of your files (except Document Timeline view, which I explain later in this chapter) is organized in rows and columns. Each row contains the information for one file, and each column contains one type of information about each file listed. You can sort the entire list by the contents of one column with a single mouse click.

To sort files in a folder:

1. **Click the My Computer icon in the Outlook Bar.**

   A list of your drives appears.

2. **Double-click the icon for the C drive.**

   A list of the folders on your C drive appears.

3. **To view a list of the files in your folders, double-click the icon for the folder whose contents you wish to see.**

   You see a listing of all the files in the folder you selected.

4. **Click the name at the top of the column you want to sort by.**

If you have many files, Outlook needs a few seconds to sort them out. It fills the time by showing you a little box containing the letters A, F, and Z. Outlook juggles the letters around and then displays the list of files in the order that you suggested. I usually put my files in name order or date order (by date modified), but you can sort by any column on the screen.

Icons view

The Icons view is a way of displaying your files by simply filling the screen with icons accompanied by the names of the files they represent. Icons are bigger and friendlier-looking than plain old lists of files, but they don't give you as much information. If you don't want much information, icons are good. If you want more information about each file, such as its size and the name of the program that created it, switch to another view, such as Details view.

Here's what you do to see the Icons view:

1. **Click the My Computer icon in the Outlook Bar.**

   Your list of drives appears.

2. **Double-click the name of one of your drives, such as the C drive.**

   Your list of folders appears.

3. **Double-click the name of a folder, such as My Documents.**

   A list of the files in the folder appears.

4. **Choose <u>V</u>iew➪Current <u>V</u>iew➪Icons.**

   A list of icons appears (see Figure 4-4). In the Icons view, the toolbar includes a set of three buttons, each of which bears a small diagram of a group of icons. Clicking any of the three buttons changes the type of Icon view that you see: large icons, small icons, or a list of icons. You can change among these views any time.

Details view

Details view is a plain old list of file names, sizes, dates, and so on — in other words, it gives you all the, uh, details. Lists in Details view look just like the lists that Windows Explorer gives you, but the Outlook version can do much more (see Chapter 5 for more about views).

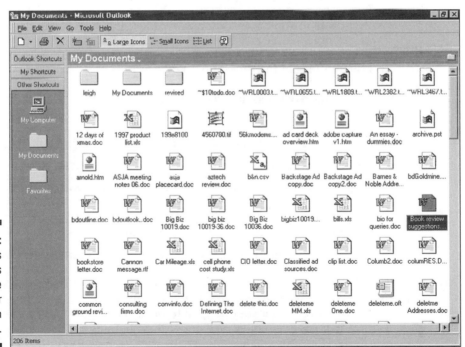

Figure 4-4: The Icons view is less informative but easier to read than other views.

To see your files in Details view:

1. **Click the My Computer icon in the Outlook Bar.**

   Your list of drives appears.

2. **Double-click the name of one of your drives, such as the C drive.**

   Your list of folders appears.

3. **Double-click the name of a folder, such as My Documents.**

   A list of the files in that folder appears.

4. **Choose View➪Current View➪Details.**

Details view is the view that I choose to use most of the time, because it shows me all the files in the folder I've chosen and gives me the most information at a glance.

By Author view

Guess how By Author view groups your files? If it's good enough for the library to organize by author, it's good enough for me.

To see your files in the By Author view:

1. **Click the My Computer icon in the Outlook Bar.**

   Your list of drives appears.

2. **Double-click the name of one of your drives, such as the C drive.**

   Your list of folders appears.

3. **Double-click the name of a folder, such as My Documents.**

   A list of the files in the folder appears.

4. **Choose View➪Current View➪By Author.**

   A list of your files appears, grouped by author (see Figure 4-5).

 If you're the only person who uses your computer, you really don't want to use the By Author view. When you're the only author, you just see all the files in whatever order they happen to be in. Viewing By Author is more useful when you share files on a network with many other people. Then questions of authorship are important. Viewing files By Author is also handy if you consolidate the work of several people; this way, you know at a glance which file came from whom.

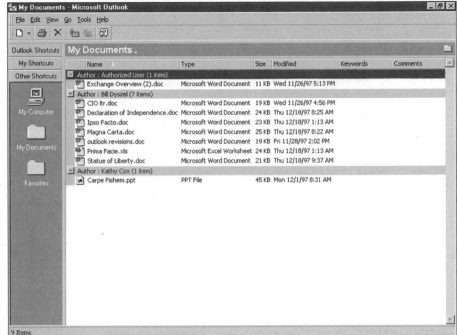

Figure 4-5:
The By
Author view
groups your
files by the
name of the
person who
created
them.

By File Type view

By File Type view groups your files according to what kind of program created the file. Files created by Microsoft Word are one file type; files created by Excel are another file type. Some file types can be created by more than one program, but Windows always associates files of a certain type with only one program.

To use the By File Type view:

1. **Click the My Computer icon in the Outlook Bar.**

   Your list of drives appears.

2. **Double-click the name of one of your drives, such as the C drive.**

   Your list of folders appears.

3. **Double-click the name of a folder, such as My Documents.**

   A list of the files in the folder appears.

4. **Choose View⇨Current View⇨By File Type.**

   A list of your files appears, with the files grouped according to the program that created them (see Figure 4-6).

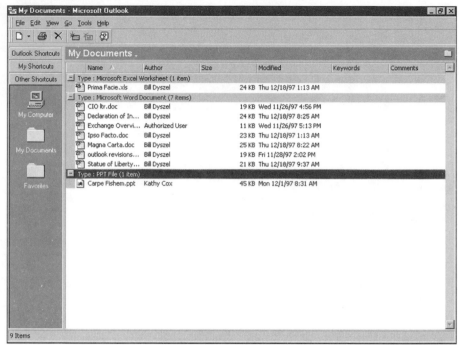

Figure 4-6:
See your
files By File
Type.

You can use By File Type view to give yourself a shorter list to look at when you're trying to find a file in a folder. If you're looking for an Excel file in a folder that has two Excel files and 98 Word files, it's easier to find one of two files in the Excel group than one of 100 in the entire folder, right?

Document Timeline view

The Document Timeline view is an interesting way to view your files according to the last date on which they were modified. Because you can click the heading of the Date Modified column to sort your files by date, you actually don't need Document Timeline view. But the Document Timeline is much cooler to look at than a simple list of filenames. That's good enough for me.

To use the cool Document Timeline view:

1. **Click the My Computer icon in the Outlook Bar.**

   Your list of drives appears.

2. **Double-click the name of one of your drives, such as the C drive.**

   Your list of folders appears.

3. **Double-click the name of a folder, such as My Documents.**

   A list of the files in the folder appears.

4. **Choose <u>V</u>iew➪Current <u>V</u>iew➪Document Timeline.**

   The Document Timeline appears with icons representing each of your files, organized by the date when they were last modified (see Figure 4-7).

Four buttons appcar in the toolbar when you use Document Timeline view. The Go to Tod<u>a</u>y button centers the timeline on today's date. You can also scroll left and right to see files modified on earlier and later dates. The Da<u>y</u> button shows you just one day; clicking a date in the top line of the timeline takes you to that date. The <u>W</u>eek button shows you seven days' worth of documents. The <u>M</u>onth button shows a month's worth of documents.

The Document Timeline is helpful when you can't remember what you called a file, but you know when you used it last. You can just look at the date you remember using the file in the timeline, and you'll find your document.

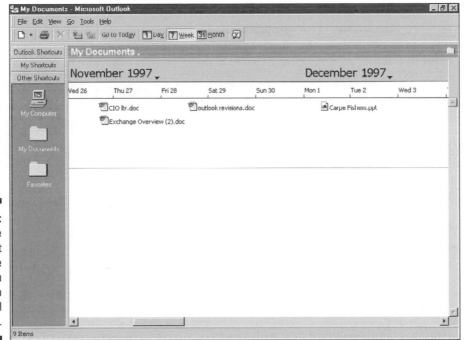

Figure 4-7:
The Document Timeline shows you your files in chronological order.

Programs view

Way back at the beginning of this chapter, I discuss the fact that some files are programs; they make the computer do actual work. Sometimes, the programs are useful (games and cool screen savers). Other times, they just create boring stuff like letters and spreadsheets. Either way, be careful when you delete or rename program files — you may lose a program you need. Windows warns you when you're deleting a program file, so you'll know to be careful.

To see your files in Programs view:

1. **Click the My Computer icon in the Outlook Bar.**

   Your list of drives appears.

2. **Double-click the name of one of your drives, such as the C drive.**

   Your list of folders appears.

3. **Double-click the name of a folder, such as Windows.**

   A list of the files in the folder appears.

4. **Choose View➪Current View➪Programs.**

   A list of the program files in the directory you're viewing appears (see Figure 4-8).

Figure 4-8:
The Programs view shows you the program files in the folder you've chosen.

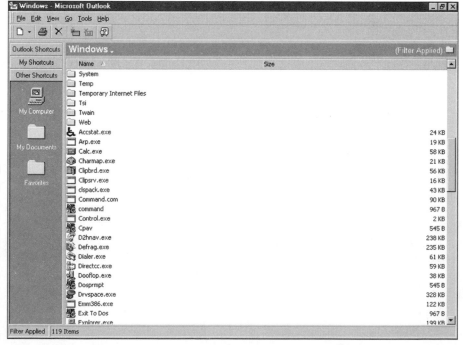

Many folders don't have any programs in them, so don't be surprised if you get a blank screen when you try Programs view. If you don't see any files that end in the letters .EXE or .COM, you don't have any program files.

Installing Outlook's File Management Tools

Unfortunately, the Outlook 98 file management tools don't automatically set themselves up when you install Outlook. You have to make a point of adding them to Outlook. Here's how:

1. **Insert the Outlook CD in your CD-ROM drive.**

   The Outlook CD install screen appears.

2. **Click the words** *Install Outlook 98 Add-On Components.*

   Internet Explorer opens, revealing a page called Microsoft Outlook 98 Component Install.

3. **Click the check box next to the words** *Integrated File Management.*

   A check mark appears next to the words *Integrated File Management.*

4. **Click Next.**

Why manage files at all?

You can also use Windows Explorer in Windows 95 to deal with files and folders, but I believe that Outlook does the job much more sensibly. You also have options for arranging your view of your files and folders in Outlook that simply don't exist in Windows Explorer.

Windows 95 has started hiding the inner workings of the computer just to make you more comfortable, but you can peek behind the scenes if you really want to see how things happen. Windows 95 also allows you to give your files sensible names that have more than eight characters, which you could not do with older versions of Windows. Sensible filenames make record-keeping easier. But many people still find the concepts of drives and folders to be nonsensical.

People work on computers every single day, and many still don't understand the machines too well, but they get along fine anyway. So don't worry — you will, too. On the other hand, if you understand how your drives and folders are organized, the knowledge can help in a pinch. The system of files and folders is like a road map that seems complicated at first, but after you've learned to use the map, you can get where you're going faster. Because Outlook presents your system of files and folders more understandably than Windows Explorer, the whole issue of keeping track of your files seems much simpler.

The Component Confirmation and Installation screen appears.

5. Click Install Now.

The Integrated File Management component is installed, and then the Install Complete dialog box appears.

6. Click OK.

After you install the File Management tools, a new Outlook Bar group named Other Shortcuts appears. You can open the Other Shortcuts group to find the My Computer icon, which is where you look for tools to manage your files.

Final Facts on Filing

If you like to get down to the nitty-gritty in dealing with files and folders, you'll like using Outlook because its file management tools (including the capability to add fields and save custom views) are very powerful. If you move or copy files only on pain of death or when bribed with chocolate, you'll like using Outlook because you can create a few simple views (or have someone else create and save some simple views for you) and not be bothered with all the ugly details of files, folders, and whatnot. You can have it both ways — but only in Outlook. The other Office 97 programs can't do the tricks that Outlook can!

The 5th Wave By Rich Tennant

"YES, WE STILL HAVE A FEW BUGS IN THE WORD PROCESSING SOFTWARE. BY THE WAY, HERE'S A MEMO FROM MARKETING."

Chapter 5

How You See It: Views and New Views

In This Chapter

▶ Using views

▶ Changing columns

▶ Sorting lists

▶ Grouping items in your table

▶ Saving your own views

When you boil it down, the two biggest things that you do in Outlook are entering information and viewing it. This chapter is about viewing information any way you want to look at it, which makes the information easier for you to use and understand.

Any body of information can have a variety of looks. Each look is referred to as a *view* in Outlook parlance. You don't have to think much about views if you'd rather not, because when you buy Outlook, dozens of views are included. Simply choose the one you want. I describe the main views in this chapter.

Types of Views

Choosing a view is like renting a car. You can choose a model with the features you want, whether the car is a convertible, a minivan, or a luxury sedan. All cars are equipped with different things — radios, air conditioning, power cup holders, and so on — that you can use or not use, as you please. Some rental agencies offer unlimited free mileage. Outlook views are much more economical, though. In fact, they're free.

Every module in Outlook has its own selection of views. The Calendar has (among others) a view that looks calendar-like. The Contacts module includes a view that looks like an address card. The Journal and the Tasks modules include a Timeline view. All modules allow you to use at least one type of Table view, which organizes your data in the old-fashioned row-and-column arrangement.

Each type of view is organized to make something about your collection of information obvious at first glance. You can change the way that you view a view by sorting, filtering, or grouping.

You don't have to do anything to see a view; Outlook is *always* displaying some kind of view. The view is the thing that takes up most of the screen most of the time. The view (or the Information Viewer, in official Microsoftese) is one of only two parts of Outlook that you can't turn off. (You also can't turn off the menu bar.)

Each view has a name, which is displayed in the Current View menu. A check mark appears next to the name of whichever view you're using. To see the Current View menu, choose View➪Current View. The Current View menu also lists other views that are available to you in the module that you're using.

Table view

All modules contain some version of the Table view. A Table view is rectangular — all rows and columns. If you create a new item by adding a new task to your Tasks list, for example, a new row turns up in the Table view. You see one row for each task in Table view (see Figure 5-1).

The names of Table views often contain the word *list,* as in Simple List, Phone List, or just List. That word means that they're a plain-vanilla table of items, just like a grocery list. Other Table view names start with the word *By,* which means that items in the view are grouped by a certain type of information, such as by entry type or by name of contact. I discuss grouped views later in the chapter and show you how to group items your own way.

Icons view

Icons view is the simplest view — just a bunch of icons with names thrown on the screen (see Figure 5-2).

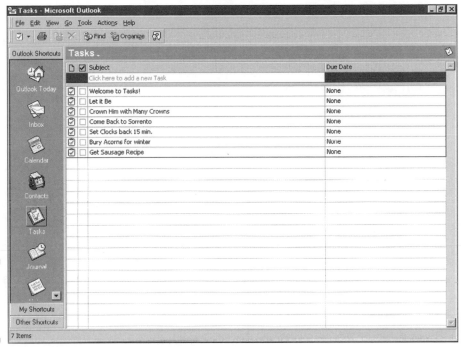

Figure 5-1:
The Tasks module in a Table view.

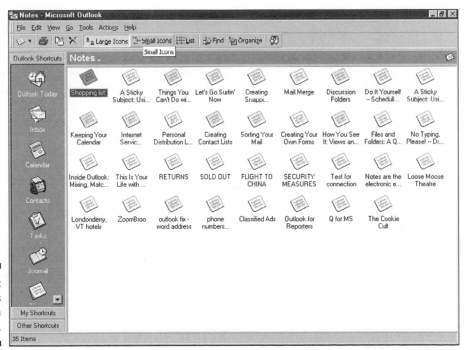

Figure 5-2:
The Notes module in Icons view.

The only Icons views that come with Outlook are used for viewing notes and file folders. Icons view doesn't show a great deal of information, and some people like it that way. I like to see more detailed information, so I stay with Table views. There's nothing wrong with using Icons view most of the time; you can easily switch to another view if you need to see more.

Timeline view

Timeline views show you a set of small icons arranged across the screen. Icons that are higher on the screen represent items that were created or tasks that were begun earlier in the day. Icons that are farther to the left were created on an earlier date (see Figure 5-3).

The Task Timeline in the Tasks module also draws a line that represents the length of time that it takes to perform an item if the start and end times of a task have been specified previously.

A Timeline view includes four toolbar buttons that allow you to change the length of time you want to view. Your choices are Go to Today, Day (not necessarily today), Week, and Month. As you can do in all other view settings, you can click to move between one-day and seven-day views and back, like changing television channels.

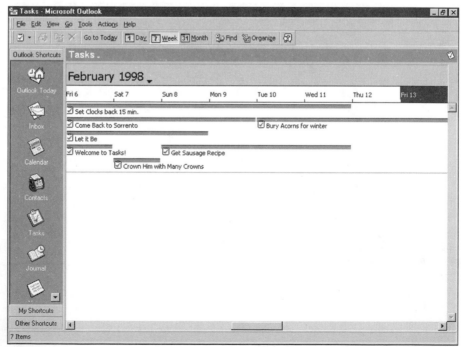

Figure 5-3:
Tasks arranged in the Timeline view.

Card view

Card views are designed for the Contacts module. Each Contact item gets its own little block of information (see Figure 5-4). Each little block displays a little or a lot of information about the item, depending on what kind of card it is. (See Chapter 10 for more about the different views in the Contacts module.)

The Address Cards view shows you only a few items at a time, because the cards are so big. To make it easier to find a name in your Contact list that's not displayed on the screen, you can type the first letter of the name that your contact is filed under to see that person's address card.

Day/Week/Month view

Day/Week/Month view is another specialized view, designed particularly for the Calendar.

Like a Timeline view, Day/Week/Month view adds Go to Today, Day, Work Week, Week, and Month buttons to the toolbar to allow you to switch between views easily. The Day, Work Week, and Week views also display a monthly calendar. You can click any date in the monthly calendar to switch your view to that date (see Figure 5-5).

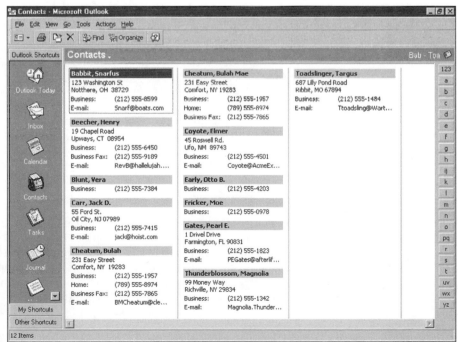

Figure 5-4:
See your
Contacts in
Address
Cards view.

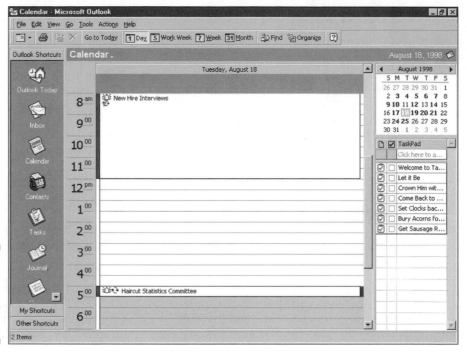

Figure 5-5:
Starting a
day in the
life of your
calendar.

Playing with Columns in Table View

Table views show you the most detailed information about the items that you've created; these views also allow you to organize the information in the greatest number of ways with the least effort. Okay, Table views look a little dull, but they get you where you need to go.

Table views are organized in columns and rows. Each row displays information for one item — one appointment in your Calendar, one task in your Tasks list, or one person in your Contact list. Adding a row is easy. Just add an item, press Ctrl+N, and then fill in the information you want for that item. Getting rid of a row is easy, too. Just delete the item. Click your mouse to select the item and then press the Delete key.

The columns in a Table view show you pieces of information about each item. Most Outlook modules can store far more pieces of information about an item than you can display onscreen in row-and-column format. The Contact list, for example, holds more than 90 pieces of information about every person in your list. If each person is represented by one row, you would need more than 90 columns to display everything.

Adding a column

Outlook starts you out with a limited number of columns in the Phone List view of your Contact list. (Remember that the names of Table views usually have "list" in them somewhere.) If you want more columns, you can easily add some. You can display as many columns as you want in Outlook, but you may have to scroll across the screen to see the information that you want to see.

To add a column in any Table view:

1. **Right-click the title of any column in the gray header row of the column.**

   A shortcut menu appears.

2. **Pick Field Chooser from the shortcut menu.**

   The Field Chooser dialog box appears.

3. **Select the type of field that you want to add.**

   The words `Frequently-Used Fields` appear in the text box at the top of the Field Chooser. Those words mean that the types of fields most people like to add are already listed. If the name of the field that you want to add isn't listed in one of the gray boxes at the bottom of the Field Chooser dialog box, pull down the menu that `Frequently-Used Fields` is part of and see what's available.

4. **Drag the field into the table.**

You have to drag the new item to the top row of the table, where the heading names are (see Figure 5-6). Notice that the names in the Field Chooser are in the same kind of gray box as the headers of each column of your table. (If they look alike, they must belong together, like Michael Jackson and Lisa Marie. Right? . . . Maybe that's not the best example.)

Moving a column

Moving columns is even easier than adding columns. Just drag the heading of the column to where you want it (see Figure 5-7).

Two little red arrows appear as you're dragging the heading to show you where the column will end up when you release the mouse button.

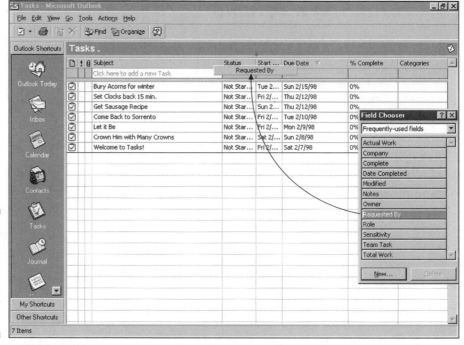

Figure 5-6:
The
Requested
By field is
dragged to
the top row
of the table.

Figure 5-7:
Moving the
Business
Phone
column.

Columns = fields

I promised to tell you how to add a column, and now I'm telling you about fields. What gives? Well, columns are fields, see? No? Well, think of it this way.

In your checkbook, your check record has a *column* of the names of the people to whom you wrote checks and another *column* that contains the amounts of those checks. When you actually write a check, you write the name of the payee in a certain *field* in the check; the

amount goes in a different *field*. So you enter tidbits of information as *fields* in the check, but you show them as *columns* in the check record. That's exactly how it works in Outlook. You enter somebody's name, address, and phone number in *fields* when you create a new item, but the Table view shows the same information to you in *columns*. When you're adding a column, you're adding a field. Same thing.

Formatting a column

Some fields contain too much information to fit in their columns. Dates are prime offenders. Outlook normally displays dates in this format: Fri 7/4/97 4:14 PM. I normally don't care which day of the week a date falls on, so I reformat the column to 7/4/97 4:14 PM and save the other space for something that I really want to know.

To change the formatting of a column:

1. **Right-click the heading of a column.**

   A menu appears.

2. **Choose Format Columns.**

   The Format Columns dialog box appears (see Figure 5-8).

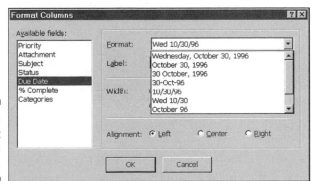

Figure 5-8:
The Format
Columns
dialog box.

3. Choose a format type from the _F_ormat menu.

Pick whatever suits your fancy. Some columns contain information that can be formatted only one way, such as names and categories. Information in number columns (especially dates) can be formatted in a variety of ways.

4. Click OK.

Your column is reformatted.

Changing a column format affects only that column in that view of that module. If you want to change the formats of other views and modules, you have to change them one at a time.

Widening or shrinking a column

Widening or shrinking a column is even easier than moving a column. Here's how:

1. Move the mouse pointer to the right edge of the column that you want to widen or shrink until the pointer becomes a two-headed arrow.

Making that mouse pointer turn into a two-headed arrow takes a bit of dexterity. If you find the procedure to be difficult, you can use the Format Column procedure that I describe in the preceding section. Type a number in the Width box — bigger numbers for wider boxes and smaller numbers for narrower boxes.

2. Drag the edge of the column until the column is the width that you desire.

The two-headed arrow creates a thin line that you can drag to resize the column (see Figure 5-9). What you see is what you get.

If you're not really sure how wide a column needs to be, just double-click the right edge of the column header. When you double-click that spot, Outlook 98 does a trick called _size-to-fit,_ which widens or narrows a column to exactly the size of the widest piece of data in the column.

Removing a column

You can remove columns that you don't want to look at.

To remove a column:

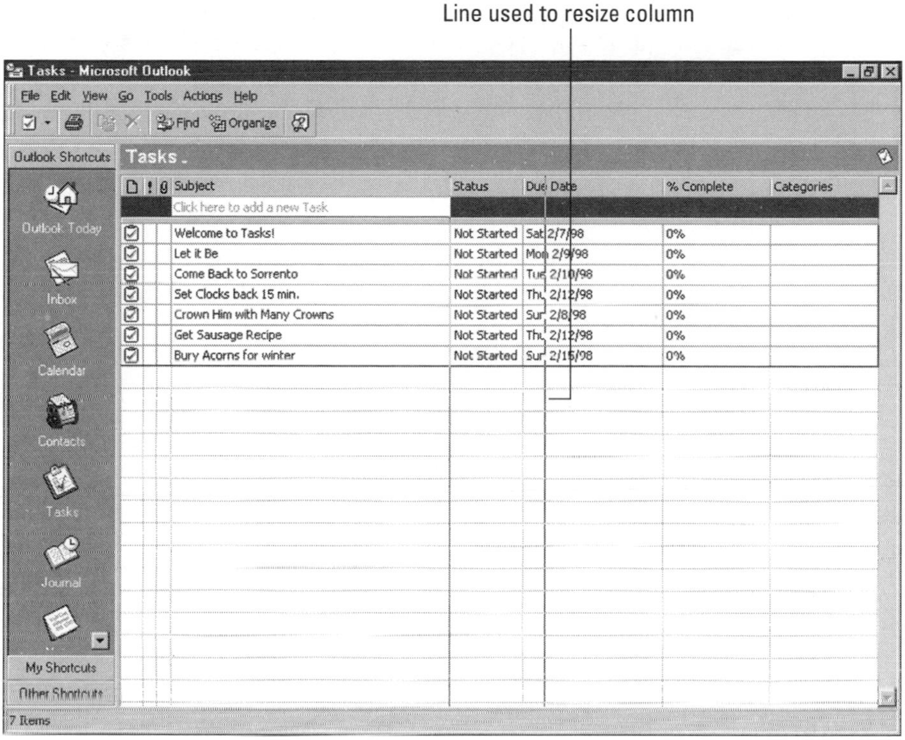

Line used to resize column

Figure 5-9:
Widening
the Status
column.

1. **Right-click the heading of the column that you want to remove.**

   A menu appears.

2. **Choose Remove This Column.**

   Zap! It's gone!

Don't worry too much about deleting columns. When you zap a column, the field remains in the item. You can use the column-adding procedure (which I describe earlier in this chapter) to put it back. If you're confused by this whole notion of columns and fields, see the sidebar "Columns = fields" in this chapter.

Sorting

Sorting just means putting your list in order. In fact, a list is always in some kind of order. Sorting just changes the order.

You can tell what order your list is sorted in by looking for triangles in headings. A heading with a triangle in it means that the entire list is sorted by the information in that column. If the column has numbers in it, and if the triangle's large side is at the top, the list begins with the item that has the largest number in that column, followed by the item that has the next-largest number, and so on, ending with the smallest number. Columns that contain text get sorted in alphabetical order. *A* is the smallest letter, and *Z* is the largest.

From Table view

By far the easiest way to sort a table is simply to click the heading of a column that you want to sort. The entire table is sorted on the column that you clicked.

From the Sort dialog box

Although clicking on a column is the easiest way to sort, it allows you to sort on only one column. You may want to sort on two or more columns.

To sort on two or more columns:

1. **Choose View⇨Current View⇨Edit Current View.**

   The View Summary dialog box appears.

2. **Click the Sort button.**

   The Sort dialog box appears.

3. **From the Sort Items By menu, choose the first field that you want to sort by.**

   Choose carefully; a much larger list of fields is in the list than is usually in the view. It's confusing.

4. **Choose Ascending or Descending sort order.**

   That means to choose whether to sort from smallest to largest or largest to smallest.

5. **Repeat Steps 3 and 4 for each additional field that you want to sort.**

   As the dialog box implies, the first thing that you select is the most important. The entire table is sorted according to that field and then by the fields that you pick later, in the order in which you select them. If you sort your phone list by company first and then by name, for example, your list begins with the names of the people who work for a certain company, displayed alphabetically, followed by the names of the people who work for another company, and so on.

6. **Click OK.**

   Your list is sorted.

Grouping

Sorting and grouping are similar. Both procedures organize items in your table according to the information in one of the columns. Grouping is different from sorting, however, in that it creates bunches of similar items that you can open or close. You can look at only the bunches that interest you and ignore all the other bunches.

For example, when you balance your checkbook, you probably *sort* your checks by check number. At tax time, you *group* your checks; you make a pile of the checks for medical expenses, another pile of checks for charitable deductions, and another pile of checks for the tax-deductible money that you spend on ...*For Dummies* books. Then you can add up the amounts that you spent in each category and enter those figures in your tax return.

Grouping views with drag-and-drop

The simple way to group items is to open the Group By box and drag a column heading into it (see Figure 5-10).

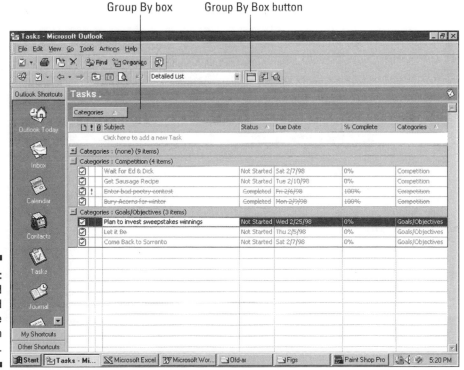

Figure 5-10: A grouped view based on one column heading.

Here's how you group items by dragging and dropping a column heading:

1. **Open the Advanced Toolbar by choosing View⇨Toolbars⇨Advanced.**

   The Advanced Toolbar appears.

2. **Click the Group By Box button in the Advanced toolbar.**

   The table drops down slightly and a box appears above the table saying, `Drag a column header here to group by that column`.

3. **Drag to the Group By box the header of the column that contains the data you want to group by.**

   You can drag several fields up to the Group By box to create groups based on more than one column (see Figure 5-11).

Using the Group By dialog box

Just as you have a second way to sort your listing, you have a second way to group your listing. Just use the Group By dialog box.

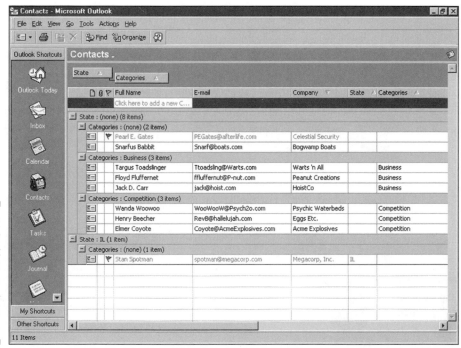

Figure 5-11:
Your
Contact list
grouped
by two
headings —
State and
Category.

To group your list:

1. **Choose View⇨Current View⇨Edit Current View.**

   The View Summary dialog box appears.

2. **Click the Group By button.**

   The Group By dialog box appears.

3. **Choose the first field that you want to group the view by.**

   The list has more fields than are showing in the table. If you choose to group by a field that's not showing in your table, you can check the Show Field in View check box (see Figure 5-12). You may also want to choose whether you want your groups to be sorted in Ascending or Descending alphabetical order, although that's less important when you're grouping.

4. **Choose any other fields that you want to group the view by.**

   If you group by too many columns, your list will be harder to use, rather than easier.

5. **Click OK.**

   Your list is grouped by as many fields as you want.

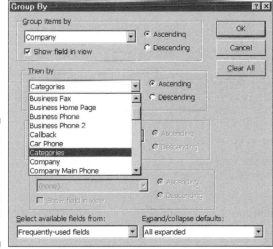

Figure 5-12:
The Group
By dialog
box with the
Show Field
in View box
checked.

Viewing grouped items

A grouped view shows you the names of the columns that you used to create the group view. If you click the Contacts icon and choose By Company view (which is a grouped view), you see gray bars with an icon at the right. The word `Company` appears next to the icon because that's the column that the view is grouped on. A company name appears next to the word `Company` — the grouped view includes a gray bar for each company in the list.

The icon at the left end of the gray bar contains either a plus sign or a minus sign. A plus sign means that there's more to be seen. Click the plus sign, and the group opens, revealing the other items that belong to the group. A minus sign means that there's no more to see; what you see is what you get in that group.

If you click the gray bar itself but not the icon, you select the entire group. You can delete the group if you select the gray bar and press the Delete key. When a group bar is selected, it's dark gray rather than light gray, like all the others.

Viewing headings only

You can click the plus and minus signs one at a time to open and close individual groups, or you can open or close all the groups at the same time.

To open or close groups:

1. **Simply choose View⇨Expand/Collapse Groups.**

   I think Expanding and Collapsing are dramatic words for what you're doing with these groups. It's not like Scarlett O'Hara getting the vapors; it's just hiding or revealing the contents of a group or all the groups.

2. **To open a single group that you have selected, choose Collapse This Group or Expand This Group.**

3. **To expand or collapse all the groups, choose Expand All Groups or Collapse All Groups.**

What could be easier?

Creating Custom Table Views

If you're used to saving documents in your word processor, then you're familiar with the idea of saving views. When you make any of the changes to a view that I describe earlier in this chapter and then change to another view, Outlook asks whether you want to discard the changes to the view, save the changes as a new view, or make the changes the new way to see the current view. If you plan to use a certain view over and over, it's worth saving.

You can create any view you like by using the Define Views dialog box. Choose View⇨Current View⇨Define Views and follow the prompts. This procedure is a little more complicated than simply changing and saving views, but you have more detailed control of the results. When you're comfortable with Outlook, you may want to give the Define Views method a try, but I think that you can do most of what you need to do just by changing the views you already have.

A Bridge from the Views

You can create an endless number of ways to organize and view the information that you save in Outlook. How you decide to view information depends on what kind of information you have and how you plan to use what you have. You can't go too wrong with views, because you can easily create new views if the old ones get messed up. So feel free to experiment.

Chapter 6

Creating Your Own Forms

. . . .

In This Chapter

▶ Understanding forms

▶ Adding standard fields to a form

▶ Adding your own fields to a form

▶ Using a custom form

. . . .

Christmas cookies come in all kinds of shapes — stars, reindeer, Christmas trees, and so on. The cookies get their shapes from a cookie cutter. If you ever make cookies for the holidays, you know how it works. Even though the cookies are different shapes and colors, they're still made of the same ingredients, and they all have a similar taste.

The data that you put in an Outlook item is shaped by a form, which does the same job on data as a cookie cutter does on cookie dough. The form shapes the data and gives it a certain appearance — a standardized format of lines, boxes, text blocks, and so on.

Every time you choose File➪New in Outlook or double-click an item to open it, a form pops up. Forms allow you to create a new item or edit information in an old item. You can customize forms to suit your needs (or at least your taste). The forms that come with Outlook are shaped and designed to handle the information that most people use most of the time. But you can create your own forms that allow you to deal with the data you want in the shape in which you want it.

You can't create forms from scratch in Outlook (the way you can with a database program like Microsoft Access), just as most people can't create their own cookie cutters. But you can bend a cookie cutter that you already have into a shape you want, and you can adjust one of the existing Outlook forms to meet your needs. Actually, you'll get much better results from customizing Outlook forms than you would by bending your cookie cutters out of shape.

After you customize a form, you can give it a different name from the old form so that you have two forms: the original Outlook form and your new, customized form. You can make the forms look entirely different when you use them, even though they're based on the same form.

The best reason to customize a form is to add fields that aren't available in the original form. Fields are categories of information that you need to use, such as phone numbers, names, and addresses. In the following section, I show you an example of a form customized to suit a car salesperson. The customized form uses all the information from the original Outlook form and adds a few fields that are specific to the needs of someone who sells cars.

Adding a Standard Field to a Form

When you first install Outlook, hundreds of standard fields are already set up for you to use. Standard fields are made to store the kind of information that people often need to use, like names, addresses, dates, and so on. You can choose to add any of them to your forms, or you can create custom fields. I discuss how to create custom fields later in this chapter (see the section "Adding a User-Defined Field to a Form").

To add a standard field to an Outlook form:

1. **Choose View➪Folder List.**

   The Folder List appears (see Figure 6-1), giving you a more detailed view of your Outlook folders. You use the Folder List to create a new folder. I suggest that you create a new folder for this example.

2. **Right-click the folder in which you want to create the new subfolder.**

   For this example, right-click the Contacts folder. A shortcut menu appears. The commands in the menu allow you to create a subfolder, as well as move, copy, rename, or delete an existing folder.

3. **Choose New Folder.**

   The Create New Folder dialog box appears (see Figure 6-2).

4. **Type a name for the folder.**

   I use **Prospects** for this example.

5. **Click OK.**

   The new folder that you created appears in the Folder List.

6. **Click the new folder.**

   If the Contacts folder has a plus sign next to it, click the plus sign. Subfolders of the Contacts folder appear.

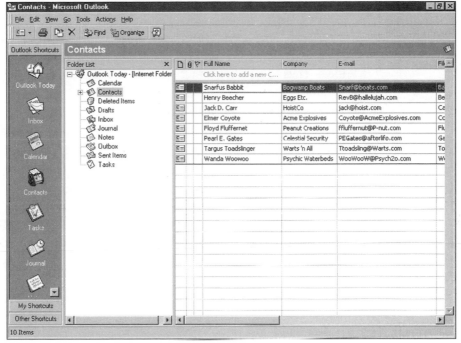

Figure 6-1:
The Folder
List,
with the
Contacts
folder
highlighted.

Figure 6-2:
The Create
New Folder
dialog box.

7. Choose File⇨New⇨Contact.

The Contact form appears.

8. Choose Tools⇨Forms⇨Design This Form.

The form switches into Forms Designer mode (see Figure 6-3). The form looks similar to what it looked like before you chose Tools⇨Forms⇨ Design This Form, but five new pages — called P.2 through P.6 — appear. These pages are blank pages that you can customize with new fields, new colors, and so on.

9. Click (P.2) or any other blank page.

It's your choice; you can add fields to any of the new pages.

10. (Optional) To make this page visible, choose Form⇨Display This Page.

The parentheses disappear from around P.2. The new pages that appear when you choose Tools⇨Forms⇨Design This Form are in parentheses, whereas the ones that appear in the form before you choose this command aren't in parentheses. That's how you can tell which pages will be visible when you finish customizing the form.

If you want, you can leave all pages visible. But one reason to create a custom form is to reduce the number of steps required to view, enter, or edit the information on the form. You also may be creating this form for other people to use, so you want to keep your form clear and simple. One-page forms are clearer and simpler than multipage forms.

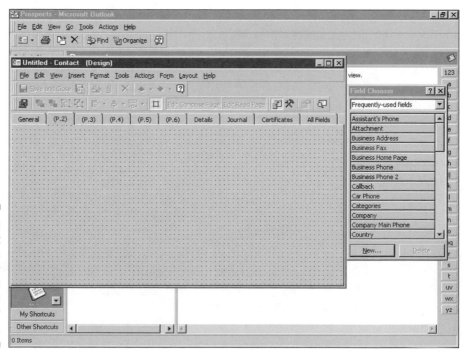

Figure 6-3:
The Contact Forms Designer with the Field Chooser showing.

You can click any page and make the page invisible to the user. You can't edit the first page, but you can make it invisible and add the same fields to a different page that you design. You can have a page with just name, address, and home phone, and then make the first page invisible to the user by clicking the General tab and then choosing Form⇨Display This Page. (The command toggles the page on and off.)

11. **Choose Form⇨Rename Page.**

    The Rename Page dialog box appears (see Figure 6-4).

Figure 6-4:
The
Rename
Page dialog
box.

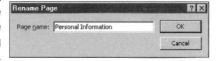

12. **Type a new name for the page.**

    I use **Personal Information** as a good name for this page, but any name you choose will work.

13. **Click OK.**

    The page tab now has the name that you entered in the Rename Page dialog box.

    Now it's time to add some fields to the new page. That's what customizing a form is all about. The Field Chooser is the place to find fields to add to your form.

    I think that the Field Chooser is confusing. You never see all the fields that are available; you see only a certain subset. The words below `Field Chooser` tell you which subset you're seeing. In this case, I use the Personal fields subset (see Figure 6-5).

    You can choose Frequently-Used fields to limit what Outlook shows you to a small range of fields, or All Contact fields to choose from every kind of field that Outlook allows in this type of form.

14. **Select a category from the drop-down list at the top of the Field Chooser and then select the name of a field in that category.**

    For this example, select the Personal fields category and then select the Referred By field, which the car salesperson can use to store the name of the person who referred the customer.

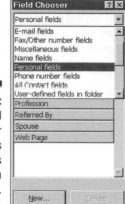

Figure 6-5:
The Field
Chooser
contains
more fields
than you
can see.

15. Drag the selected field onto the page.

When you drag a field onto the page in Forms Designer mode, it auto-matically aligns properly on the page. To add more fields to your form, keep dragging them in from the Field Chooser (see Figure 6-6).

Publish button

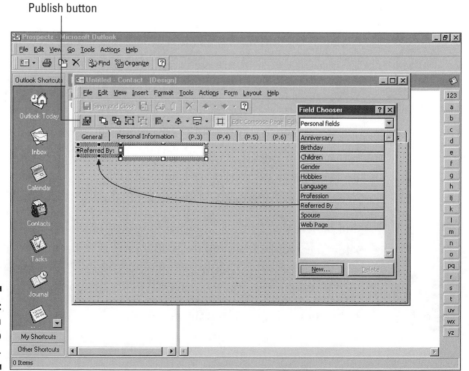

Figure 6-6:
Dragging a
field into
a form.

16. Choose Tools⇨Forms⇨Publish Form As.

The Publish Form As dialog box appears. *Publishing* is the Outlook term for making a form available in a certain folder or group of folders. Outlook will publish your new form to whichever folder you clicked before beginning to design your form unless you click the Look In button and choose a different folder.

17. Type a name for your new form.

The name **New Prospect** is a good one for this form. The form name will appear in the menus when you create a new item for this folder.

18. Click Publish.

Nothing visible happens, but your form is published to the folder that you designated — in this case, the Prospects folder.

19. Choose File⇨Close.

A dialog box appears, asking Do you want to save changes?

20. Click Yes to save changes.

A dialog box appears, asking Do you want to save this contact with an empty file as field?

21. Click Yes.

The Forms Designer closes.

The form now contains your additional standard field.

Adding a User-Defined Field to a Form

You can choose from hundreds of standard fields when you first use Outlook, but that's just the beginning. User-defined fields let you add types of information to your forms that weren't included with Outlook.

Here's how to create a user-defined field and add it to a form:

1. Choose File⇨New⇨Contact.

The Contact form appears.

2. Choose Tools⇨Forms⇨Design This Form.

The form switches into Forms Designer mode. The form looks similar to what it looked like before you chose Tools⇨Forms⇨Design This Form, but five new pages — called P.2 through P.6 — appear. These pages are blank pages that you can customize with new fields, new colors, and so on.

3. Click the tab of an unused page.

You can add fields to any of the new pages.

4. Choose Form⇨Display This Page.

The parentheses disappear from the name of the page in the tab, showing you that this page will be visible when you finish customizing the form.

5. Click New in the Field Chooser dialog box.

The New Field dialog box appears (see Figure 6-7).

Now to create a User-Defined field: A *User-Defined field* is a field that you dream up to put in your form because you need to add a type of data for which Outlook doesn't have a standard field.

Figure 6-7:
The New
Field dialog
box.

6. Type a name for a new field.

Outlook doesn't include a field called Make of Auto, so type **Make of Auto**. You can use any name up to 32 characters.

7. Click OK.

Your new field appears in the Field Chooser, and the words `User-Defined Fields` appear at the top of the Field Chooser as the field type.

8. Drag the new field onto the form page.

The new field aligns itself automatically.

9. Click the Publish button at the far left of the Design Form toolbar.

The Publish button appears at the left end of the lower Forms toolbar (refer to Figure 6-6). You can also choose File⇨Publish Form As. The Publish Form As dialog box appears, with the current name of the form already filled in.

10. Click Publish.

Changes that you made to your form are now stored and will appear the next time you use the form.

Using the Form You've Designed

It's easy to use a form you've designed in any folder to which you published the form. The name you gave to the form will turn up on the Outlook main menu whenever you choose the Outlook folder that you published the form to.

Here's how you use a custom form:

1. **Click the Actions menu.**

   That's the menu immediately to the left of Help in the menu bar.

2. **Choose the custom form name that appears at the bottom of the menu.**

   If you created the form called New Prospect earlier in this chapter, when you choose the Contacts menu, the name New Prospect appears at the bottom of the menu (see Figure 6-8); choose it.

3. **Fill out the form.**

4. **Click Save and Close.**

You can have more than one custom form assigned to a folder. You can create a Vacation Request folder, for example, and store Vacation Request, Vacation Approved, and Vacation Denied forms in the same folder.

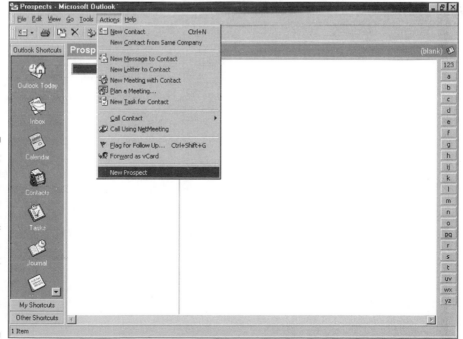

Figure 6-8:
When you publish a custom form, the name of your form appears at the bottom of the Actions menu.

Making a Custom Form a Folder's Default Form

Every time you choose a folder in Outlook and choose File⇨New, a form pops up to invite you to enter the kind of data that is used in that folder. You can also pick another form to use by choosing the form by name from the menus. If you want your custom form to be the one that Outlook offers when you choose File⇨New, you need to designate the form to be the default form for that folder.

Here's how you designate a form to be the default form for a folder:

1. **Choose View⇨Folder List.**

   The Folder List opens if it was closed. This command toggles like a light switch, opening the Folder List if it was closed and closing the list if it was open.

2. **Click the folder for which you want to change the default form.**

   For this example, that folder is the Prospects folder.

3. **Choose File⇨Folder⇨Properties for *Name of folder.***

   The folder's Properties dialog box appears (see Figure 6-9).

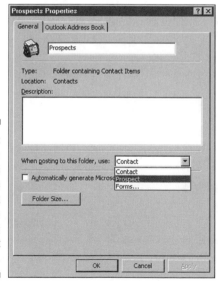

Figure 6-9:
Use the folder's Properties dialog box to set the folder's default form.

4. Click the When Posting to This Folder, Use drop-down list.

Select the name of your custom form.

5. Click OK.

Now every time you choose File➪New in that folder, your customized form appears.

Part II
E-Mail and Contacts: Not Just Playing Post Office

The 5th Wave   By Rich Tennant

"QUICK KIDS! YOUR MOTHER'S FLAMING SOMEONE ON THE INTERNET!"

In this part . . .

Office boundaries can extend worldwide and keeping in touch with coworkers at home and away can be difficult without an integrated message-sending and contact-tracking system like Outlook. This part shows you many ways to dress up your e-mail, stay in touch with your contacts, and span the globe through the Internet without leaving your desktop.

Chapter 7

E-Mail: Basic Delivery

In This Chapter

▶ Sending messages

▶ Opening and replying to messages

▶ Previewing message contents

▶ Forwarding messages

▶ Deleting messages

▶ Saving an unfinished message

▶ Saving messages as files

▶ Setting message sensitivity and importance

*1*f you're as lazy as I am, electronic mail — e-mail — is a dream. I love getting mail — fan mail, junk mail, official mail, anything except bills. But regular paper mail stacks up in ugly piles, and I always lose the important stuff. E-mail is quick to read, easy to find, and simple to answer. Outlook makes e-mail even easier to read, create, and answer. You don't even have to organize your e-mail in Outlook; it organizes itself!

Front Ends and Back Ends

You need two things to send and receive e-mail:

✔ A program that helps you create, save, and manage your messages

✔ A program that actually transports the messages to or from the other people with whom you exchange messages

Some technical people call these two parts the front end and the back end, respectively. Outlook is a front end for e-mail; It helps you create, format, store, and manage your messages, but it has very little to do with actually getting your messages to your destination. That work is done by a back-end service (such as Microsoft Exchange Server, cc: Mail, or Lotus Notes in your office), by your Internet Service Provider (ISP), or by an online service like CompuServe or The Microsoft Network (MSN).

If you feel that you're the last person on earth without Internet e-mail capability, you've got that capability now with Outlook. To run Outlook, you must have Windows 95. The Windows 95 Desktop has an icon for The Microsoft Network. If you don't have an Internet e-mail service, it's easy to get one — just click the Microsoft Network icon. The friendly Microsoft prompts then welcome and guide you through the process of collecting your credit card number and, of course, collecting your money. A few keystrokes, and voilà — you have e-mail service faster than you can say "billionaire Bill Gates."

I don't want to give too much hype to MSN. Although Microsoft has made it fiendishly simple to sign up for MSN, the price it charges for monthly access is no better than any of the other popular online services, and the service it offers is no great shakes. For a long time, representatives of The Microsoft Network wouldn't support Microsoft Outlook. Go figure. You can use CompuServe or AT&T WorldNet for Internet access and e-mail or any of a thousand other services, but MSN is the easiest to join. I tell you more about online services in Chapter 12.

You may already be set up on an office e-mail system, such as Microsoft Mail or cc:Mail. If so, I assume that you have a computer guru around to set you up on those systems, because that stuff can get kind of messy. You can definitely use Outlook to exchange e-mail via nearly any regular Internet Service Provider. Usually the ISP's technical support people can help you set up Outlook.

In many ways, electronic mail is better than regular paper mail (also known as snail mail). E-mail is delivered much faster than paper mail — almost instantaneously. I find that speedy delivery is really handy for last-minute birthday greetings. E-mail is also incredibly cheap; in fact, it's free much of the time.

Creating Messages

If you can type a name, you can send an e-mail message. But if you type just the name, your recipient gets an e-mail message containing nothing but a name. So you really need to type a name and a message.

To create a new e-mail message, follow these steps:

1. **Choose <u>G</u>o▷Out<u>b</u>ox (or press Ctrl+Shift+O).**

   The e-mail Outbox appears. You can also go to the Inbox (Ctrl+Shift+I).

2. **Choose <u>F</u>ile▷<u>N</u>ew▷<u>M</u>ail Message (or press Ctrl+N).**

   The New Message form appears (see Figure 7-1).

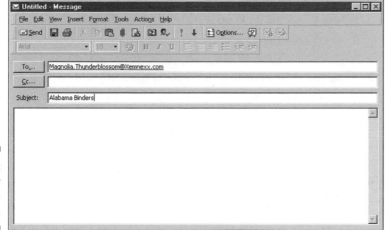

Figure 7-1:
The New
Message
form.

3. **Click the To text box and type the e-mail address of the person to whom you're sending your message.**

You can also click the To button itself, find the name of the person to whom you're sending the message in the Address Book, and then click OK. Or you can use the AutoName feature, which I describe in the "What's in a name? AutoName!" sidebar in this chapter.

What's my e-mail address?

When you have an e-mail account, you want to tell other people your e-mail address so that they can send stuff to you. E-mail addresses are a little like long-distance telephone numbers. If you live in Chicago, and you're calling someone in New York, you tell that person that your number is (312) 555-9780; if the other person lives in Chicago, you leave off the (312) and just tell him or her to call you at 555-9780. If you work in the same office, you say that you're at extension 9780; the other person knows the rest.

Likewise, your e-mail address comes in short, medium, and long versions for different people, depending on how much of the address they share with you. If you use The Microsoft Network and your account name is Jane_Doe, your e-mail address to the world

at large is Jane_Doe@msn.com. (Don't_forget_that_punctuation; computers still aren't smart enough to know that Jane_Doe with the underscore and Jane Doe with no underscore are the same person.) Other members of The Microsoft Network address mail to you as Jane_Doe. (The underscore isn't required; I'm just using it as an example of things that stop a computer cold but that you and I wouldn't notice.)

The same is true if you're on an office e-mail system. If you work for International Widgets Corporation, you may be Jdoe@widgets.com. (Check with your company's computer guru about your corporate e-mail address.) Your coworkers can send you messages at Jdoe.

4. **Click the C̲c text box and type the e-mail addresses of the people to whom you want to send a copy of your message.**

   If you're sending messages to multiple people, separate their addresses with either a comma or a semicolon.

5. **Type the subject of the message in the Subject box.**

   Your subject can be up to 256 characters long, but keep it shorter. A snappy, relevant subject line makes someone want to read your message; a long or weird subject line doesn't. (Well, you never know with a weird subject line — but don't send weird e-mail at the office, unless everybody does.)

6. **Type the text of your message in the text box.**

   If you use Microsoft Word 97 as your word processor, you can also set up Outlook to use Word 97 as your e-mail editor. You can include formatting, graphics, tables, and all the tricks available in Word to make your e-mail more attractive. When you use Word as an e-mail editor, you don't do anything different — you just see the Word toolbars in the Outlook e-mail form when you're creating e-mail. You can use all the tools you see to add formatting to your e-mail. I've listed in Chapter 20 a few formatting tricks you can use. You can also read Dan Gookin's *Word 97 For Windows For Dummies* (IDG Books Worldwide, Inc.) for more complete information about using Word 97.

   Be careful how you format e-mail to send to people on the Internet. Not all e-mail systems can handle graphics or formatted text like boldface or italics, so the masterpiece of correspondence art that you send to your client on the Internet may arrive as gibberish. If you don't know what the other person has on his or her computer, go light on the graphics. When you're sending e-mail to your colleagues in the same office, or if you're sure that the person you're sending to also has Outlook, the formatting and graphics should look fine.

7. **Click the S̲end button.**

   Your mail is sent to the Outbox. If you're on an office network, your mail automatically goes from your Outbox to the Inbox of the person to whom you're sending the message. If you're using an online service like MSN or CompuServe, you need to press F5 to send the e-mail message along.

Setting the priority of a message

Some messages are more important than others. The momentous report that you're sending to your boss demands a different level of attention than the wisecrack that you're sending to your friend in the sales department. Setting the importance level to High tells the person getting the message that your message requires attention.

What's in a name? AutoName!

One neat feature of Outlook is that you can avoid memorizing long, confusing e-mail addresses of people to whom you send mail frequently. If the person to whom you're sending a message is entered in your Contact list (see Chapter 10 for more information about contacts) and you've included an e-mail address in the Contact record, all you have to type in the To box of your e-mail form is the person's name or even just a part of the person's name. Outlook helps you fill in the rest of the person's name and figures out the e-mail address. You know that you got it right when Outlook underlines the name with a solid black line after you press the Tab key or click outside the To box. If Outlook underlines the name with a red wavy line, Outlook thinks that it knows the name you're entering, but the name isn't spelled quite right, so you need to correct the spelling. If Outlook doesn't put any underline below the name, it's telling you that it has no idea to whom you're sending the message but that it will use the name that you typed as the literal e-mail address. So you have to be doubly sure that the name is correct.

Here's how you set the priority of a message:

1. Choose Go➪Outbox (or press Ctrl+Shift+O).

The Outbox screen opens, showing your outgoing mail (see Figure 7-2).

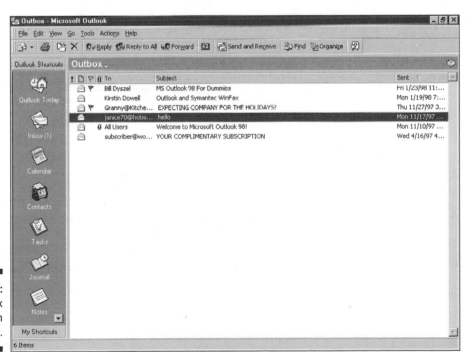

Figure 7-2:
The Outbox with messages.

2. **Double-click the title of the message for which you want to set the importance level.**

   The Message form opens, looking just like it did when you created the message. You can also set the importance level while you're writing the message. You can use either of two buttons in the Message form toolbar to designate the importance of the message as High or Low. Just click one of the importance buttons and then choose File⇨Close (or press Alt+F4) to close. If the toolbar is turned off or missing, follow the rest of these steps.

3. **Click the Options button in the toolbar.**

   The Message Options dialog box (see Figure 7-3) allows you to define qualities about your message that are optional (clever name, eh?).

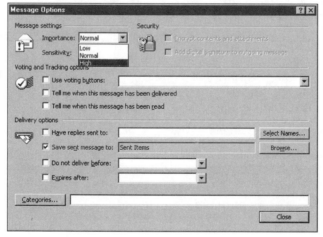

Figure 7-3:
Use the
Message
Options
dialog box
to set the
priority
of your
message.

4. **Click the triangle at the right end of the Importance box.**

   A menu appears.

5. **Choose High, Normal, or Low.**

   Normally, Importance is set to Normal, so you don't have to do anything. Putting a Low importance on your own messages seems to be silly, but you can also assign importance to messages that you receive in your Inbox, to tell yourself which messages can be dealt with later, if at all.

6. **To close the Message Options dialog box, click Close (or press Esc).**

7. **If the Office Assistant asks** Do you want to save changes?, **click Yes.**

I've told you how to change the priority of a message by opening it from the Outbox, so Outlook sees what you've done as a change to the message and asks permission to save the changes. You can also set the priority of your message as you create it by clicking the Options button and choosing the priority before clicking Send. Remember, if you're using Outlook on a network using Microsoft Exchange, your mail doesn't stay in the Inbox very long, so your best bet is to set the priority of the message while composing the message.

Setting the sensitivity of a message

You may want your message to be seen by only one person, or you may want to prevent your message from being changed by anyone after you send it. Sensitivity settings allow you to restrict what someone else can do to your message after you send it and who that someone else can be.

To set the sensitivity of a message:

1. **Choose Go⇨Outbox (or press Ctrl+Shift+O)**

   The Outbox screen opens, showing your outgoing mail.

2. **Double-click the title of the message for which you want to set the sensitivity level.**

   The Message form opens. You can set the sensitivity while you write the message or change the sensitivity after you write the message but before you send it.

3. **Click the Options button in the toolbar.**

   The Message Options dialog box appears (see Figure 7-4).

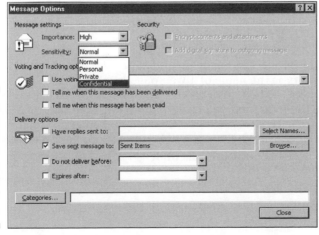

Figure 7-4:
Click the
Options
button to
set the
sensitivity
of your
message.

4. **Click the scroll-down button (the triangle) at the right end of the Sensitivity box.**

   A menu scrolls down with the words Normal, Personal, Private, and Confidential. Most messages you send will have Normal sensitivity, so that's what Outlook uses if you don't say otherwise. The Personal and Confidential settings only notify the people getting the message that they may want to handle the message differently from a Normal message. Some organizations even have special rules for dealing with Confidential messages. Marking a message Private means that no one can modify your message when they forward it or reply to it.

5. **Choose Normal, Personal, Private, or Confidential.**

6. **To close the Message Options dialog box, click Close (or press Esc).**

7. **If the Office Assistant asks** Do you want to save changes?, **click Yes.**

   Outlook sees what you've done as a change to the message and asks permission to save the changes.

You can also set the sensitivity of your message as you create it by clicking the Options button and choosing the sensitivity from the Message Options dialog box before clicking Send.

Setting the sensitivity of a message to Private or Confidential doesn't make the message any more private or confidential than any other message; it just notifies the recipient that the message contains particularly sensitive information. Many corporations are very careful about what kind of information can be sent by e-mail outside the company. If you use Outlook at work, check with your system administrators before presuming that the information you send by e-mail is secure.

Adding an Internet link to an e-mail message

All Office 97 programs automatically recognize the addresses of items on the Internet. If you type the name of a Web page, such as www.pcstudio.com, Outlook changes the text color to blue and underlines the address, making it look just like the hypertext you click to jump between different pages on the World Wide Web. That makes it easy to send someone information about an exciting Web site; just type or copy the address into your message. If the recipient is also an Outlook user, he or she can just click the text to make the Web browser pop up and open the page you told them about.

Reading and Replying to E-Mail Messages

Outlook has a couple of ways to tell you when you receive an e-mail message. In the Outlook Bar, a number in parentheses next to the Inbox icon tells you how many unread e-mail messages you have (see Figure 7-5). The word *Inbox* in the Folder List changes to boldface type when you have unread e-mail, and if you look in the Inbox, the titles of unread messages are in bold as well.

To open and read an e-mail message, follow these steps:

1. Choose Go⇨Inbox (or press Ctrl+Shift+I).

The Inbox screen opens, showing your incoming mail.

2. Double-click the title of the message that you want to read.

The message opens, and you can see the text of the message (see Figure 7-6). If the message is really long, press the down-arrow key or the PgDn key to scroll through the text.

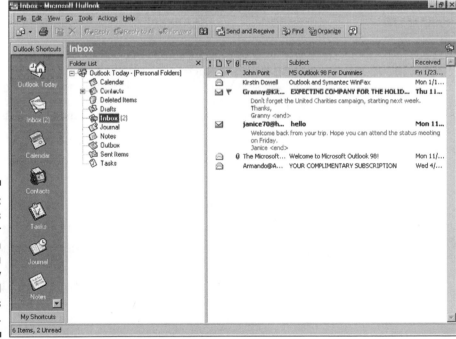

Figure 7-5: Numbers next to your Inbox icon tell you how many unread messages are there.

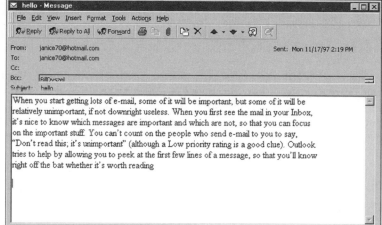

Figure 7-6:
Double-
click a
message to
open it and
read the
contents.

3. **To close the Message screen, choose File⇨Close (or press Alt+F4).**

The Message screen closes, and you see the list of messages in your Inbox.

Previewing message text

When you start getting lots of e-mail, some of it will be important, but some of it will be relatively unimportant, if not downright useless. When you first see the mail in your Inbox, it's nice to know which messages are important and which are not, so that you can focus on the important stuff. You can't count on the people who send e-mail to you to say, "Don't read this; it's unimportant" (although a Low priority rating is a good clue). Outlook tries to help by allowing you to peek at the first few lines of a message, so that you know right off the bat whether it's worth reading.

To see previews of your unread messages:

1. **Choose Go⇨Inbox (or press Ctrl+Shift+I).**

The Inbox screen opens, showing your incoming mail.

2. **Choose View⇨Current View⇨Messages with AutoPreview (see Figure 7-7).**

The list of messages in your Inbox appears with the first few lines of each unread message displayed in blue.

Every module in Outlook has a collection of views that you can use to make your information easier to use. The view called Messages with AutoPreview is the best way to look at your incoming e-mail. In Chapter 9, I show you some of the other views that can make your collection of e-mail messages more useful.

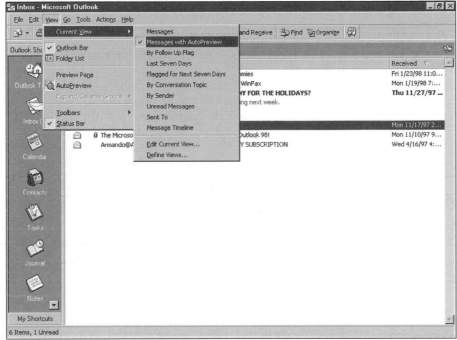

Figure 7-7:
You can
see a
preview
of your
messages
with Auto-
Preview.

Sending a reply

The thing I love about e-mail is that it's so easy to send a reply. You don't even need to know the person's address when you're sending a reply; just click the Reply button, and Outlook takes care of it for you.

Here's how you reply to a message:

1. Choose Go⇨Inbox (or press Ctrl+Shift+I).

The Inbox screen opens, showing your incoming mail.

2. Double-click the title of the message to which you want to reply.

The message you double-clicked opens, and you can see the contents of the message.

If the message is already open, you can skip the first two steps and go directly to Step 3.

3. To reply to the people who are named in the From line, click the Reply button.

I'm seeing a preview of Internet gobbledygook

If you receive a great deal of e-mail from the Internet, the first few lines of your messages may be nothing but computerese. That's because Internet e-mail bounces between computers all over the country — and sometimes all over the world — before it gets to you. The lines of gibberish at the beginning of your Internet e-mail messages are directions used by the computers that the messages bounced among so that the message ends up bouncing to you successfully. Because the opening lines are computerese, Outlook's AutoPreview is less helpful with Internet e-mail; instead, use it for messages on your corporate network.

4. **To reply to the people who are named in the Cc line as well as the From line, click the Reply to All button.**

The Reply screen appears (see Figure 7-8).

You may get (or send) e-mail that's addressed to a whole bunch of people all at once. At least one person must be named in the To line; more than one person can be in the Cc line, which is for people to whom you're sending only a copy. Very little difference exists between what happens to mail that's going to people in the To line and mail that's going to the people in the Cc line — all of them can reply to, forward, or ignore the message. You don't always need to reply to the people on the Cc line, or you may want to reply to only some of them. If you do that, you must click the Reply button (not Reply to All) and add them again to the Cc line.

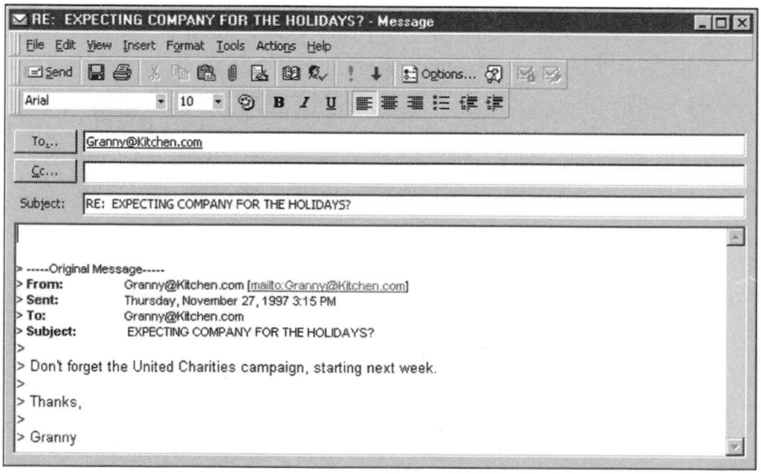

Figure 7-8:
The Reply
screen.

RE: EXPECTING COMPANY FOR THE HOLIDAYS? - Message

File Edit View Insert Format Tools Actions Help

To... Granny@Kitchen.com

Cc...

Subject: RE: EXPECTING COMPANY FOR THE HOLIDAYS?

> -----Original Message-----
> **From:** Granny@Kitchen.com [mailto:Granny@Kitchen.com]
> **Sent:** Thursday, November 27, 1997 3:15 PM
> **To:** Granny@Kitchen.com
> **Subject:** EXPECTING COMPANY FOR THE HOLIDAYS?
>
> Don't forget the United Charities campaign, starting next week.
>
> Thanks,
>
> Granny

5. Type your reply in the Message box.

Don't be alarmed that text is already in the text box — that's the text of the message to which you're replying. Your blinking cursor is at the top of the screen, so anything that you type precedes the other person's message. (This arrangement means that the person who gets your message can review the original message, which helps them remember exactly what they said when they get your reply.)

6. Click the Send button.

On your office network, clicking Send speeds the message to its intended recipient.

If you're a stand-alone user who's sending mail on an online service like The Microsoft Network or CompuServe, you must also press F5 to send your message.

7. Choose File➪Close (or press Esc) to close the Message screen.

The Message form disappears and your Inbox reappears.

Using a link to the Web from your e-mail

When you open a message, sometimes you see blue, underlined text with the name of a Web page or other Internet resource, such as www.pcstudio.com. If you want to look at that page, all you have to do is double-click the text and, if everything is installed correctly, your Web browser pops up and opens the Web page whose name you've clicked.

After you open the page, you can save the page to your Favorites folder to allow you to find it again easily.

That's Not My Department: Forwarding Mail

You may not always have the answer to every e-mail message that you get. You may need to pass a message along to somebody else to have it acted upon, so pass it on.

To forward a message:

1. Choose Go➪Inbox (or press Ctrl+Shift+I).

The Inbox screen opens, showing your incoming mail.

2. Double-click the title of the message that you want to forward.

The Message screen opens (see Figure 7-9). You can forward the message as soon as you read it. If you've already opened the message, you can skip the first two steps.

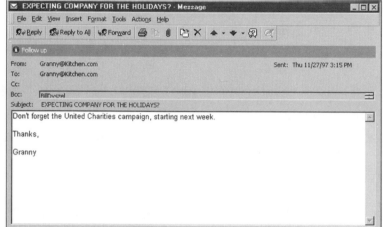

Figure 7-9:
The message you want to forward is opened.

3. Click the For_ward button.

The Forward screen appears (see Figure 7-10). The subject of the original message is now the subject of the new message, except that the letters *FW:* (for Forward) are inserted at the beginning.

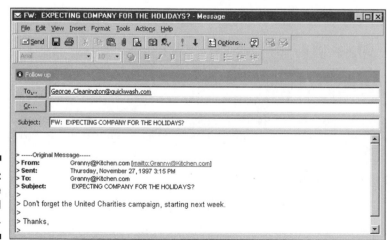

Figure 7-10:
The Forward screen.

4. **Click the To text box and type the e-mail address of the person to whom you're forwarding the message.**

   If the person to whom you're forwarding is entered in your Contact list, just type the person's name — Outlook figures out the e-mail address for you.

5. **Click the Cc text box and type the e-mail addresses of the people to whom you want to forward a copy of your message.**

   Many people forward trivia, such as jokes of the day, to scads and scads of their friends by e-mail. Most recipients are included as Cc addresses.

   Remember, business e-mail etiquette is very different from home e-mail etiquette. Many employers have strict policies about appropriate use of their corporate e-mail systems. If you work for such a company, be aware of your company's policies.

   If you want to pester your friends by sending silly trivia from your home computer to their home computers (like I do), that's your own business.

6. **In the text box, type any comments that you want to add to the message.**

   The text of the original message appears in the text box, preceded by the words `Original Message` and a couple of blank lines. You can preface the message that you're forwarding if you want to give that person a bit of explanation — for example, **This is the 99th message I've had from this person.**

7. **Click the Send button.**

   Your message is on its way.

Deleting Messages

You can zap an e-mail message without a second thought; you don't even have to read the thing. As soon as you see the Inbox list, you know who's sending the message and what it's about, so you don't have to waste time reading Burt's Bad Joke of the day. Just zap it.

If you accidentally delete a message you didn't want to lose, click the Deleted Items icon; you'll find all the messages you've deleted in the last few months. To recover a deleted message, just drag it from the Deleted Items list to either the Inbox icon or the Outbox icon.

Here's how you delete a message:

1. **Choose Go⇨Inbox (or press Ctrl+Shift+I).**

   The Inbox screen opens, showing your incoming mail.

2. **Click the title of the message that you want to delete.**

   You don't have to read the message — you can just delete it from the list.

3. **Choose Edit⇨Delete (or press Delete).**

When you delete messages, Outlook doesn't actually eliminate deleted items; it moves them to the Deleted Items folder. If you have unread items in your Deleted Items folder, Outlook annotates the Deleted Items icon with the number of unread items, the same way that it annotates the Inbox with the number of unread items. You can get rid of the annotation by choosing Tools⇨Empty "Deleted Items" Folder. Or you can just ignore the annotation.

Saving Interrupted Messages

If you get interrupted while writing an e-mail message, all is not lost. You can just save the work that you've done and return to it later. Just choose File⇨ Save (or press Ctrl+S), and your message is saved to the Drafts folder as shown in Figure 7-11 (unless you had reopened the message from the Outbox — in that case, Outlook saves the unfinished message to the Outbox).

When a message is ready to be sent, its name appears in the Outbox in italics. If you've saved it to work on later, its name appears in normal text, not italics. If you're not finished with the message and plan to return to it later, save it (press Ctrl+S). If the message is ready for prime time, send it (press Alt+S).

Saving a Message as a File

You may create or receive an e-mail message that's so wonderful (or terrible) that you just have to save it. You may need to print out the message and show it to someone else, save it to a floppy disk, or export it to a desktop-publishing program.

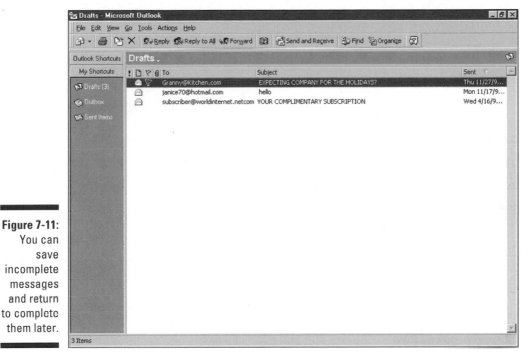

Figure 7-11:
You can save incomplete messages and return to complete them later.

To save a message as a file, follow these steps:

1. **Choose File⇨Save As (or press F12).**

   The Save As dialog box appears.

2. **Click the triangle at the end of the Save In box (called the scroll-down button) to choose the drive to which you want to save your file.**

   If you do all your work on drive C, Outlook chooses drive C first, so you don't have to do anything. To save to a floppy disk, choose the A drive.

3. **Click the name of the folder in which you want to save the file.**

   A list appears of all files in the folder that you select.

4. **Click the File Name text box and type the name that you want to give the file.**

   Type any name you want, up to 256 characters.

5. **If you want to change the type of the file, click the triangle at the end of the Save as Type box and choose a file type.**

   If you're using Word as your e-mail editor, you see the entire range of file types that you can create in Word. If not, the list offers text, the Outlook message format, Outlook Template, and the Internet standard format, HTML (see Figure 7-12). Use HTML. The Outlook Template format is for a message you want to use over and over again in Outlook.

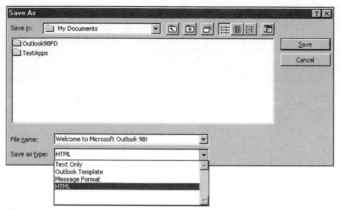

Figure 7-12:
The Save As
dialog box.

6. **Click Save (or press Enter).**

The message is saved to the file and folder you specified in Steps 2 through 4.

Postscript

Sending e-mail is simple. Keeping track of all the tens of millions of people to whom you want to send e-mail is a bigger task. Fortunately, Outlook does both things, so you can go to one program to get the names of the people you know, to find the things that you know about them, and to send them e-mail asking them to tell you more.

Chapter 8

E-Mail: Special Delivery

In This Chapter

▶ Using flags with messages

▶ Saving copies of messages you send

▶ Including your name with your remarks in replies

▶ Setting options for replies

▶ Attaching files to messages

▶ Setting up a signature

*O*utlook can do all sorts of tricks with the mail you send out, as well as with the messages you receive. You can flag messages with reminders, customize your messages with a signature, or add special formatting to the messages you send as replies.

As the automobile ads say, "Your mileage may vary." Outlook is just the pretty face on an elaborate arrangement of other items that make e-mail work. Outlook is like the dashboard of your car; you can use the dashboard to make the car do what you want it to do, but the things that your car can do depend more on what's under the hood than what's on the dashboard. In the same way, some features of Outlook work only if the system that's backing it up supports those features, too. Some features work only if the person to whom you're mailing uses a system that supports advanced features as well.

Microsoft Exchange Server is the name of a program that runs on many corporate networks and adds a number of features to Outlook, such as delaying delivery of messages or diverting messages to someone else. In this book, I don't discuss features you may not have. Feel free to explore the Options dialog boxes and give some of the slicker features a try. If the features work, you'll know that everything's lined up right and you have the necessary bells and whistles. If the features don't work, no loss — Outlook can do plenty, even without the help of Microsoft Exchange Server.

Nagging by Flagging

Some people like to use their list of e-mail messages as a to-do list. You can flag messages to remind yourself about things that you have to do. You can also plant a flag in a message you send to others to remind them of a task that they have to do.

Adding a flag to an e-mail message

You can add flags to e-mail messages for the same reason that you add reminders to tasks and appointments — to help you remember to do something. Reminders can be set for a specific time of day, while flags are set by day, but not time of day.

To attach a flag to your e-mail messages (ones you send and ones that you're sent):

> **1. Choose Go⇨Inbox (or press Ctrl+Shift+I).**
>
> The Inbox screen opens, showing your incoming mail (see Figure 8-1).

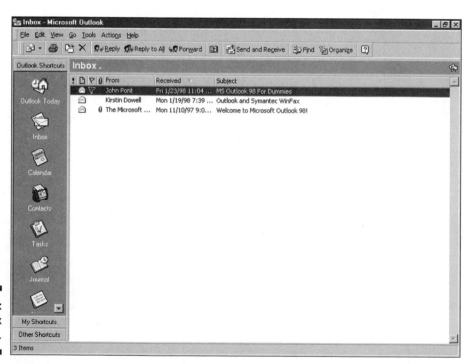

Figure 8-1:
The Inbox
screen.

2. Double-click the message that you want to flag.

The Message dialog box appears.

3. Choose Actions⇨Flag for Followup (or press Ctrl+Shift+G).

The Flag for Follow Up dialog box appears (see Figure 8-2).

Figure 8-2:
Need to add
a flag?

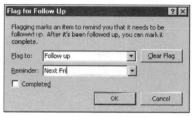

4. Click the triangle at the right end of the Flag To text box and choose one of the menu items or type your own choice.

A handy flag is "Follow Up," to remind you to confirm an appointment or other arrangement.

5. Click the Reminder box and type the date on which you want the reminder flag to appear.

You can type the date **3/3/99**; Outlook understands. You can type **first wednesday of march**; Outlook understands. You can type **a week from Wednesday**; Outlook understands that to mean "seven days after the Wednesday that comes after today." You don't even have to worry about capitalization. Don't type **I hate mondays**, though; Outlook doesn't understand that. (But I do.)

6. Click OK.

When the date you entered in the Flag for Follow Up dialog box arrives, a reminder dialog box pops up to help jog your memory.

Changing the date on a flag

Procrastination used to be an art; Outlook makes it a science. When someone nags you with flags, you can still put it off. Yes, dear, you *can* do it later.

To change the date on a flag:

1. Choose Go⇨Inbox (or press Ctrl+Shift+I).

The Inbox screen opens, showing your incoming mail (see Figure 8-3).

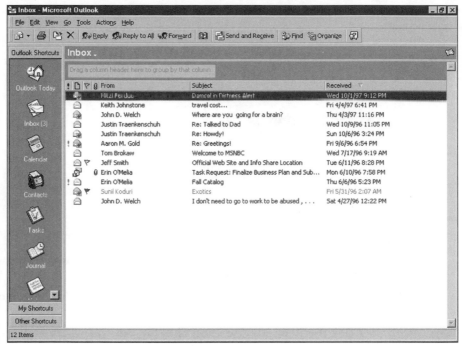

Figure 8-3:
A mass of
messages,
ready for
flags.

2. Double-click the message whose flag you want to change.

The Message dialog box appears.

3. Choose Actions➪Flag for Followup (or press Ctrl+Shift+G).

The Flag for Follow Up dialog box appears (see Figure 8-4).

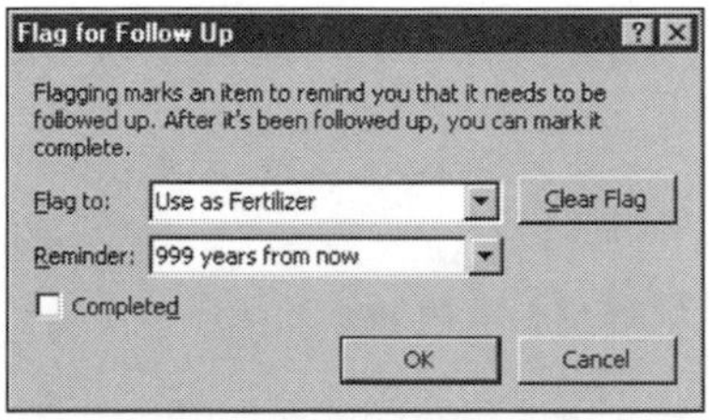

Figure 8-4:
The Flag for
Follow Up
dialog box.

4. Click the Reminder box and type the new date when you want the reminder flag to appear.

Type the date when you'll feel ready to be flagged again. **999 years from now** will work — really!

5. Click OK.

Of course, there's a catch. You can always change the date on the flags that you've set, but if someone sends you a message, flags it, and marks it "Private," you can't change the contents of the flag. Rats!

Saving Copies of Your Messages

Nothing is handier than knowing what you've sent and when you sent it. You can save all your outgoing mail in Outlook so that you can go back and look up the messages you've sent. Outlook starts out saving sent items when you first install the program, but you can turn this feature on and off, so before you go changing your options, look in your Sent Messages folder to see whether it contains messages.

To save copies of your messages:

1. **Choose Tools⇨Options.**

   The Options dialog box appears.

2. **Click the E-Mail Options button.**

   The E-Mail Options dialog box appears (see Figure 8-5).

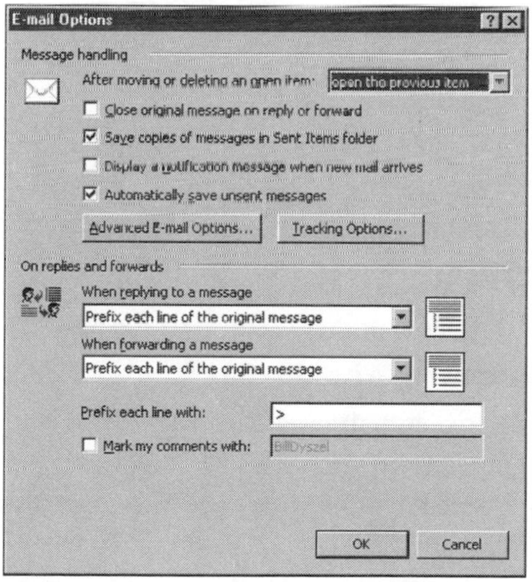

Figure 8-5: You can decide whether to save copies of the messages you send to the Sent Messages folder by using the E-Mail Options dialog box.

3. Click the Save Copies of Messages in Sent Items Folder check box.

If the box already contains a check mark, leave it alone. If you click the box when it's already checked, you turn off your "vote" for saving messages. Don't worry if you make a mistake; you can always change it back. Just make sure a check appears in the box if you want to save messages.

4. Click OK.

Outlook saves two months' worth of saved messages and sends older messages to an archive file to save memory in your computer.

Automatically Adding Your Name to the Original Message When Replying

When you reply to a message, it helps to include parts of the original message that you're replying to, so that the person reading your message knows exactly what you're responding to. The trick is: How will the reader know which comments are his or hers and which are yours?

Outlook allows you to preface your comments with your name or any text that you choose. If you want to be understood, it's best to use your name. If you want to confuse the issue, use a phrase like "Simon says."

To tag your replies with your name:

1. Choose Tools⇨Options.

The Options dialog box appears.

2. Click the E-Mail Options button.

The E-Mail Options dialog box appears (see Figure 8-6).

3. Click the Mark My Comments With check box.

Be sure that the check box isn't already checked or you will remove the check.

4. In the Mark My Comments With text box, enter the text that you want to accompany your annotations.

Your best bet is to enter your name here. Whatever you enter will be used as the prefix to all text you type when replying to messages.

5. Click OK.

Figure 8-6:
To use your
name as a
prefix to all
text you
type in your
message
replies,
check the
Mark My
Comments
With box
and enter
your name
in the text
box to the
right.

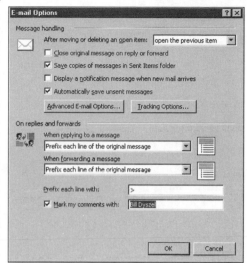

You can select and delete the text of the original message when you create a reply, but including at least a part of the message you're replying to makes your response easier to understand. You also have the option of selecting and deleting the parts of the original text that aren't relevant to your reply.

Setting Your Options

You can control the appearance of the messages that you forward, as well as your replies. If all your e-mail stays in your office among other Office 97 users, you can make your text look pretty incredible in messages you send to one another by adding graphics or wild-looking fonts or special effects like blinking text. If you're sending mail to poor ol' Internet users or to people on an online service such as CompuServe (see Chapter 12 for more about e-mail to online services and the Internet), you need to pay attention to how messages look to those people.

To set your options:

1. **Choose Tools➪Options.**

   The Options dialog box appears.

2. **Click the E-Mail Options button.**

   The E-Mail Options dialog box appears (see Figure 8-7).

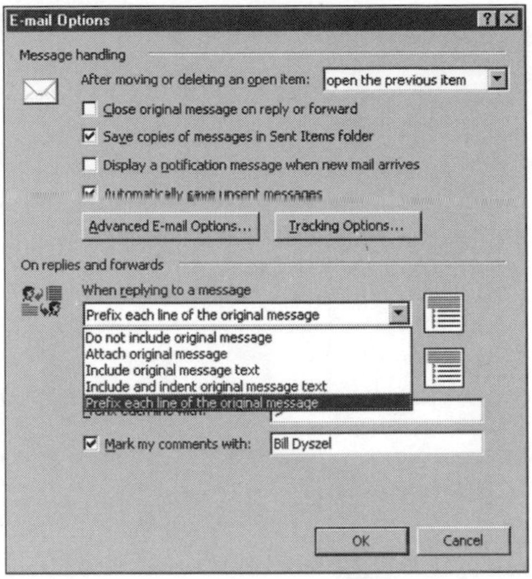

Figure 8-7:
Change the appearance of your outgoing messages by selecting what you need in the E-Mail Options dialog box.

3. Click the scroll-down button (triangle) at the right end of the When Replying to a Message box.

A menu of options drops down. When Outlook is first installed, Include and Indent Original Message Text is the default option. The diagram to the right of the scroll-down menu illustrates how the message will be laid out when you choose each option.

4. Choose the style that you prefer to use for replies.

The little diagram to the right of the menu changes when you make a choice to show you what your choice will look like. If you don't like the choice that you've made, try another and see how it looks in the diagram.

5. Click the triangle at the right end of the When Forwarding a Message box.

The When Forwarding a Message box has one choice fewer than the When Replying to a Message box does, but the two menus work the same way, and they both have that little diagram of the page layout off to the right.

6. Choose the style that you prefer to use for forwarding messages.

Just pick one; you can always change it.

7. Click OK.

You can do all sorts of fancy, exciting, and even useful tricks with e-mail by taking advantage of Outlook's options. If the advanced options seem confusing, you can easily ignore them. Just click Reply and type your answer.

Sending Attachments

If you've already created a document that you want to send to somebody, you don't have to type the document all over again in a message; just send the document as an attachment to an e-mail message. You can attach any kind of file — word-processing documents, spreadsheet files, and presentations from programs such as PowerPoint, for example. Any kind of file can be sent as an attachment.

To send an attachment:

1. **Choose Go➪Inbox (or press Ctrl+Shift+I).**

   The Inbox screen opens, showing your incoming mail.

2. **Choose File➪New➪Mail Message (or press Ctrl+N).**

   The New Message form appears.

3. **Choose Insert➪File or click the paper-clip button in the Message form toolbar.**

   The Insert File dialog box appears (see Figure 8-8). It looks just like the dialog box that you use for opening files in most Windows 95 programs, and it works like opening a file, too. Just click the name of the file you want to send and press Enter.

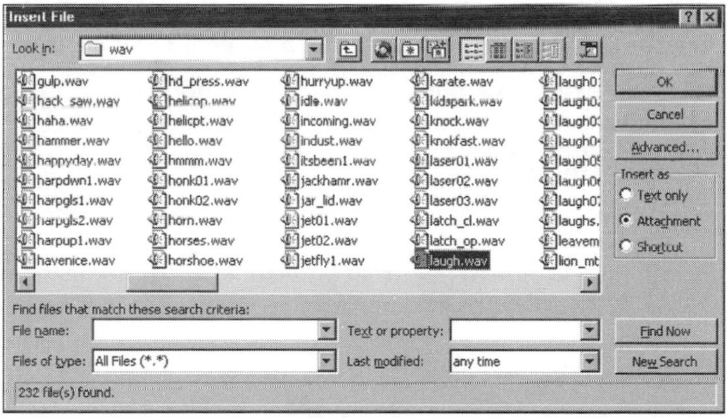

Figure 8-8:
The Insert
File dialog
box.

4. **In the list of files, click the name of the file that you want to send.**

   An icon appears in your text representing the file you've attached to your message.

5. **Click OK.**

   Your Message form now contains an icon. The name of the icon is the same name as the file that you selected, which means that the file is attached. When you send this e-mail message, a copy of the file that you selected will go to your recipient.

6. **Type your message (if you have a message to send).**

   You may not have a message; perhaps you only want to send the attachment. If what you want to say is in the attachment, that's fine, but remember that the contents of an attachment don't show up on the recipient's screen until he or she double-clicks to open the attachment.

7. **Click the To button.**

   The Select Names dialog box appears.

8. **Select a name from your mailing list.**

   If the name of the person to whom you want to send your message isn't in the list, you can click the Cancel button and return to the Message form. Then just type the person's e-mail address in the To text box.

9. **Click the To button.**

   The name of the selected person appears in the To box of the Select Names dialog box.

10. **Click OK.**

    The name of the selected person is now in the To box of the message.

11. **Click the Subject text box and type a subject for your message.**

    Subjects are optional, but if you want somebody to read what you sent, including a subject helps.

12. **Click the Send button.**

    Your message and its attachment are sent.

Those are just a few of the tricks that you can do with the mail you send. You can also do tricks with the mail you get; I cover those tricks in Chapter 9.

Creating Signatures for Your Messages

Many people like to add something called a *signature* to the end of every message they send. A signature is usually a small piece of text that identifies you to everyone reading your message and tells something you want everyone to know. Many people include their name, the name of their business, their motto, a little sales slogan, or some squib of personal information.

You can tell Outlook to automatically add a signature to all your outgoing messages, but first you must create a signature file. Here's how to create your signature file:

1. **Choose Tools⇨Options.**

   The Options dialog box appears.

2. **Click the Mail Format tab.**

   The Mail Format dialog box appears.

3. **Click the Signature Picker button.**

   The Signature Picker dialog box appears (see Figure 8-9).

Figure 8-9:
The
Signature
Picker
dialog box.

4. **Click the New button.**

   The Create New Signature dialog box appears.

5. **Type a name for your new signature.**

   The name you type appears in the Signature box. You can name a signature anything you want.

6. **Click the Next button.**

   The Edit Signature dialog box appears.

7. **Type the text of the signature you want to create.**

   The text you type appears in the Signature Text box. You can put anything you want in a signature, but try to be brief. You don't want your signature to be longer than the message to which it's attached.

8. **Click the Finish button.**

   The Signature Picker dialog box appears.

9. Click OK.

The Mail Format dialog box appears.

10. Click OK.

The Options dialog box appears.

11. Click OK.

Your new signature will now appear on every message you send. If you create more than one signature, you can switch between signatures by following Steps 1 and 2 and then choosing the signature you want from the scroll-down menu next to the words *Use this signature by default.*

Chapter 9

Sorting Your Mail

. . . .

In This Chapter

▶ Setting up a new mail folder

▶ Filing messages in folders

▶ Using and customizing stationery

▶ Looking at your messages

▶ Previewing your messages

▶ Using the Rules Wizard

▶ Sorting junk e-mail

▶ Using Remote Mail

. . . .

1 have good news and bad news about e-mail. The good news is that e-mail is free; you can send as much as you want for virtually no cost. The bad news is that e-mail is free; anybody can easily send you more e-mail than you can possibly read. Before long, you need help sorting it all out so you can deal with messages that need immediate action.

Outlook has some handy tools for coping with the flood of electronic flotsam and jetsam that finds its way into your Inbox. You can create separate folders for filing your mail, and you can use Outlook's view feature to help you slice and dice your incoming messages into manageable groups.

Even better than the view feature is the Rules Wizard, which automatically responds to incoming messages according to your wishes. You can move all messages from certain senders to the folder of your choice, send automatic replies to messages about certain subjects, or delete messages that contain certain words that offend you.

An even more effective way to deal with offensive messages is to use the new junk e-mail filters that are built into Outlook 98. You only need to turn the filters on once — after you do, you'll have a lot less junk mail cluttering up your Inbox.

Creating a New Mail Folder

The simplest way to manage incoming mail is just to file it. Before you file a message, though, you need to create at least one folder in which to file your messages. You have to create a folder only once; it's there for good after you create it. You can create as many folders as you want; you may have dozens or just one or two.

I have folders for filing mail from specific clients, for example. All the e-mail I've received in connection to this book is in a folder called Outlook For Dummies (clever title, eh?). Another folder called Personal contains messages that aren't business related.

To create a folder for new mail:

1. Click the Inbox icon.

The list of messages in your Inbox appears.

2. Choose File⇨New⇨Folder (or press Ctrl+Shift+E).

The Create New Folder dialog box appears.

3. Click the word Inbox in the list of folders at the bottom of the Create New Folder dialog box.

The word Inbox is highlighted (see Figure 9-1).

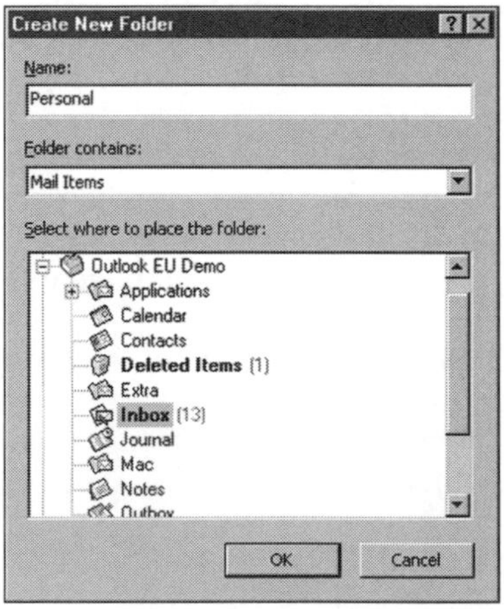

Figure 9-1:
The Create New Folder dialog box with the word Inbox highlighted.

4. In the <u>N</u>ame text box, type a name for your new folder, such as Personal.

You can name the subfolder anything you like. You can also create many folders for saving and sorting your incoming e-mail. Leaving all your mail in your Inbox gets confusing. On the other hand, if you create too many folders, you may be just as confused as if you had only one.

5. Click OK.

You now have a new folder named Personal (or whatever name you entered) for filing messages you want to save for future reference. I like to use three or four mail folders for different types of mail to make it easier to find what I'm looking for.

Moving messages to another folder

Filing your messages is as easy as dragging them from the folder they're in to the folder where you want them. Just click the Inbox to look at your messages when they arrive, and then drag each message to the folder where you want your messages to stay.

To move messages to another folder:

1. Choose <u>Go</u>⇨Inbox (or press Ctrl+Shift+I).

Your list of incoming mail messages appears.

2. Click the title of the message that you want to move.

The message is highlighted.

3. Drag the message to the icon on the Outlook Bar for the folder in which you want to store it.

Your message is moved to the folder to which you dragged it. If you created a folder named Personal (or anything else) in the preceding section of this chapter, you can drag the message there.

The Outlook toolbar has a button called Move to Folder that you can click to move a selected message to the folder of your choice. The best thing about the Move to Folder button is that it remembers the last half-dozen folders to which you moved messages. That feature makes it easy to move messages to folders that may not even appear on your Outlook Bar.

Using stationery

It's only been a few centuries now since preprinted stationery came into fashion for paper mail, so I suppose it's not too early for the same idea to catch on for electronic mail as well.

Stationery is designed to convey a visual impression about your message. With the right choice of stationery, you can make your message look uniquely important, businesslike, or just plain fun.

Unlike paper stationery, you can have an unlimited selection of stationery for your e-mail messages without spending any money on printing and paper. Just pick the design you want from a menu, and there you are! Correspondence Art!

To use stationery:

1. Choose Actions➪New Mail Message Using➪Stationery.

The Select a Stationery dialog box appears, containing a list of each type of stationery you can choose (see Figure 9-2). Each time you click the name of a type of stationery, you see what that stationery looks like in the Preview window.

If the New Mail Message Using command on the Actions menu isn't black and doesn't work when you click it, you need to turn the feature on. Choose Tools➪Options, click the Mail Format tab, and choose HTML from the scroll-down menu at the top of the Mail Format page.

Figure 9-2:
The Select a Stationery dialog box.

2. Double-click the stationery that you want.

The stationery you choose appears. For this example, I chose the Balloon Party Invitation stationery (see Figure 9-3).

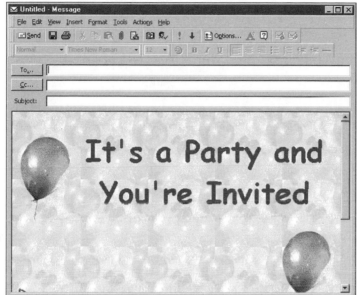

Figure 9-3:
Balloon
Party
Invitation
Stationery.

3. Fill in the information in the form.

You can customize stationery to fit any need. Just click any box where you can put information and enter your desired text. You can replace any existing text on a piece of stationery; just select the text you want to replace by dragging the mouse pointer over the text, and then type the text you want.

4. Click the To button.

The Select Names dialog box appears (see Figure 9-4).

5. Select the name of the person to whom you want to send the message.

The name you click is highlighted to show that you've selected it.

6. Click the To button.

Yes, I know, you clicked the To button before. This one enters the person's name in your e-mail message.

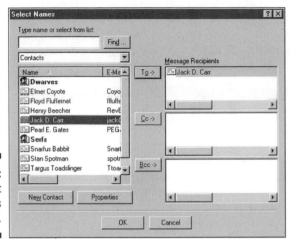

Figure 9-4:
The Select
Names
dialog box.

7. **Click OK.**

   The Select Names dialog box disappears, and the stationery reappears.

8. **Click Send.**

   If your computer is on a network at your office, your message is on its way. If you're using Outlook at home, you have to send your message by choosing Tools➪Check for New Mail. (I know that "Check for New Mail" doesn't sound like what you'd do to send mail, but that's the name for the command.) You can also press F5.

Viewing Your Messages

You can use at least ten views of your messages, beginning with the set that comes with Outlook. You can modify each view by sorting on any column of information in any view by clicking the title of that column. Any of these views works in any mail folder, and the mechanics of using views of your mail are the same as the mechanics of using views in other Outlook modules. For an overview of views in Outlook, see Chapter 5.

I'm describing the menu method of changing views here simply for reliability. You can also click the Organize button in the toolbar, then click Views, and pick a view from there. You can turn off the toolbar, but the menus are always there.

Messages view

Messages view is the no-frills picture of your Inbox — From, To, Subject, just the basics. Messages that you haven't read yet are listed in boldface type; the others are listed in plain type.

To see your Inbox in Messages view:

1. From the Inbox, Choose View⇨Current View.

The list of views available in the current module appears. You need to be in the Inbox to view your incoming messages.

2. Choose Messages.

The Messages view of your Inbox appears, listing your messages by author, date, and subject (see Figure 9-5). You can view any of them by double-clicking the title, or you can get a short preview by switching to AutoPreview.

I like to leave my Inbox in the Messages view or the AutoPreview view. Because I've set up folders for sorting other personal mail, I normally move incoming messages to other folders where I manage them by applying different views.

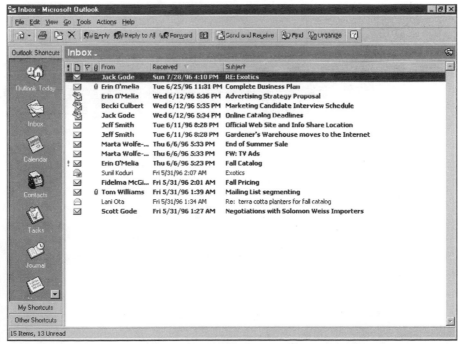

Figure 9-5:
The Messages view of your Inbox.

AutoPreview view

When you don't have time to read all the messages you get, a preview is helpful. The first few lines can give you a hint as to which messages you want to read. AutoPreview shows you these first few lines. To use AutoPreview:

1. **Choose View⇨Current View.**

   The list of available views appears.

2. **Choose Messages with AutoPreview.**

   Your messages appear with AutoPreview (see Figure 9-6).

Normally, you see previews only of messages that you haven't read yet. You see only the titles of messages that you have read. Actually, Outlook assumes that you've read any message you've opened. You can also mark a message read or unread by right-clicking it and choosing Mark as Read or Mark as Unread. I sometimes mark messages as Read and then delete them when I've judged from their preview or return address that I'm not interested in reading them. Sometimes I mark a message Unread after I read it if it's a long message that I'd like to devote more time to later. Marking a message unread makes the blue AutoPreview text appear, which helps jog my memory.

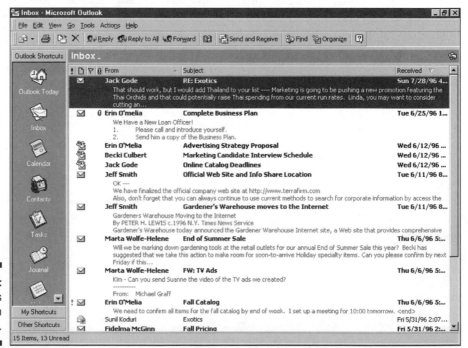

Figure 9-6:
Messages
with
AutoPreview.

Flagged view

You can flag incoming messages to help you keep track of what you have to do in response to each message. Flagged view groups your messages according to whether flags are set on the messages, and lists what kinds of flags are set and when they're due. For more about flagging, refer to Chapter 8.

To use the Flagged view (also called the By Follow Up Flag view):

1. Choose View⇨Current View.

The list of current views appears.

2. Choose By Follow Up Flag.

Your messages appear organized in two groups, Flagged and Normal (see Figure 9-7). Normal in this case means it's not flagged.

Some experts say that the most efficient way to deal with all your incoming messages is to file them according to what you need to do with them and then act upon them according to each message's priority and timing. Message flags are one handy way of getting a handle on what you have to do with the messages that you get. By Follow Up Flag view automatically organizes your messages according to the action that they demand, making you instantly efficient, right?

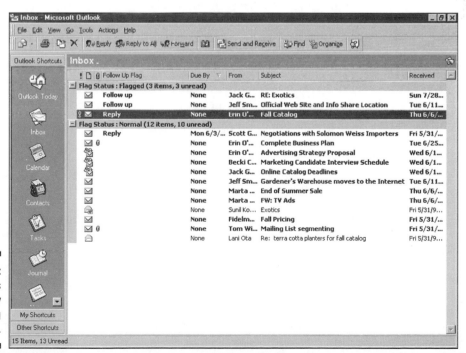

Figure 9-7:
Messages
in By Follow
Up Flag
view.

Last Seven Days view

When you're asked to take immediate action on a message you received a few days ago, it's not always easy to find the message that told you what to do, especially if you get lots of e-mail. Last Seven Days view shows you only the messages that you got within the past week. Finding an item in a short list is easier than in a long one.

To use the Last Seven Days view:

1. **Choose View⇨Current View.**

   The list of current views appears.

2. **Choose Last Seven Days.**

   You see the messages you received during the last seven days.

The Last Seven Days list limits your view to messages that arrive in a seven-day time period. It does not sort messages according to what's in them or who sent them. You can sort your messages according to the name of the sender or the subject of the message by clicking the titles at the top of the columns in the view.

Flagged for Next Seven Days view

If you're flagging messages that are really important, the messages that you've flagged to get your attention in the next few days are likely to require your attention first. For a quick look at the hottest of the hot items, use Flagged for Next Seven Days view.

To see the Flagged for Next Seven Days view:

1. **Choose View⇨Current View.**

   The list of current views drops down.

2. **Choose Flagged for Next Seven Days view.**

   Your messages appear in Flagged for Next Seven Days view (see Figure 9-8).

Like Flagged view, Flagged for Next Seven Days view cuts to the essentials: who sent the message, the subject of the message, and when action is due on the message that is marked.

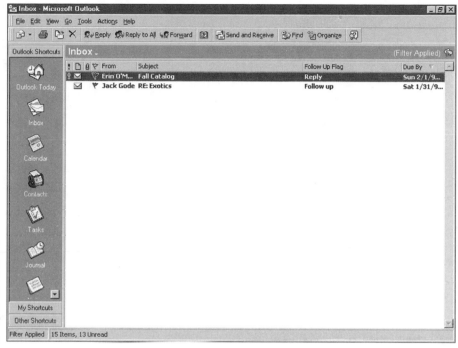

By Conversation Topic view

You should always include a subject line that's easy to understand, so that the person who gets your message will know at first glance the topic of your message and what to do about it. With any luck, other people will do the same thing for you. Then you can really get some mileage from your messages by sorting them in By Conversation Topic view.

To sort messages By Conversation Topic:

1. **Choose View⇨Current View.**

    The list of current views appears.

2. **Choose By Conversation Topic view.**

    Your messages appear in By Conversation Topic view (see Figure 9-9).

When you select By Conversation Topic view, Outlook groups your messages according to their subject lines and puts a plus or minus sign next to their titles. Plus signs tell you that more messages will appear under that title if you click on the plus. A minus sign next to a title means that no more messages are to be seen under that title.

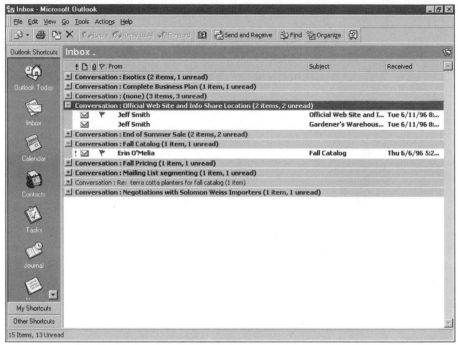

Figure 9-9:
The By
Conversation
Topic view.

When groups of people carry on discussions by e-mail, they normally just click the Reply button and type their two-cents' worth, so all the messages have the same subject line. After a while, the messages resemble a conversation, with each message responding to the contents of one or more of the earlier messages. These e-mail conversations are often called *threads*.

When you participate in an e-mail conversation, it's best if you don't edit the subject line unless you plan to change the subject. That way, everybody else in the conversation knows that you're participating in the same conversation.

By Sender view

When the boss calls and asks, "Did you get the e-mail message about bonuses that I sent you three weeks ago?" you probably don't want to spend a great deal of time sorting through everybody else's messages from the past three weeks. The quickest way to answer the boss's question promptly is to switch to By Sender view.

To use the By Sender view:

1. **Choose <u>V</u>iew⇨Current <u>V</u>iew.**

    The list of current views appears.

2. **Choose By Sender view.**

    Your messages appear in the By Sender view (see Figure 9-10).

You can instantly find the boss's name in By Sender view. Double-click the message titled Bonuses. Then you can tell the boss, "I certainly did; it's right here in front of me." You'll be able to reply so quickly that the boss will be glad to give you that bonus.

Unread Messages view

You don't have to read every message that comes across your screen, but Murphy's Law says that the most important information will be in a message that you haven't read yet. The Unread Messages view gives you a quick peek at the things you haven't taken a quick peek at yet.

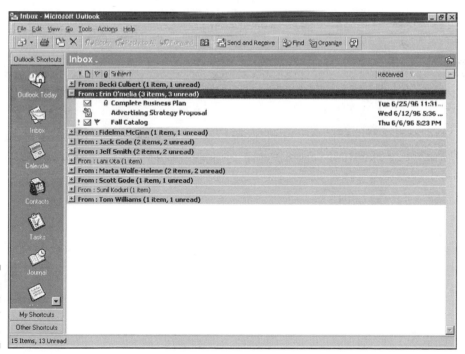

Figure 9-10:
The By
Sender
view.

To see the Unread Messages view:

1. **Choose View⇨Current View.**

   The Current View menu appears.

2. **Choose Unread Messages view.**

   Your unread messages appear (see Figure 9-11).

Don't leave your Inbox in the Unread Messages view all the time because messages will seem to vanish when you finish reading them. It's easier to use Messages view most of the time and switch to Unread Messages view now and then as a strategy for finding things.

Sent To view

It may seem silly to have a view of your Inbox sorted according to the name of the person each message is sent to. After all, it's your Inbox; everything should be sent to you, or it wouldn't be here, right?

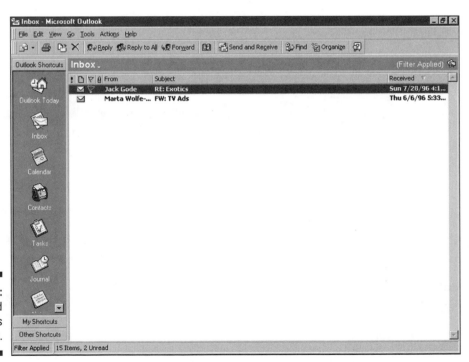

Figure 9-11:
The Unread
Messages
view.

You have two reasons for using Sent To view. Some messages that come to you are addressed to everybody at your company, for example, so it's good to know that certain messages shouldn't be taken personally. The second reason is that the same set of views is available in the Inbox and the Sent Items folder. The Sent Items folder is where Outlook keeps copies of messages that you've sent to other people. Knowing what you sent to whom can come in very handy.

To use the Sent To view:

1. Choose <u>V</u>iew⇨Current <u>V</u>iew.

The list of current views appears.

2. Choose Sent To view.

Your list is rearranged according to whom the message was sent (see Figure 9-12).

Sent To view is only sorted, not grouped, which means that the messages appear in order of the names of the people who sent them. A grouped view would display as the heading of a group the name of each person who has sent you mail. If you click the Subject column, you lose the benefit of having the list sorted by sender. If your Sent To list appears to be sorted incorrectly, just click the word To at the top of the To column.

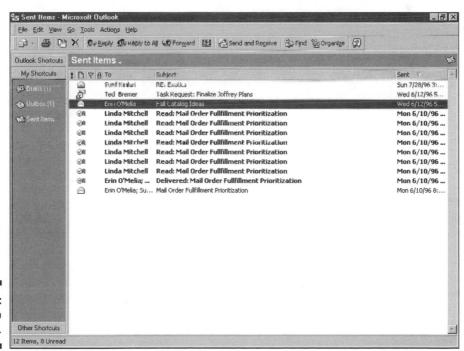

Figure 9-12:
The Sent To
View.

Message Timeline view

Message Timeline view is one of the most interesting views in Outlook; it draws you a graph of all your messages according to when they arrived. Message Timeline view is designed to help you find messages when you can remember when they arrived but not why they arrived or who sent them.

To use Message Timeline view:

1. **Choose View➪Current View.**

    The list of current views appears.

2. **Choose Message Timeline view.**

    The Message Timeline view appears (see Figure 9-13).

The little icons that represent the messages are actually shortcuts to the messages that they represent. You can open a message by double-clicking the icon for that message. You can also right-click the message icon to reply to a message, delete a message, or move a message to another folder.

Figure 9-13:
The
Message
Timeline
view.

Using the Preview Pane

If you need to skim through a whole bunch of messages quickly, the Preview Pane can help. When you choose View➪Preview Pane, the Inbox screen divides into two sections. The top section shows your list of messages; the bottom shows the contents of the message you've selected in the top section (see Figure 9-14). To move from one message to the next, just press the down-arrow key. You can also view any message in your Inbox by clicking the title of the message.

The difference between looking at messages in the Preview Pane and looking at them in AutoPreview mode is that you can see graphics and formatting in the Preview Pane, but you can only see the text of a message in the AutoPreview mode. If your friends send you messages using Outlook Stationery, for example, you can appreciate their graphic genius by viewing their messages in the Preview Pane.

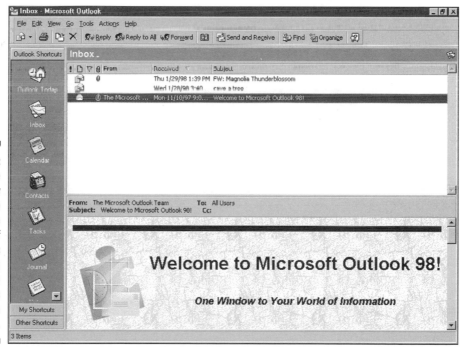

Figure 9-14: The Preview Pane displays the list of messages along with the contents of one message.

Using Rules

Rules are probably my favorite feature in Outlook. I get tons of e-mail messages, and I can easily waste the whole day sorting through them. Outlook uses rules to automatically sort my incoming mail into different folders so that I can waste a little less time wading through all the messages.

I don't know exactly how many different rules you can create with the Rules Wizard, but I'm sure that you can create more rules than you and I will ever need.

The Rules Wizard is called a Wizard because of the way the program leads you step by step to create each rule. The process is pretty simple. Here's how you create a simple rule to move an incoming message from a certain person to a certain folder:

1. **Choose Go➪Inbox (or press Ctrl+Shift+I).**

   The list of messages in your Inbox appears.

2. **Choose Tools➪Rules Wizard.**

   The Rules Wizard dialog box appears (see Figure 9-15).

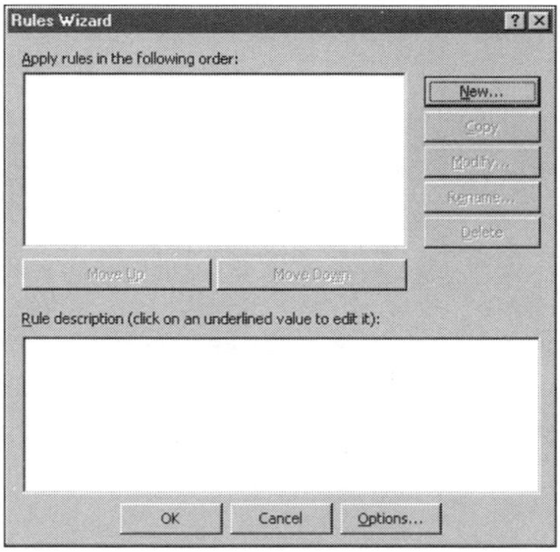

Figure 9-15:
The Rules Wizard dialog box lets you make the rules.

3. **Click the New button.**

   A dialog box for creating new rules appears. The dialog box contains a list of the types of rules you can create.

4. Choose the type of rule you want to create.

The Rules Wizard offers several common types of rules that you may want to create, such as `Move new messages from someone`, `Assign categories to sent messages`, or `Notify me when important messages arrive` (see Figure 9-16). Another choice is `Build as I go`, when you want to create rules that don't quite fit the Rules Wizard's predefined types. For this example, I suggest choosing `Move new messages from someone`. The words `Apply this rule after the message arrives from people or distribution list move it to the specified folder` appear in the Rule Description box at the bottom of the dialog box.

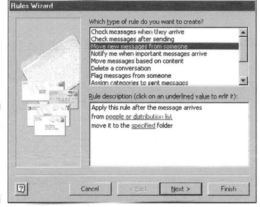

Figure 9-16:
Choose the type of rule you want to create.

5. Click the first piece of underlined text in the Rule Description box, which says *people or distribution list*.

Your address book appears.

6. Double-click the name of the person whose messages you want to move to a new folder.

The name of the person you choose replaces the words `people or distribution list`.

7. Click the next piece of underlined text in the Rule Description box, which is the word *specified*.

Another dialog box opens to let you choose the folder to which you want to move the message (see Figure 9-17).

Figure 9-17:
Choose the folder to which your messages will go.

8. **Double-click the name of the folder to which you want to move messages.**

   The dialog box closes, and the name of the folder you choose appears in the sentence in the Rule Description box.

9. **Click Finish.**

   The first Rules Wizard dialog box appears with a list of all your rules. Each rule has a check box next to it. You can turn rules on and off by clicking the check boxes. If a check mark appears next to a rule, it's turned on; otherwise, the rule is turned off.

10. **Click OK to close the Rules Wizard.**

Rules can do much more than just sort incoming messages. You can create rules that automatically reply to certain messages, flag messages with a particular word in the subject, delete messages about specific topics . . . the sky's the limit.

Filtering Junk E-Mail

The Junk E-Mail filter is a special kind of rule that looks over all your incoming mail and automatically moves anything that looks like junk e-mail to a special folder. You can delete everything that gets moved to your Junk E-Mail folder now and again after checking to make sure that Outlook didn't mistakenly move real e-mail to your Junk E-Mail folder.

I don't entirely know how Outlook figures out which messages are junk and which are real. I find that some junk e-mail still gets through, but Outlook catches more than half of the junk messages I get. Once or twice I've seen it dump items from real people into the Junk E-Mail folder. Outlook once sent a message from my father to the Junk E-Mail folder; I've been checking the Junk E-Mail folder regularly every since.

You need to turn Junk E-Mail filtering on so that Outlook knows that you want the junk e-mail moved. You also need to make separate choices about whether you want to get rid of plain junk mail and adult-oriented junk mail. Some folks like junk mail; who's to say?

To turn on Junk E-Mail filtering:

1. **Choose <u>T</u>ools⇨Organi<u>z</u>e (or click the Organize button on the Toolbar).**

   The Organize window appears.

2. **Click the Junk E-Mail link in the Organize window.**

   The text in the right portion of the Organize window changes to reveal controls related to Junk E-Mail.

3. **Click the scroll-down button next to the word Automatically in each line of the Organize window and choose Move from the list.**

   The word *Move* appears in the scroll-down menus (see Figure 9-18).

4. **Click the top Turn ON button to the right of the scroll-down menu that says Junk E-Mail.**

   If you've never created a Junk E-Mail folder before, a dialog box appears, asking whether you want to create one.

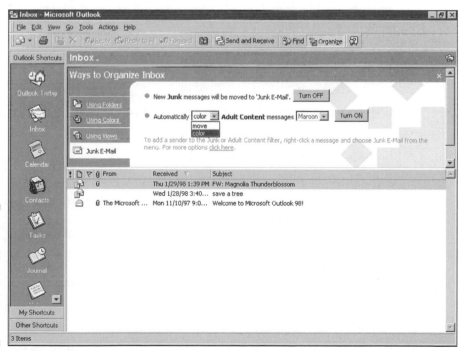

Figure 9-18: Junk E-Mail filters let you give color to off-color messages, too.

5. **Click Yes.**

   The Turn ON button that you clicked changes to a button called Turn OFF.

6. **Click the lower Turn ON button.**

   Both buttons now say Turn OFF.

7. **Choose Tools⇨Organize (or click the Organize button on the Toolbar).**

   The Organize window closes.

Using Remote Mail

Lots of people get lots of e-mail messages every day. If you get messages by the bushel but you only really need to see one or two things, Outlook's Remote Mail feature can help you cull through your mess of messages and pick out the few that you really want to see. Remote Mail dials your online service and shows you the names of the messages that are waiting for you. You can mark the messages that you think are important and have Outlook just get the messages you marked.

Remote Mail is especially helpful when you're checking e-mail from a laptop computer while traveling. Messages that are especially long or have big fat files attached can take a long time to send over a telephone connection. Remote mail lets you skip the messages you don't want to wait for and focus on the messages you really need.

Here's how to use Remote Mail to pick and choose your messages:

1. **Choose Go⇨Inbox (or press Ctrl+Shift+I).**

   The list of messages in your Inbox appears.

2. **Choose Tools⇨Remote Mail⇨Connect.**

   The Remote Mail dialog box appears (see Figure 9-19).

3. **Click the name of the online service on which you want to see titles of your waiting messages.**

   A check mark appears next to the names of the services you select.

4. **Click Next.**

   The Remote Connection Wizard dialog box appears.

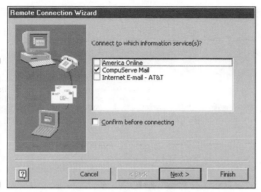

Figure 9-19:
Check off
the services
you want to
check with
Remote
Mail.

5. Click the button that says Do only the following.

The button is colored black when you choose it. A line for each message service you choose appears in the box saying something like `Retrieve new message headers via the Microsoft Network`. Be sure that a check mark appears next to each service that you want to check.

6. Click Finish to start the Remote Mail session.

The Remote Mail status box remains on the screen until the session is complete. When the Remote session is complete, the titles of any messages you have waiting on your online service appear in your Inbox with a special icon, indicating that the message is still at the online service, waiting for you to retrieve it. You can't read messages until you retrieve them. A new toolbar, called Remote, also appears.

7. Right-click each message that you want to retrieve.

A shortcut menu appears (see Figure 9-20).

8. Choose Mark to Retrieve.

A second icon appears next to each message that you mark to retrieve.

9. Click the Connect icon on the Remote toolbar.

The Remote Connection Wizard dialog box appears again. Check to see that a check mark is next to the name of the service from which you want to retrieve messages. The last service you used is normally still checked.

10. Click Next.

The dialog box for the next step of the Remote Connection Wizard appears.

11. Click Finish.

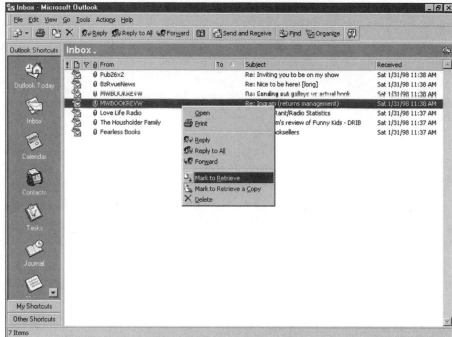

Figure 9-20:
Picking by
clicking;
right-
click the
messages
you want to
mark for
retrieval.

Although Remote mail can save you some time now, you may find the process a bit too complicated to use every day. If you really get scads and scads of messages, you'll find Remote Mail necessary from time to time. Normally, however, you're better off just pressing F5 to send and receive all messages.

Chapter 10

Your Little Black Book: Creating Contact Lists

• •

In This Chapter

▶ Storing names and addresses

▶ Checking out the view

▶ Sorting and rearranging views

▶ Using grouped views

▶ Finding names in your Contact lists

▶ Sending a vCard

• •

*H*ardly anybody works alone. Even if you work at home, you always have people you need to keep track of — people you sell things to, buy things from, have lunch with, or any of dozens of things you need to do with other people. All that personal information can be hard to store in a way you can find and use again quickly when you need it. And you need to know different things about people in different parts of your life. So you need a tool that's flexible enough to let you organize names, addresses, and all that other information in ways that make sense in different contexts.

For example, I work as a computer consultant and write for computer magazines. The information I need to keep about consulting clients (systems, software, hours, locations, and networks) differs from the information I need for dealing with people in the publishing business (editors, deadlines, topics, and so on). I'm also still active as a professional singer and actor, and my contacts in those businesses are two entirely different kettles of fish. But when someone calls on the phone, or when I want to do a mailing to a group from one world or another, I need to be able to look up the person right away, regardless of which category the person fits in.

Outlook is flexible enough to let me keep all my name and address information in a single place but sort, view, find, and print it differently, depending on what kind of work I'm doing. You can also keep lists of family and friends stored in Outlook right alongside your business contacts and still distinguish them from one another quickly when the need arises.

Storing Names, Numbers, and Other Stuff

Storing lots of names, addresses, and phone numbers is no big trick, but finding them again can take magic unless you have a tool like Outlook. You may have used other programs for storing names and related numbers, but Outlook ties the name and number information together more tightly with the work you do that uses names, addresses, and phone numbers, such as scheduling and task management.

If you've ever used a little pocket address book, you pretty much know how to use Outlook's contacts feature. Simply enter the name, address, phone number, a few juicy tidbits, and there you are!

To store a name in the Outlook Contacts module, follow these steps:

1. **Choose <u>G</u>o⇨<u>Co</u>ntacts.**

   The Contact list appears (see Figure 10-1).

2. **Choose <u>Fil</u>e⇨<u>N</u>ew⇨<u>C</u>ontact.**

   The New Contact form appears.

   To be really quick about it, press Ctrl+Shift+C instead to see the form shown in Figure 10-2.

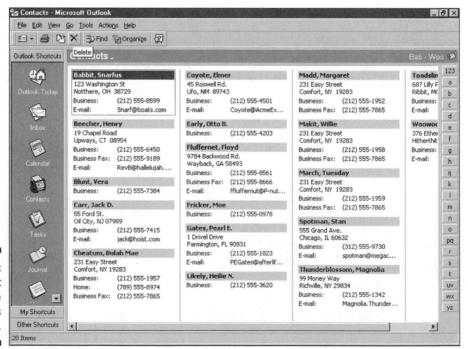

Figure 10-1:
The Contact list in the Contacts module.

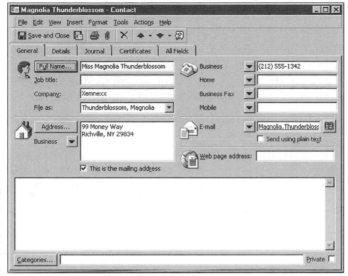

Figure 10-2:
The New
Contact
form.

3. **Click the Fu̲ll Name button.**

   The Check Full Name dialog box appears (see Figure 10-3):

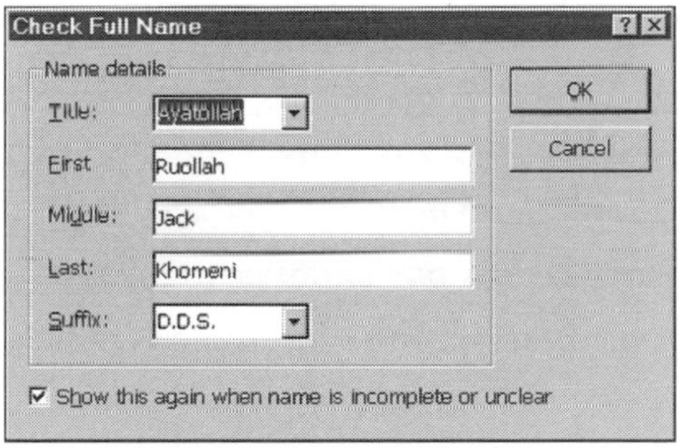

Figure 10-3:
The Check
Full Name
dialog box.

- Click the triangle (called the scroll-down button) on the right edge of the Title text box and choose a title from the list that drops down, such as Mr., Ms., or Dr., or type one in, such as **Rev.**, **Ayatollah**, or whatever.

- Click in the Fi̲rst text box and enter the contact's first name.

- Click in the Mi̲ddle text box and enter the contact's middle initial (if any). If there's no middle initial, you can leave this box blank.

- Click in the <u>L</u>ast text box and enter the contact's last name.

- Click in the <u>S</u>uffix drop-down list and choose a suffix, such as Jr., III, or type one in the box, such as **Ph.D.**, **D.D.S.**, or **B.P.O.E.**

- Click OK. The Check Full Name dialog box closes, and you are back in the New Contact form, where the name you entered is now shown in both the F<u>u</u>ll Name and Fi<u>l</u>e As text boxes.

4. **Click in the appropriate box and enter the information requested on the New Contact form.**

   If the information is not available — for example, if the contact has no job title — leave the box blank. A triangle after the box indicates a drop-down list with choices you can select. If your choice is not listed, enter your choice into the box.

   - If you've entered a name in the F<u>u</u>ll Name box, the Fi<u>l</u>e As box will already contain that name.

   - If you want this person filed under something other than his or her name, click in the Fi<u>l</u>e As box and type in your preferred designation. For example, you may want to file your dentist's name under the term *Dentist* rather than by name. If you put Dentist in the Fi<u>l</u>e As box, the name turns up under Dentist in the alphabetical listing rather than under the name itself. Both the F<u>u</u>ll Name and the Fi<u>l</u>e As designation exist in your Contact list. That way, for example, you can search for your dentist either by name or the word *Dentist*.

5. **Click the A<u>d</u>dress button to open the Check Address dialog box.**

   - Click the <u>S</u>treet text box and type in the contact's street address.

   - Click the <u>C</u>ity text box and type in the contact's city.

   - Click the St<u>a</u>te/Province text box and type in the contact's state.

   - Click the <u>Z</u>IP/Postal Code box and type in the contact's postal code.

   - Click the triangle at the right end of the C<u>o</u>untry box and choose the contact's country if Outlook has not already chosen the correct one.

   See Figure 10-4 for a look at a completed Check Address dialog box.

6. **Click OK.**

   The Check Address dialog box closes.

7. **Click the check box on the New Contact form next to** This Is the Mailing Address, **if the address you've just entered is the address you plan to use for sending mail to the contact.**

8. **Click in the text box to the right of the Business phone box, and type in the contact's business phone number.**

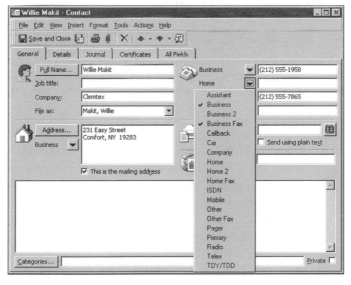

Figure 10-4:
The Check
Address
dialog box.

9. Click in the text box to the right of the Home phone box, and type in the contact's home phone number.

For numbers other than Business and Home phones, click the triangle to the right of the phone number type block and choose the kind of number you're entering. Then enter the number.

The New Contact form has four phone number blocks. Any of them can be used for any of the 19 phone number types that are available in the drop-down list. You can also add custom fields so that you can include more than four phone numbers for a single contact. For the person who has everything, you can create custom fields for that person's Ski Phone, Submarine Phone, Gym Phone — as many as you want. For more about Custom Fields, see Chapter 24.

You can choose any of 19 phone number types to enter, depending on what types of phone numbers your contacts have (see Figure 10-5).

Figure 10-5:
You can
always get
your
contact at
one of
these types
of phone
numbers.

10. Click in the E-Mail text box and enter your contact's e-mail address.

If your contact has more than one e-mail address, click the triangle at the left edge of the E-Mail box (see Figure 10-6), select E-mail 2, and then click in the text box and enter the second address.

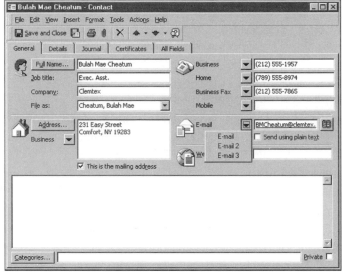

Figure 10-6:
You can enter more than one e-mail address for each person in your Contact list.

11. Click in the Web Page text box if the contact has a Web page, and enter the URL address for that page if you want to be able to link to that page directly from the Address Card.

URL is a fancy name for the address of a page on the World Wide Web. When you see ads on TV that refer to www.discovery.com or www.dummies.com, what you're seeing is a *Uniform Resource Locator,* or URL. You can view a Web page by entering the URL for the page in the Address box of your Web browser. If a person or company in your Outlook Contact list has a Web page, you can enter the URL for that page in the Web Page box. To view the Web page for a contact, select the contact and choose Contact➪Explore Web Page (or press Ctrl+Shift+X); your Web browser opens and loads the contact's Web page.

12. Click in the large text box at the bottom of the form and type in anything you want.

You can enter directions, details about meetings, the Declaration of Independence — anything you want (preferably something that can help you in your dealings with the contact).

Format the text in the big text box (see Figure 10-7) by using the buttons on the formatting toolbar, if you want. The tools on the formatting toolbar are just like the ones all the other word-processing programs use: font, point size, bold, italic, justification, and color. Select the text you want to format and change formatting. You can change the formatting of a single letter or the whole text box. You can't format the text in the smaller data text boxes in the other parts of the Contact form — only in the big text box at the bottom of the form. If your formatting toolbar isn't showing, choose View➪Toolbars➪Formatting from the Contact form menu.

13. Click the Categories button at the bottom left of the screen to assign a category to the contact, if you want.

Assigning categories is another trick to help you find things easily. For an example of how to use categories with any Outlook item, see Chapter 14. After you assign categories to Outlook items, you can easily sort or group the items according to a category you've assigned.

Choose one of the existing categories if one suits you, and then click OK (see Figure 10-8).

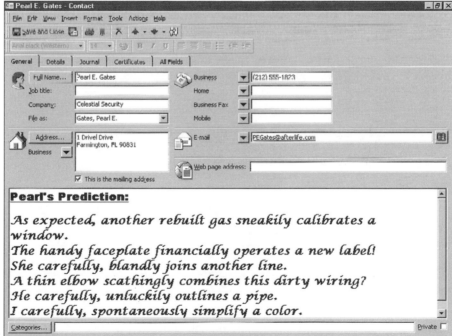

Figure 10-7:
Have fun with formatting in the Contact text box.

Figure 10-8:
Put your
contact in a
category
for easy
reference.

14. **If none of the existing categories suits you, click Master Category List in the lower-right corner to see the Master Category list box.**

    Type a category of your choice in the New box (see Figure 10-9). Be sure not to add too many new categories, because doing that could make it hard to find things.

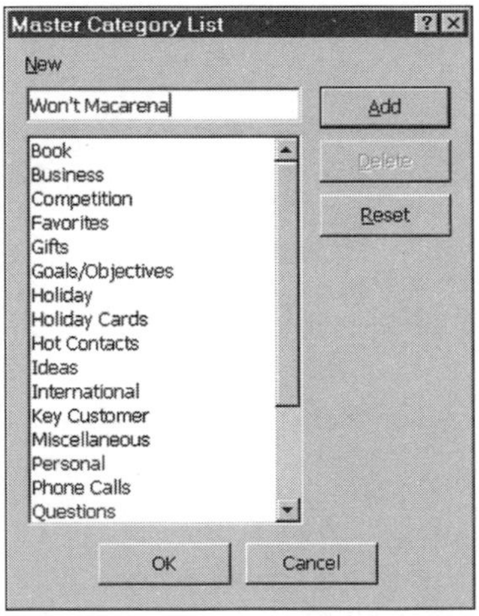

Figure 10-9:
Enter
your own
category in
the Master
Category
List.

15. **Click Add and then click OK to return to the Categories list.**

    Choose the new category from the list if you want. You can choose more than one category at a time.

16. **Click the Private box in the lower-right corner of the New Contact form if you're on a network and you don't want others to know about your contacts.**

17. **Click the Journal tab at the top left of the form to open the Journal page and set your Journaling Preferences.**

    Journaling is a handy feature that lets you keep track of all your activities with any person, place, or thing you deal with on your computer. You may as well turn Journaling on in case you want to use it later:

    • To activate your journal, click in the check box that says Automatically Record Journal Entries for This Contact.

    • When you're first entering a contact, it's best to leave the Show Journal Entries choice as All (see Figure 10-10). If you don't want to show all Journal entries related to the contact, click the triangle (scroll button) at the right of the Show Journal Entries menu and choose an entry you'd like to display.

18. **When you're done, click Save and Close.**

After you enter anything you want or need (or may need) to know about people you deal with at work, you're ready to start dealing.

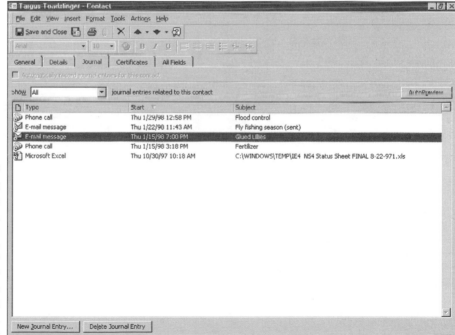

Figure 10-10:
With the Journal on, you have a complete record of all your activities with this contact.

Viewing Contacts

After you enter your contact information, Outlook lets you see the information arranged in many different and useful ways, called *views*. Viewing your contact information and sorting the views are quick ways to get the big picture of the data you've entered (see Chapter 5 for more information on views). Outlook comes with anywhere from five to 12 predefined views in each module. You can easily alter any predefined view. Then you can name and save your altered view and use it just like the predefined views that come with Outlook.

To change the view of your Contact list:

1. **Choose Go⇨Contacts.**

   The Contact list box appears.

2. **Choose View⇨Current View and pick the view you want.**

   You can shift between views like you can switch television stations, so don't worry about changing views and changing back. Figure 10-11 shows the Current View menu and its list of views for Contacts. The Detailed Address Cards view is selected.

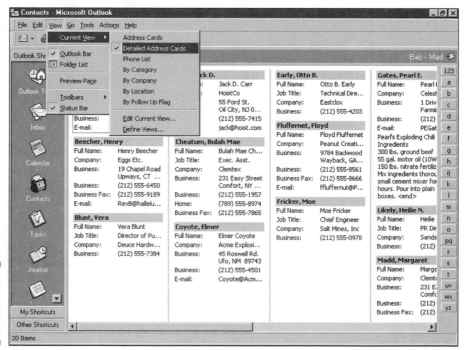

Figure 10-11:
The Detailed
Address
Cards view.

3. **Choose Address Cards from the drop-down menu (or whatever other view you want).**

   You can also choose Detailed Address Cards, Phone List, By Category, By Company, By Location, or whatever other views are listed.

4. **You see the Address Cards view as shown in Figure 10-12 (or whatever other predefined view you select).**

To use one of the other views, repeat the preceding steps and choose the view you want.

Sorting a view

Some views are organized as simple lists, such as the Phone List view of the Contacts module. Figure 10-13 shows the Phone List: a column of names on the left, followed by a column of company names, and so on.

If you're missing one view that is arranged in columns, all you have to do to sort that column is to click once on the title of the column. For example, suppose you want to see the names of the people who work for IBM who are entered in your Contact list. One easy way to see all their names at once is to sort on the Company column:

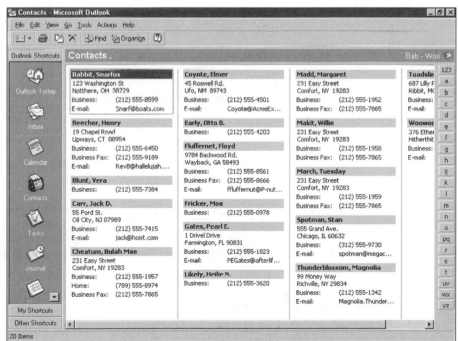

Figure 10-12: Your contacts in Address Cards view.

Figure 10-13:
The Phone
List view.

1. **Choose View⇨Current View.**

   The list of views appears.

2. **Choose the Phone List view.**

   Your list of contacts appears in the Phone List view.

3. **Click the head of the Company column.**

   You see a little icon with the letters AFZ and an arrow. That tells you that Outlook is sorting the column in alphabetical order. If you only have a few items to sort, the icon may flash by so quickly you don't notice it. When you have a really long list to sort, the icon may stay there for several seconds as Outlook sorts your list.

After you've sorted your list, it's easier to find the name of somebody by scrolling down to that part of the alphabet. If you sort by company, all the contacts line up in order of company name, so you can scroll down to the section of your list where all the people from a certain company are listed.

Rearranging views

You can rearrange views simply by dragging the column title and dropping the title where you want it. For example, to move the Business Phone column in the Phone List view:

1. Choose View⇨Current View⇨Phone List.

The Phone List view of your contacts appears.

2. Click on the Business Phone heading and drag it on top of the column to its left.

You see a pair of red arrows pointing to the border between the two columns to the left of the Business Phone column. The red arrows tell you where Outlook will drop the column when you release the mouse button (see Figure 10-14).

3. Release the mouse button.

The Business Phone column is now to the left of the File As column rather than the right. If it makes more sense to you to have File As to the right of Business Phone, you can set up your view in Outlook to do just that.

You can use the same process to move any column in any Outlook view. Because the screen is not as wide as the list, you may need to move columns around at times to see what you really want to see. For example, the Phone List in Figure 10-14 shows eight columns, but the list in that view really has 12 columns. You must use the scroll bar at the bottom of the list to scroll to the right to see the last column, Categories. If you want to see the Categories column at the same time as the Full Name column, you have to move the Categories column to the left.

Figure 10-14:
You can rearrange columns in any Outlook view by dragging the column heading to the location you desire.

Using grouped views

Sometimes sorting just isn't enough. Contact lists can get pretty long after awhile — you can easily collect a few thousand contacts in a few years. Sorting a list that long means that, if you're looking for stuff starting with the letter *M,* the item you want to find will be about three feet below the bottom of your monitor screen, no matter what you do.

Groups are the answer, and I don't mean Outlook Anonymous. Outlook already offers you several predefined lists that use grouping.

You can view several types of lists in Outlook: A sorted list is like a deck of playing cards laid out in numerical order, starting with the deuces, then the threes, then the fours, and so on up through the picture cards. A grouped view is like seeing the cards arranged with all the hearts in one row, then all the spades, then the diamonds, and then the clubs. Outlook also has several other view types that don't apply to contacts, like Timeline and Address Cards.

Gathering items of similar types into groups is handy for tasks like finding all the people on your list who work for a certain company when you want to send congratulations on a new piece of business. Because grouping by company is so frequently useful, the By Company view (see Figure 10-15) is set up as a predefined view in Outlook.

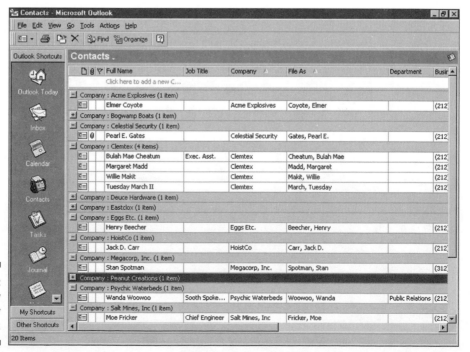

Figure 10-15:
The By Company view.

To use the By Company view:

1. **Choose Go⇨Contacts.**

   The Contacts module opens with its current view displayed.

2. **Choose View⇨Current View⇨By Company.**

   If you've made any changes in the view you were just using, a dialog box appears, asking you to Discard, Save, or Update the Current View. Choose Discard.

   Each gray bar labeled Company: (name of company) has a little box at the left with a plus or minus sign on it. Click a plus sign to see additional names in that category; a minus sign indicates that no more entries are available.

3. **Click the plus icon to see entries for the company listed on the gray bar.**

This grouping thing gets really handy if you've been assigning categories to your contacts as you've created items. If you're clever about how you use and add categories that fit the work you do, grouping by category can be a huge time-saver.

If the predefined group views don't meet your needs, you can group items according to just about anything you want, assuming that you've entered the data.

To see the By Category view:

1. **Choose Go⇨Contacts.**

   The Contacts view appears.

2. **Choose View⇨Current View⇨By Category.**

   If you've made changes to the current Contacts view, a dialog box appears, asking you to Discard, Save, or Update the Current View. Choose Discard.

   Each gray bar has an icon on the left side with a plus or a minus, followed by Category: *name of Category*. A minus means that no entries are hidden under that company's heading; a plus means that more entries are available (see Figure 10-16).

3. **Click a plus icon to see more entries for the Category listed on the gray bar.**

Grouping is a good way to manage all Outlook items, especially contacts. After you get a handle on using groups, you'll save a lot of time when you're trying to find things.

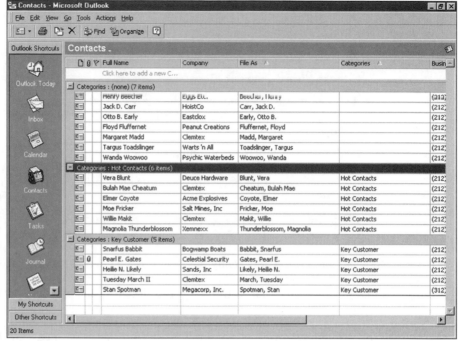

Flagging Your Friends

Sometimes you need a reminder to do something involving another person. For example, if you promise to call someone a month from now, the best way to help yourself remember is to flag that person's name in the contact list. A reminder will pop up on the appointed date and prompt you to make the call.

Adding a flag to a contact

E-mail messages aren't the only items that you can flag. You can add reminders to tasks and appointments to achieve the same effect. Reminders can be set for a specific time of day, while flags are set by day, but not time of day.

To attach a flag to your e-mail messages (ones that you send and ones that have been sent to you):

1. Choose Go⇨Contacts.

The Contacts screen opens, showing your collection of contacts.

2. Right-click the contact that you want to flag.

A Shortcut menu appears (see Figure 10-17).

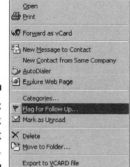

Figure 10-17:
Right-click
any contact
to add a flag.

3. Choose Flag for Follow Up.

The Flag for Follow Up dialog box appears (see Figure 10-18).

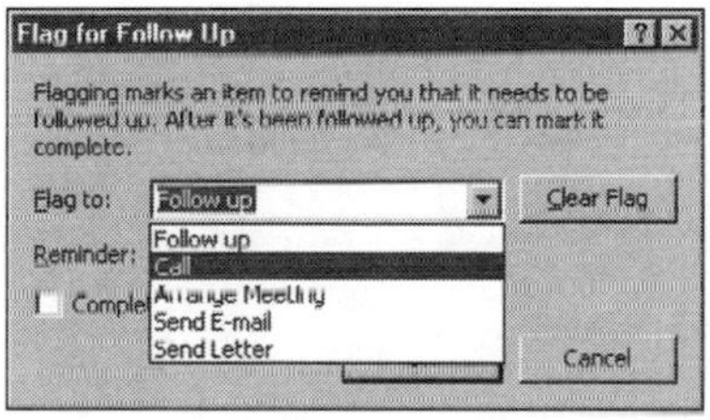

Figure 10-18:
Want to flag
a friend?

4. Click the triangle at the right end of the Flag To text box and choose one of the menu items or type your own choice.

A handy flag is "Follow up," to remind you to confirm an appointment or other arrangement.

5. Click the Reminder box and type the date on which you want the reminder flag to appear.

You can either enter the exact date by typing something like **11/12/98** or you can type **12 days from now** or **the first Friday of February**. Outlook can even figure out some holidays. If you type **Christmas** or **Valentine's Day**, it knows what you mean and substitutes the date. If you type **Thanksgiving** or **Bastille Day**, Outlook doesn't understand. Maybe Outlook only remembers holidays that involve gifts. I know people like that.

6. Click OK.

When the date you entered in the Flag for Follow Up dialog box arrives, a reminder dialog box pops up to help jog your memory.

Hitting the Snooze button

Even after you've instructed Outlook to nag you to pieces with flags and reminders, you can always wait just a teeny bit longer by hitting the Snooze button when your flag pops up. If you usually hit the snooze button on your alarm clock a few dozen times each morning, you'll understand just how satisfying this feature can be. Unfortunately, Outlook can't play the radio for you while you snooze.

To set a flag to snooze:

1. **Click the scroll-down menu that says "Click Snooze to be reminded again" on the Reminder dialog box.**

   The range of available choices appears, starting at 5 minutes and ending at 1 week (see Figure 10-19).

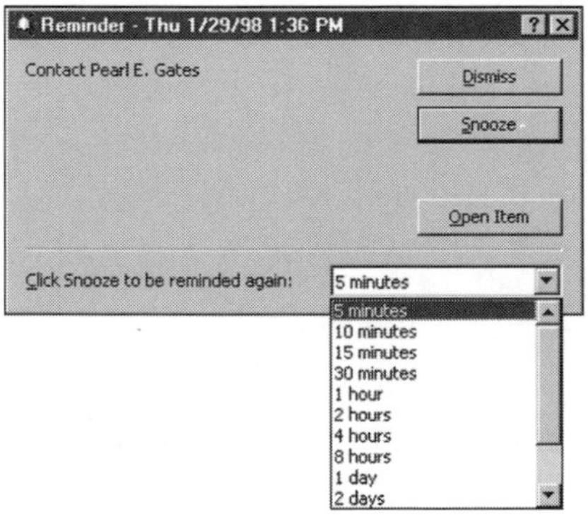

Figure 10-19: A flag reminder popping up to remind you to do something.

2. **Choose the length of time by which you want to delay the reminder.**

   The time you choose appears in the text box.

3. **Click the Snooze button (or press Alt+S).**

   The Reminder dialog box disappears.

It may seem silly to set a flag to remind you to do something and then put the job off by hitting snooze. I find it helpful to keep things on the agenda, even while I'm putting them off. I don't really know if it helps me get more done. I'll check it out and get back to you . . . later.

Finding Contacts

The whole reason for entering names in a Contact list is so that you can find them again. Otherwise, what's the point of all this rigmarole?

Finding names in the Outlook Contacts module is child's play. The easiest way is to look in the Address Cards view under the last name.

To find a contact by last name:

1. **Choose Go⇨Contacts.**

   Your list of contacts appears.

2. **Choose View⇨Current View⇨Address Cards.**

   The Address Cards view appears (see Figure 10-20).

The Address Cards view has a set of lettered tabs along the right edge. You can click a tab to go to that lettered section, but there's an easier way: Simply type the first letter of the name you're looking for. For example, if you're looking for Magnolia Thunderblossom (and you've let Outlook make her File As name Thunderblossom, Magnolia), type the letter T. You see the names that start with T.

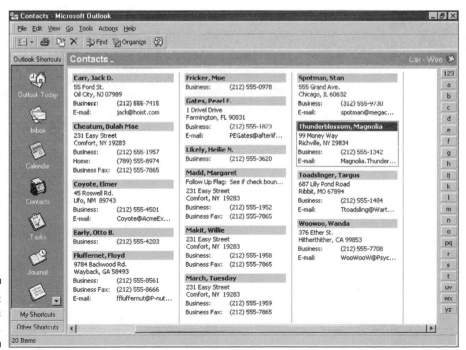

Figure 10-20:
The Address
Cards view.

Of course, you may need to search for a contact name based on something like the company the contact works for. Or you may want to find all the people on your list who live in a certain state. Or people who put you in a certain state of mind (if you've included that in their Contact record). To do this, you use the Find Items tool.

To search for a contact using the Find Items tool:

1. **Click Tools⇨Find on the menu bar (or click the Find button on the Toolbar).**

   The Find window appears (see Figure 10-21).

2. **Type the text you want to find.**

   If you're looking for your friend George Washington's phone number, type **Washington**.

3. **Click the Find Now button.**

   If your search is successful, a list of contacts that match the text you entered appears below the Find window.

4. **Double-click the name of the contact in the list at the bottom of the screen to see the Contact record.**

   If you get nothing, check to see whether the thing you're searching for is spelled exactly right.

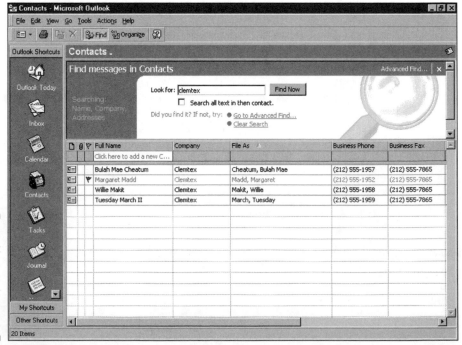

Figure 10-21:
Choose what kind of item you're looking for with the Find tool.

Remember, it's hard to be as stupid as computers — close doesn't count with them. If you saw Grge Wshngtn, you'd know to look for George Washington. Not a computer — George would have to have his vowels removed before a computer would see those two words the same way.

On the other hand, if you only have a scrap of the name you're looking for, Outlook can find that scrap wherever it is. A search for "Geo" would turn up George Washington as well as any other Georges in your Contact list, including Phyllis George and George of the Jungle (if they're all such close, personal friends of yours that they're in your Contact list).

Sending a Business Card

One new feature in Outlook 98 is the capability to forward an electronic "business card," or vCard, to any other person who uses Outlook 98 or any other program that understands how to use a vCard. You can easily send any contact record in your list to anybody by e-mail.

The most obvious thing you'd want to send this way is your own contact information. All you need to do is create a contact record for yourself that contains all the information you want to send someone. Then follow these steps:

1. **Choose Go⇨Contacts.**

   Your list of contacts appears.

2. **Double-click the contact record containing the information you want to send.**

   The contact record you double-clicked opens.

3. **Choose Actions⇨Forward as vCard.**

   A new message form opens with a vCard file attached to the message (see Figure 10-22).

4. **Type the address of the person to whom you want to send the message in the To text box.**

   You can also click the To button and pick a name from the Address Book.

5. **Click the Send button (or press Alt+S).**

   Your message and the attached vCard are sent to your recipient.

When you receive a vCard in an e-mail message, you can add the vCard to your Contact list by double-clicking the icon in the message that represents the vCard.

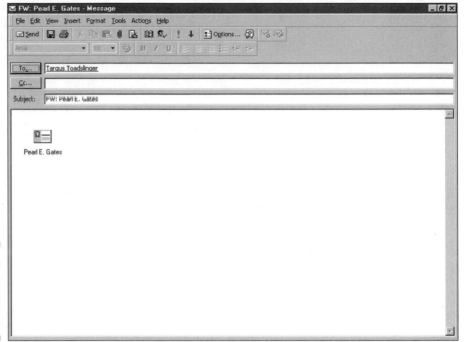

Figure 10-22:
A message
form with
a vCard
attached.

Chapter 11

Personal Distribution Lists and Address Books

· ·

In This Chapter

▶ Figuring out which Outlook you have

▶ Sorting all those Address Books

▶ Creating a Personal Distribution List

▶ Adding names to your Personal Address Book

▶ Making changes to your Personal Distribution List

▶ Importing a Schedule+ Address Book

· ·

*I*f you send regular messages to the same groups of people, Personal Distribution Lists save time. Whether you regularly harangue all the members of Congress or all the members of your company softball team, you can create a list of names and e-mail addresses and then address those people as a unit — that's what a Personal Distribution List is.

This chapter covers features that exist only in the Corporate version. I think the fact that two different versions of Outlook 98 exist is weird, so I don't blame anyone for finding this issue confusing. I hope that Microsoft finds a way to recombine the two versions of Outlook in the next year or so. If you use Outlook at home and get your e-mail from an online service or Internet Service Provider, skip to Chapter 12 for details that relate to you.

Figuring Out Whether You Have Corporate Outlook or Internet Outlook

Outlook 98 comes in two distinct flavors: the Corporate version and the Internet Mail Only version. As you may guess, the Corporate version is aimed at people who use Outlook in large businesses on big networks. The Internet Mail Only version is best for the home and small office user.

If you're not sure which version of Outlook you're using, choose Help⇨ About Microsoft Outlook from the Outlook menu bar. The second line of the About Outlook dialog box says either *Corporate* or *Internet Mail Only.*

About Address Books

The Corporate version of Outlook 98 still uses the crazy quilt of Address Books that it inherits from Outlook 97 and from the Exchange Inbox program that preceded both programs. The Address Books are a nutty arrangement of several separate, independent lists of names and e-mail addresses — it's pretty confusing. Microsoft simplified the issue of dealing with Address Books in the Internet Mail Only version, but that doesn't help if you use Outlook on a large corporate network. I'll try to help you make sense of it all anyway.

The Outlook Contact list contains all kinds of personal information, whereas an Address Book focuses on e-mail addresses. An Address Book can also deal with the nitty-gritty details of actually sending your message to your corporate e-mail system, especially if that system is Microsoft Exchange Server.

Here's the lowdown on your plethora of Address Books:

✔ **The Personal Address Book:** The Personal Address Book is your very own list of e-mail addresses of the people to whom you send mail. It is not the same as the Outlook Contact list; you can include individual names in either, neither, or both the Personal Address Book and the Contact list.

✔ **The Contacts Address Book:** The Contacts Address Book is really the list of e-mail addresses from the Contact list. Outlook automatically creates the Contacts Address Book to allow you to add the names of people in your Contact list to a Personal Distribution List.

✔ **The Global Address List:** If you're using Outlook on a corporate network, the Global Address List, which is maintained by your system administrator, normally contains the names and e-mail addresses of all the people in your company. The Global Address List makes it possible to address an e-mail message to anybody in your company without having to look up the e-mail address.

✔ **Additional Address Books:** If you create additional folders for Outlook contacts, those folders also become separate Address Books. Your system administrator can also create additional Address Books.

If you're lucky, you'll never see the Address Book. All the addresses of all the people you ever send e-mail to are listed in the Global Address List that somebody else maintains, such as on a corporate network. Under those circumstances, Outlook is a dream. You don't need to know what an Address Book is most of the time — you just type the name of the person you're mailing to in the To box of a message. Outlook checks the name for spelling and takes care of sending your message. You'd swear that there's a tiny psychic inside your computer who knows what you need.

Under less-than-ideal conditions, when you try to send a message, Outlook either complains that it doesn't know how to send the message or can't figure out whom you're talking about. Then you have to mess with the address. That situation happens only when the address isn't listed in one of the Address Books or isn't in a form that Outlook understands. In that case, you must either enter the full address manually or add your recipient's name and address to your Address Book.

Creating a Personal Distribution List

The other situation in which you need to deal with Address Books is when you want to create a Personal Distribution List, as you do in this chapter, to save yourself the trouble of adding addresses to a message one by one.

You can create Personal Distribution Lists only in the Personal Address Book. You can't clump people up in the Contacts module and address them as one person. You can send a single e-mail message to a group of people by adding all their names in the To box of a message, but only the Personal Address Book can store a Personal Distribution List. This arrangement is left over from Exchange Inbox — the Microsoft program that came before Outlook. The Personal Address Book isn't as pretty as the Outlook Contact list, but it gets the job done.

To create a Personal Distribution List:

1. **Choose Tools⇨Address Book (or press Ctrl+Shift+B).**

   The Address Book dialog box appears. You can also bring up the Address Book by clicking the Address Book button in the toolbar.

2. **Choose File⇨New Entry.**

   The New Entry dialog box appears.

3. **Choose Personal Distribution List from the Select the Entry Type box.**

4. **Click OK.**

   The New Personal Distribution List Properties dialog box appears (see Figure 11-1).

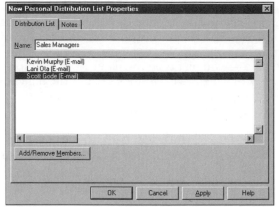

Figure 11-1:
The New
Personal
Distribution
List
Properties
dialog box.

5. Type a name for your new distribution list.

Pick a memorable name that describes what's in the group. Try Sales Managers, Art Directors, or Serfs — whatever describes the members of the group.

6. Click Add/Remove **Members**.

The Edit Members Of dialog box appears (see Figure 11-2). The Edit Members Of dialog box is really a different version of the Address Book, including the names of all the people listed in a certain Address Book; the name of the Address Book that they're listed in appears in the top-right corner of the dialog box.

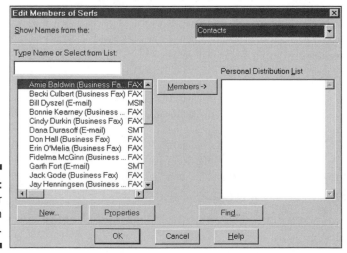

Figure 11-2:
Editing your
distribution
list.

7. Click the name of a person you want to add to your Personal Distribution List.

You can select multiple names by holding down the Ctrl key while clicking each name. You can select a series of consecutive names by clicking the first name that you want to select and then holding down the Shift key while clicking the last name.

8. Click the <u>M</u>embers button.

The name or group of names that you selected appears in the Personal Distribution List box on the right side of the dialog box.

9. Click OK.

Your Personal Distribution List is available for your use.

 You can also add one Personal Distribution List to another. You can have groups called Hourly Employees and Salaried Employees, for example, and add them both to a group called All Employees. Then you can send only one message to reach all members of both groups. You only have to edit the smaller group when a new employee is hired or some other change is made; the larger group, such as the All Employees group, automatically includes whatever changes you make in any smaller groups that belong to it.

Using a Personal Distribution List

Suppose that you want to send a message to the members of the All Employees group that I discuss in the preceding section of this chapter. If you've created a Personal Distribution List, you can send a single message and reach everybody.

To send a message to your Personal Distribution List:

1. Choose <u>F</u>ile⇨New⇨<u>M</u>ail Message.

The Untitled Message form appears.

2. Click the T<u>o</u> button.

The Select Names dialog box appears (see Figure 11-3), showing the list of names from your Contacts module.

3. Select Personal Address Book from the <u>S</u>how Names From The drop-down list.

The names in your Personal Address Book appear in the left window of the Select Names dialog box, as do the names of any Personal Distribution Lists that you've created. You can store a Personal Distribution List only in the Personal Address Book, not the Contact list. If you think that's nonsensical, you're right; I do, too.

A Personal Distribution List

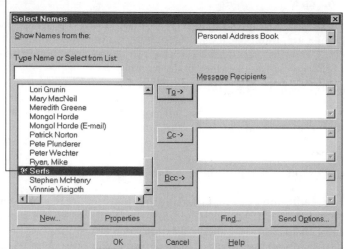

Figure 11-3:
The Select
Names
dialog box.

Your Personal Distribution Lists appear in the list in boldface, with a little two-faces icon.

4. Click the name of the Personal Distribution List that you want to use.

You can choose more than one list at a time or include several lists by holding down the Ctrl key while clicking.

5. Click the To button.

If you want to send a copy of the message to members of a list, click the Cc or Bcc button. (Bcc stands for blind copies — copies sent to folks that you don't want to appear on the open copy list.)

6. Click OK.

The New Message form appears, with the list you selected displayed in the To box. Now you can type your subject and message and then send your e-mail.

A quick way to get Outlook to complete any name in the To line of a message is to type the first four or five letters of the name and click the Check Names button in the toolbar (or press Ctrl+K). That goes for Personal Distribution Lists as well. If you want to send a message to a Personal Distribution List named Hourly Employees, type Hourly in the To box of the Message Form and then press Ctrl+K. The name Hourly Employees appears in the To box in bold underlined text to show that Outlook knows what you mean and has addressed the message properly.

Editing a Personal Distribution List

People come and people go in Personal Distribution Lists, just like everywhere else. It's a good thing that you can edit the lists.

To edit your Personal Distribution List:

1. **Choose Tools⇨Address Book.**

   The Address Book dialog box appears.

2. **Select Personal Address Book from the Show Names From The dropdown list.**

   The names of the people and Personal Distribution Lists that you've entered appear in the Names column of the dialog box (see Figure 11-4).

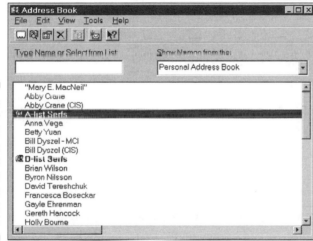

Figure 11-4: Your Personal Distribution Lists show up in the Address Book dialog box.

3. **Double-click the name of the Personal Distribution List that you want to edit.**

   The Properties dialog box appears, displaying the names of the people in the distribution list.

4. **Click Add/Remove Members.**

   The Edit Members Of dialog box appears. The current names of members are listed on the right side of the dialog box; people in your Address Book who are not members of the list are on the left.

5. **Click the name of a person you want to add to the Personal Distribution List.**

   You can choose more than one person by holding down the Ctrl key while clicking each name.

6. **Click the Members button.**

   The names of the people you selected now appear in the Personal Distribution List column.

7. **In the Personal Distribution List column, click the name of anyone you want to remove from the list.**

8. **Press the Delete key.**

   The name that you selected is deleted.

9. **Click OK.**

   The Edit Members Of dialog box disappears.

10. **Click OK.**

    The Properties dialog box disappears.

11. **Choose File➪Close (or press Alt+F4).**

    The Address Book closes.

Your Address Book is now updated and corrected for the next time you need to send a message.

Importing an Address Book from Schedule+ and Other Applications

If you've been using another personal information manager, such as Schedule+, you can import your files from the old program and use the contacts that you already have. Importing is much easier than typing hundreds of contacts again.

The programs that you can import files from include

- ✔ Act!
- ✔ Ecco
- ✔ Lotus Organizer
- ✔ Schedule+
- ✔ SideKick

You can also import files from any of a number of other programs that can export standard text files.

To import a file:

1. **Choose File⇨Import and Export.**

   The Import and Export Wizard appears. A *Wizard* is a series of dialog boxes with instructions to guide you through a sequence of choices to help you complete a process that requires several parts. The process of importing files and having Outlook convert them into a Contact list varies depending on what kind of file you're importing, how the information in the file is arranged, and how you want Outlook to treat it.

2. **Follow the directions that the Wizard gives you for the program you're importing from.**

You may need to install some special tools from the Office 97 CD-ROM to import your file. Follow the prompts of the Import and Export Wizard.

Corporate Outlook: The Bottom Line

The collection of Address Books that you see in the Corporate version of Outlook is really inherited from Microsoft Exchange Server, the program at the heart of the e-mail system in many large companies. Like other things you find in large organizations, it's rather clumsy and nonsensical. But after you get used to doing it "the company way," you'll get along just fine.

Chapter 12

Internet Mail Tricks

In This Chapter

▶ Discovering ISPs

▶ Checking out the online services

▶ Choosing a service provider

▶ Setting up e-mail accounts

▶ Establishing directory services

Some folks say that Microsoft needs three tries to get any new product right. Outlook 98 is a second attempt. The program is getting better, but this version still has some very strange aspects. The strangest thing about Outlook 98 is that you must choose between two entirely different versions of Outlook 98 depending on whether you're a corporate user or a "normal" standalone user. Many aspects of the two versions look and act alike, but some parts are as different as night and day.

The biggest differences between the two versions appear when you want to set up e-mail services and use address books for sending messages. In this chapter, I discuss the features that exist only in the Internet Mail Only version of Outlook 98. If you use the Corporate version, you can skip this chapter entirely.

Everything about the Internet and online services changes quickly. When it comes to the best way to get and use an online service, what's true as I write this chapter may no longer be true when you read it. I tell you how it is as of early 1998.

What's an ISP?

If you don't work in a big company with its own e-mail system, you probably send and receive e-mail through an outside service that your computer dials up over the telephone. The general term for the kind of outfit that provides this service is *Internet Service Provider,* or *ISP.* ISPs do more than exchange e-mail messages for you; they also provide the Internet connection that enables your browser to access and display pages from the World Wide Web and lets you do nearly anything that you can do on the Internet.

Online services such as America Online, CompuServe, and The Microsoft Network function as ISPs, but they also offer a variety of features like discussion forums and file libraries. If you belong to an online service, you don't need a separate ISP. On the other hand, if all you want to do is exchange e-mail and browse the Web, you may not want a full-featured online service; an ISP may be all you need.

Online Services — Who's Who?

The biggest online service is America Online (AOL). Eleven million people call AOL their online home, and new members are joining every day. AOL subscribers can log on and take advantage of shopping, travel services, classes, and information of every type. They can also browse the Internet and exchange e-mail. Previously, you couldn't use Outlook with America Online, but AOL supports Outlook Express as of early 1998. If AOL supports Outlook Express for e-mail, you'll be able to set up the Outlook 98 Internet Mail Only version to exchange your AOL e-mail messages, too.

AOL users can get a great deal from using either Outlook Express or Outlook 98. AOL used to require you to use its own e-mail software, which was pretty weak. (You couldn't even delete more than one message at a time.) Outlook lets you sort and organize all your incoming messages and even lets you make rules so that Outlook can do the sorting and filtering for you.

CompuServe is the second biggest online service, now wholly owned by AOL. Outlook has always been able to send and receive e-mail messages via CompuServe. Technically-minded people are likely to prefer CompuServe because of that service's large collection of technical forums and file libraries. I'm a big CompuServe fan myself, although I don't spend nearly as much time reading CompuServe forums as I did before the Internet hit it big.

The Microsoft Network, or MSN, is Microsoft's own online service. As you'd guess, MSN is the easiest service to join and set up to work with Outlook. Lots of people thought that Microsoft would wipe out all the other online services when it released MSN, but that hasn't been the case. Microsoft bungled the project over and over and revamped the service three times but still can't manage to eat too much of AOL's lunch, as much as Microsoft clearly would like to. After you've joined, MSN is no easier than any other service and no better deal.

The biggest advantage to using an online service to connect you to the Internet is that these services all try to make the process of connecting as easy as possible, and most of them have plenty of staff to help you when things go wrong. Also, if you want some assurance that you or your children won't run across scary people or nasty material while exploring cyberspace, online services are well equipped to screen out things that you may find objectionable.

If you want to check out one of the online services, call one of these numbers:

America Online	www.aol.com	800-827-6364
CompuServe	www.compuserve.com	800-848-8990
The Microsoft Network	www.msn.com	800-386-5550

Picking a Provider

Literally hundreds of Internet Service Providers exist around the United States and thousands around the world. Some of them are small businesses that only serve a certain community. Others are huge global companies that can be reached from nearly anywhere on the planet Earth (and perhaps some other planets, too — I don't know).

If you do all your e-mailing and Web surfing from home or from one spot, a local ISP may be just fine for you. Check your local newspapers for ads from nearby ISPs. Local shops may be a little more personal and less inclined to censor the things you browse like the bigger operators sometimes do. Lots of nasty places exist on the Internet that some people don't want to run across accidentally, so a little bit of censorship suits some folks just fine. Other people want completely unfettered access when they surf the Web, so smaller services with no censorship suit them better. Take your pick.

If you travel a lot and need to check your e-mail while you travel, a big operator may suit you best. Table 12-1 lists ISPs with pretty wide coverage in the United States.

Table 12-1	National ISPs	
ISP	*Web Address*	*Phone Number*
AT&T WorldNet Service	www.att.com/worldnet	800-IMAGINE
Concentric Network	www.concentric.net	800-745-2747
Earthlink Network	www.earthlink.net	800-395-8410

(continued)

Table 12-1 *(continued)*

ISP	Web Address	Phone Number
GTE Internet Solutions	www.gte.net	800-927-3000
IBM Internet Connection Service	www.ibm.net	800-821-4612
IDT Internet Services	www.idt.net	201-883-2000
MCI Internet	www.mci2000.com	800-550-0930
MindSpring	www.mindspring.com	800-719-4660
Netcom	www.netcom.com	408-983-5970
SpryNet	www.sprynet.com	206-957-8998
Whole Earth Networks	www.wenet.com	415-281-6500

You can find an even more extensive list of ISPs in a magazine called *Board-watch,* or you can check the magazine's Web site at www.boardwatch.com.

Setting Up Accounts

After you've signed up with an ISP, you need to set up Outlook to send and receive e-mail from your account. You need to set up your Internet e-mail account only once, although you can set up multiple Internet e-mail accounts.

The process I describe here only works with the Internet Mail Only version of Outlook 98. If you're using the Corporate version, the process of setting up e-mail accounts is different. If you're a corporate user, your system administrators may not want you to mess around with account settings, so skip this part of the chapter.

If you're on your own, you should probably call the tech support line from your online service or ISP to get all the proper spellings of the server names and passwords that you have to enter.

To set up an e-mail account in the Internet Mail Only version of Outlook 98:

1. **Choose Tools⇨Accounts.**

   The Internet Accounts dialog box appears.

2. **Click Add.**

   A shortcut menu appears.

3. **Choose <u>M</u>ail from the shortcut menu.**

   The Internet Connection Wizard appears.

4. **Type your name in the <u>D</u>isplay Name text box.**

   Your name appears as you type. This name will appear on all your e-mail.

5. **Click <u>N</u>ext.**

   The Internet E-Mail Address screen appears.

6. **Type your e-mail address in the <u>E</u>-Mail Address text box.**

   The address you type appears.

7. **Click <u>N</u>ext.**

   The E-Mail Server Names screen appears.

8. **Type your e-mail server names in the appropriate boxes.**

   Check with your online service or ISP for the names and exact spellings of your e-mail servers.

9. **Click <u>N</u>ext.**

   The Internet Mail Logon screen appears.

10. **Type your account name and password.**

    Check with your online service or ISP to find out exactly what to type here.

11. **Click <u>N</u>ext.**

    The Friendly Name screen appears.

12. **Type the name you want to assign to this account in the text box.**

    The name you type appears.

13. **Click <u>N</u>ext.**

    The Choose Connection Type screen appears.

14. **Choose the type of connection you want to use.**

    Connect using my phone line is usually a good bet. That makes Outlook automatically dial your phone and check your e-mail whenever you ask. *I will establish my Internet connection manually* means that you'll need to start up your connection to your ISP or online service before you can exchange messages. That's a good choice if you don't want Outlook dialing your phone when you're not looking. Again, your ISP tech support people can help you choose.

15. **Click <u>N</u>ext.**

    The Congratulations screen appears! Aren't you proud?

16. **Click Finish.**

The Internet Connection Wizard closes, and your new account appears in the list of accounts in the Internet Accounts dialog box.

17. **Click Close.**

You've now set up your e-mail account.

As I mention earlier in this section, you can set up more than one Internet e-mail account, so you can have separate addresses for each member of the family. You also may want to have separate accounts for business use and personal use. Perhaps you just want to set up separate accounts so that you can send yourself messages. Whatever you like to do, the process of setting up different accounts is pretty much the same.

Setting Up Directory Services

Sending an e-mail message to somebody is easy if you know that person's e-mail address. You can find e-mail addresses for people around the world right from Outlook. Before you can use Outlook to find e-mail addresses, though, you need to set up a directory service to help you find names and addresses.

Outlook 98 is set up to check one of several popular search services to find e-mail addresses, but you need to tell Outlook which one you want to use. Here's how to tell Outlook which search service you prefer:

1. **Choose Tools⇨Accounts.**

The Internet Accounts dialog box appears.

2. **Click the Directory Service tab.**

The list of directory services you can choose appears.

3. **Click the name of the service you want to use.**

The name of the service you select is highlighted. You can choose any of them, and if you don't like your choice, you can easily switch to another one. I picked Bigfoot because it gave the most responses when I looked for my own name.

4. **Click the Properties button.**

The Properties dialog box appears.

5. **Click the box that says *Check names against server when sending mail.***

A check mark appears in the check box.

6. Click OK.

The Properties dialog box closes.

7. Click Close.

The Internet Accounts dialog box closes.

Now you can check an e-mail address while you're creating a new message. Just type the name of the person you want to find in the To box of your message, and then click the Check Names button in the message toolbar (or press Ctrl+K). If the service you picked knows your recipient's address, an underline appears beneath the person's name to show you that the message is properly addressed.

Internet, intranets — What's the difference?

As if all the hoopla about the Internet weren't enough, now the word *intranet* is being bandied about. What's the difference between *the Internet* and *an intranet*? An *intranet* is the name for an installation of Internet-style Web pages and browsers set up on a company's computer network that's intended for use by the company itself (including the employees and customers and suppliers of the company).

To people who work at the company, it's like having their own private Internet. Not all intranets are restricted from public view, but they can be if the company that created that particular intranet wants it that way. Using an intranet is exactly like using the Internet. Outlook functions the same way whether you use the Internet or an intranet.

Part III

Taking Care of Business

In this part . . .

You know whom to contact and where they are, and you can send them a message at almost warp speed. But what's all the messaging about? Business. Those things that keep you employed and the economy booming. Meetings and deadlines, schedule conflicts, and too many tasks — all crying out for your expert attention. In this part, you see how Outlook makes it easy to keep your business in line.

Chapter 13

Days and Dates: Keeping Your Calendar

In This Chapter

▶ Using the Date Navigator

▶ Finding a date (the number kind)

▶ Making and breaking dates

▶ Viewing in Calendar

▶ Printing your appointments

*A*ll those precious minutes, and where do they go? Outlook makes your computer the perfect place to solve the problem of too little time in the day. Although Outlook can't give you any extra hours, you can use it to get a better grip on the hours you've got, and it can free those precious minutes that can add up to more hours spent in productive work. If only Outlook could solve the problem of having to do productive work in order to earn a living.

No doubt you've been looking at calendars your whole life, so the Outlook Calendar will be pretty simple for you to understand because it looks like a calendar: plain old rows of dates, Monday through Friday plus weekends, and so on. You don't have to learn to think like a computer to understand your schedule.

If you want to see more information about something in your calendar, most of the time all you have to do is click the calendar with your mouse. If that doesn't give you enough information, click twice. If that doesn't give you everything you're looking for, read on; I fill you in on the fine points. I suspect that the Outlook Calendar will be so easy that you won't need much special training to find it useful.

The Date Navigator: Really Getting Around

The Date Navigator is actually the name of this feature, but don't confuse it with Warren Beatty's chauffeur. The Date Navigator is a trick you can use in Outlook to change the part of the Calendar you're seeing or the time period you want to look at (see Figure 13-1).

Figure 13-1:
The Outlook
Date
Navigator.

◀	November 1998		December 1998		January 1999	▶

```
     November 1998          December 1998           January 1999
  S  M  T  W  T  F  S     S  M  T  W  T  F  S     S  M  T  W  T  F  S
 25 26 27 28 29 30 31              1  2  3  4  5                    1  2
  1  2  3  4  5  6  7     6  7  8  9 10 11 12     3  4  5  6  7  8  9
  8  9 10 11 12 13 14    13 14 15 16 17 18 19    10 11 12 13 14 15 16
 15 16 17 18 19 20 21    20 21 22 23 24 25 26    17 18 19 20 21 22 23
 22 23 24 25 26 27 28    27 28 29 30 31          24 25 26 27 28 29 30
 29 30                                           31  1  2  3  4  5  6
```

Believe it or not, that unassuming little two- or three-month calendar scrap is probably the quickest way to change how you look at the Calendar and make your way around it. All you have to do is click the date you want to see, and it opens in all its glory. It couldn't be simpler.

To use the Date Navigator:

1. Choose Go⇨Calendar.

The Calendar appears.

2. Choose View⇨Current View⇨Day/Week/Month.

The Date Navigator appears as a small calendar in the upper-right corner.

- To see details of a single date, click that day in the Date Navigator. You see the appointments and events scheduled for the day you clicked.

- To see a full-month view, click one of the letters (SMTWTFS) at the top of the months.

- To see a week's view, move the mouse pointer just to the left of the week you want to see. When the arrow points up and to the right rather than up and to the left, click it.

  As time goes by (so to speak), you'll find that you gravitate to the Calendar view that suits you best. I happen to like the Seven Day view because it includes both Calendar and Task information in a screen that's pretty easy to read. You can leave Outlook running most of the time in order to keep the information you need handy.

Time travel isn't just science fiction. You can zip around the Outlook calendar faster than you can say Buck Rogers. Talk about futuristic; the Outlook calendar can schedule appointments for you well into the year 4500! Think about it: Between now and then are more than 130,000 Saturday nights! That's the good news. There are also more than 130,000 Monday mornings. Of course, in our lifetimes, you and I only have to deal with about 5,000 Saturday nights at most, so we have to make good use of them. Better start planning.

So when you need to find a free date fast:

1. **Choose Go⇨Go To Date (or press Ctrl+G).**

   A dialog box appears with today's date highlighted.

2. **To go to another date, type the date you want as you normally would, such as** January 15, 1998, **or** 1/15/98.

   A really neat way to change dates is to type in something like **45 days ago** or **93 days from now** (see Figure 13-2). Try it. Outlook understands simple English when it comes to dates. Don't get fancy, though — Outlook doesn't understand **Four score and seven years ago**. But who does?

Figure 13-2:
The Go To
Date dialog
box with a
tall order.

If you want to go to today's date, choose Go⇨Go To Today. No matter which date you land on, you can plunge right in and start scheduling. You can double-click the time and date when you want an appointment to occur and enter the particulars, or you can double-check details of an appointment on that date by double-clicking the date and making changes to the appointment if necessary. You can also do something silly like finding out what day of the week your birthday falls on 1,000 years from now. Mine's on Saturday. Don't forget.

Meetings Galore: Scheduling Appointments

Many people live and die by their datebooks. The paper type of datebook is still popular, being the easiest to put stuff in (although after it's in, the stuff can be a pain to find). Outlook makes it easier to add appointments than most computer calendars do, and Outlook makes it a whole lot easier to find things after you've entered them. It also warns you when you've scheduled two dates at once. (Very embarrassing!)

To schedule an appointment:

1. **Choose File⇨New from the menu bar.**

   The New Item menu appears (see Figure 13-3).

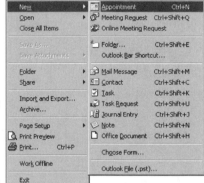

Figure 13-3:
Selecting
a new
appointment.

You may notice Ctrl+N next to the word Appointment. If you press Ctrl+N in any section of Outlook, a dialog box appears to let you create a new item in that section.

Press Ctrl+Shift+A from any section of Outlook to create an appointment. The catch is, you won't see the appointment on the calendar until you switch to the Calendar view.

2. **Choose Appointment.**

   The Appointment form opens (see Figure 13-4).

3. **Click in the Subject box and type something there to help you remember what the appointment's about.**

   Type **Dentist appointment** or **Receive Oscar** or whatever. This text will show up on your calendar.

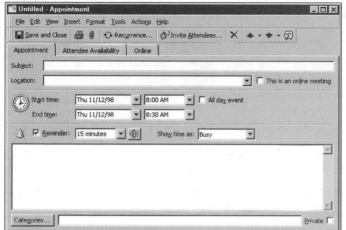

Figure 13-4:
The
Appointment
form.

4. Click in the Location box and enter the location.

Notice the little triangle (scroll bar button) at the right side of the box. If you click the triangle, you see a list of the last few locations where you scheduled appointments so that you can use the same places over and over without having to retype them. Another advantage to having this recallable list of locations is that it makes it easy to enter locations. That way you can sort your list of appointments according to location to see, for example, if conference rooms are free.

5. If you want Outlook to remind you of your appointment, click the Reminder box.

Choose how far in advance you want Outlook to notify you of an upcoming appointment. You can set the amount yourself by typing it in, or you can click the scroll-down button and choose a predetermined length from the Reminder box.

- If you want a sound to play as a reminder, click the sound icon next to the Reminder box to see the Reminder Sound dialog box (see Figure 13-5). (If you don't have a sound card, you won't be able to hear a sound.)

- If the appointment is tentative, click the scroll-down button to the right of the Show Time As menu and choose Tentative.

- You can also mark the appointment as Free, Busy, or Out of Office. (Out of Mind is not an option yet.)

If you're using Outlook on an office network, other people may be able to see your schedule in order to plan meetings with you. Designations like Free, Busy, or Out of Office let coworkers who can view your schedule know whether you're available for a meeting.

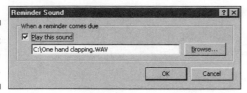

Figure 13-5:
Pick a
sound.

• If you need to remember more information about this appointment, type the information in the text box at the bottom of the dialog box: directions to a new client's office, books for school, the Declaration of Independence, whatever turns you on.

6. **Click the Categories button at the bottom left to assign a category to the appointment if you like.**

Using the Categories dialog box (see Figure 13-6) is another trick for finding things easily.

Figure 13-6:
The
Categories
box.

7. **Choose an existing category, if one suits you, and then click OK.**

8. **If none of the existing categories suits you, click the Master Category List button at the bottom right.**

The Master Category List dialog box appears (see Figure 13-7).

9. **Type a category of your choice in the New category box.**

Be sure not to add too many new categories, as you could have a hard time finding things.

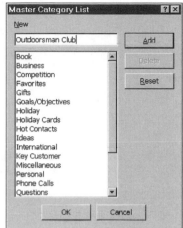

Figure 13-7:
The Master
Category List
dialog box.

10. **Click Add and click OK.**

    You're now back in the Categories dialog box, with the new category added to the list.

11. **Select the new category from the Available Categories list and then click OK.**

    You can select more than one category at a time.

12. **Click the Private box in the lower-right corner of the New Appointment form if you're on a network and you don't want others to know about your appointments.**

13. **Click Save and then Close.**

    The appointment you created appears in the Active Appointments view (see Figure 13-8).

You may have to change your view of the Calendar by clicking the Date Navigator on the date the appointment occurs so that you can see your new appointment.

If you're using reminders for all your important appointments, you must have Outlook running so that the reminder pops up. You can keep Outlook running in the background if you start up a second program such as Microsoft Word. When the reminder time arrives, you either see a dialog box or a message from the Office Assistant like the one in Figure 13-9.

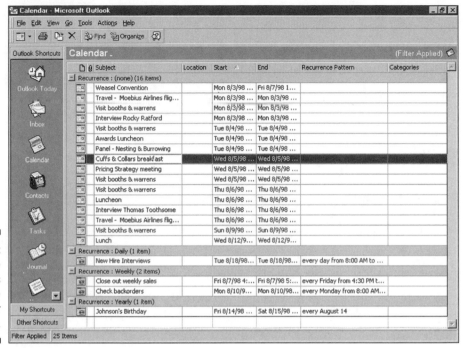

Figure 13-8:
The Active Appointments view of the Calendar module.

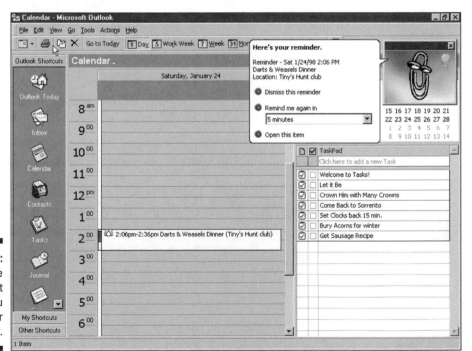

Figure 13-9:
The Office Assistant reminds you of your appointment.

Not this time: Changing dates

You can be as fickle as you want with Outlook. In fact, to change the time of a scheduled item, all you do is drag the appointment from where it is to where you want it to be (see Figure 13-10). Or back again . . . maybe . . . if you feel like it. . . .

To change an appointment:

1. Click the appointment in the Calendar view.

A blue bar appears at the left edge of the appointment.

2. Place the mouse pointer over the blue bar.

The mouse pointer turns into a little four-headed arrow.

3. Drag the appointment to the time or date where you want it to be.

If you're in the One-Day view, drag an appointment to a different date on one of the small calendars in the upper right.

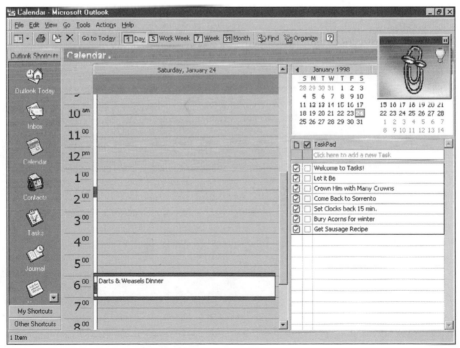

Figure 13-10:
If your appointment is a drag, drop it in a new spot.

TIP

If you want to create a copy of an appointment for another time, hold down the Ctrl key while you use the mouse to drag the appointment to another time or date. For example, if you're scheduling a Summer Intern Orientation from 9 to 11 a.m. and 1 to 3 p.m., you can create the 9 a.m. appointment and then copy it to 1 p.m. by holding Ctrl and dragging the appointment. Then you have two appointments with the same subject, location, and date, but different hours.

If you copy an appointment to a different date by dragging the appointment to a date on the Date Navigator, you retain the hour of the appointment but change the date.

If you want to change an appointment to a date you can't see on the Calendar:

1. **Double-click the appointment.**

   The Appointment dialog box opens.

2. **Click in the leftmost Start time block and then click the scroll-down button to the right of the date to pull down a calendar (see Figure 13-11).**

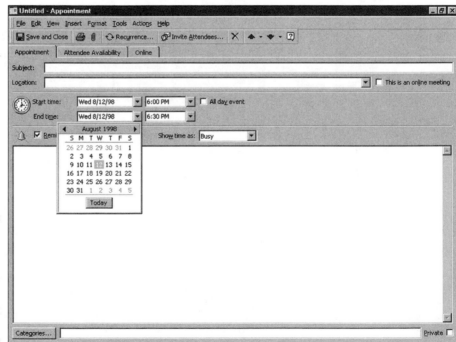

Figure 13-11:
The pull-
down
Calendar
in the
Appointment
form.

3. **Pick the month by clicking one of the triangles beside the month's name.**

   Clicking the left triangle moves you one month earlier; clicking the right triangle moves you one month later.

4. **Click the day of the month you want.**

5. **Click in the rightmost Start Time text box and enter the appointment's new time, if needed.**

6. **Make any other changes you need in the appointment by clicking on the information you want to change and typing the revised information over it.**

7. **Click Save and Close.**

To change the length of an appointment:

1. **Click the appointment.**

2. **Move the mouse pointer over the lines at the top or bottom of the appointment.**

   When it's in the right place, the mouse pointer turns into a two-headed arrow that you can use to drag the lines of the appointment box.

3. **Drag the bottom line down to make the appointment time longer; drag the bottom line up to make the appointment shorter.**

   You can only change an appointment's length by dragging in multiples of 30 minutes (see Figure 13-12).

To shorten an appointment to less than 30 minutes:

1. **Double-click the appointment and click the End Time box.**

2. **Type the ending time.**

3. **Click Save and Close.**

You can enter times in Outlook without adding colons and often without using AM or PM. Outlook translates **443** as 4:43 PM. If you plan lots of appointments at 4:43 AM, just type **443A**. Just don't call *me* at that hour, okay?

Not ever: Breaking dates

Well, sometimes things just don't work out. Sorry about that. Even if it's hard for you to forget, with the click of a mouse Outlook deletes dates you'd otherwise fondly remember. Okay, two clicks of a mouse. *C'est la Vie, C'est L'Amour, C'est la Guerre.* (Look for my next book, *Tawdry French Clichés.*)

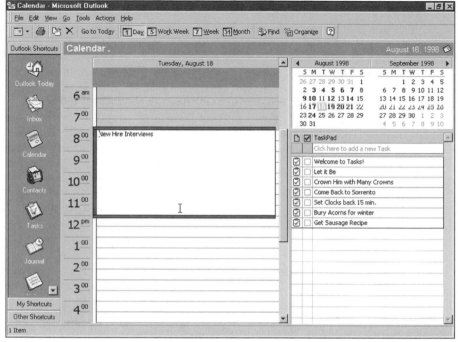

Figure 13-12:
The thick dark line shows an appointment being lengthened.

To delete an appointment (after you've called to break it, of course):

1. **Right-click the appointment (that is, click with the right mouse button).**

2. **Click D̲elete.**

   Your appointment has been canceled.

The Ctrl+D combination you see next to the Delete command means you can delete the appointment in just one keystroke. How cold.

We've got to keep seeing each other: Recurring dates

Some appointments are like a meal at a Chinese restaurant; as soon as you're done with one, you're ready for another. With Outlook, you can easily create an appointment that comes back like last night's spicy Szechwan noodles.

To create a recurring appointment (that is, an appointment that's regularly scheduled):

1. Choose Go⇨Calendar.

The Calendar appears.

2. Click the New tool icon at the left end of the toolbar (see Figure 13-13).

The Appointment form appears (refer to Figure 13-4). Yeah, I know. I do it differently earlier in the chapter when I tell you how to create an appointment the first time. This way is the *really* easy way to create a new appointment.

3. Click the Subject box and enter the subject.

4. Click the Location box and enter the location.

5. If you want Outlook to remind you, click the Reminder box.

- Choose how far in advance you want Outlook to remind you.
- If you want a sound to play as a reminder, click the sound icon.

0. Click the Actions menu.

The Actions menu drops down (see Figure 13-14).

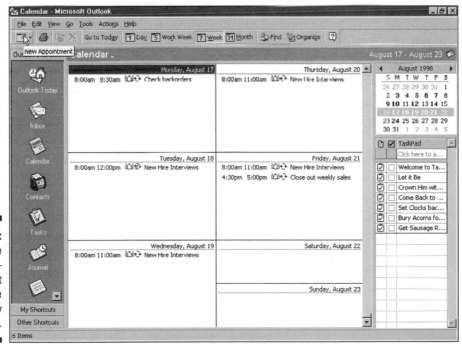

Figure 13-13:
Clicking the New tool — the easiest way to create a new appointment.

Figure 13-14:
The Actions
menu.

7. Choose Recurrence.

The letters Ctrl+G next to the Recurrence command mean that you can also create the recurring appointment with just that one keystroke.

The Recurrence dialog box appears (see Figure 13-15).

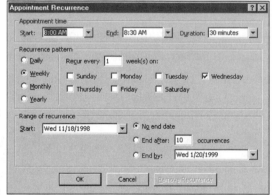

Figure 13-15:
The
Recurrence
dialog box.

8. Click the End text box and enter the ending time.

9. In the Recurrence Pattern box, click the Daily, Weekly, Monthly, or Yearly option button to select how often the appointment recurs.

10. In the next part of the Recurrence Pattern box, choose how often the appointment occurs.

11. In the Range of Recurrence box, enter the first occurrence in the Start box.

12. Choose when the appointments will stop.

You can select No End Date, End After a certain number of occurrences, or End By a certain date.

13. Click OK.

14. Click Save and Close.

Even a recurring appointment gets changed once in awhile. To edit a recurring appointment:

1. Double-click the appointment you want to edit.

The Open Recurring Item dialog box appears.

2. Choose whether you want to change just the occurrence you clicked or the whole series.

3. Click OK.

The Recurring Appointment dialog box appears (see Figure 13-16).

4. Edit the details of the appointment.

To change the recurrence pattern, click Actions➪Recurrence. Then change the recurrence pattern and click OK.

5. Click Save and Close.

I find it helpful to enter regular appointments, such as classes or regular recreational events, even if I'm sure I won't forget them. Entering all my activities into Outlook prevents me from scheduling conflicting appointments.

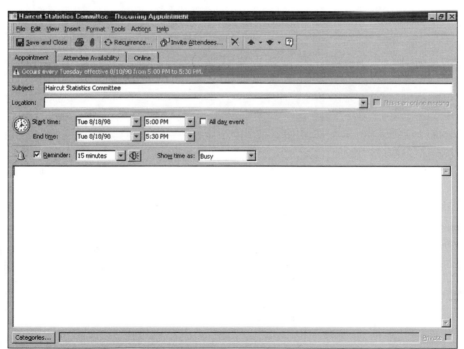

Figure 13-16:
The
Recurring
Appointment
dialog box.

Getting a Good View of Your Calendar

Outlook lets you slice and dice the information in every section nearly any way you can imagine, using different views. You could easily fill a cookbook with different views you can create, but I'm going to stick to the standard ways of looking at a calendar that most people are used to. If you want to cook up a calendar arrangement that nobody's ever thought of before, Outlook will probably let you, but you have to live with it. That's okay; if you accidentally create a Calendar view you don't like, you can delete it.

The basic Calendar views are the Daily view, shown in Figure 13-17, the Weekly view, shown in Figure 13-18, and the Monthly view, shown in Figure 13-19.

Other views of the Calendar, such as the Active Appointments view, are big helps when you're trying to figure out when you did something or when you will do something.

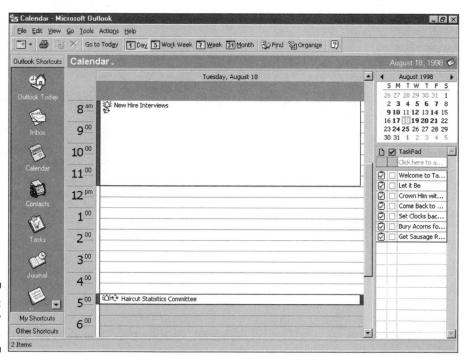

Figure 13-17: The Daily view.

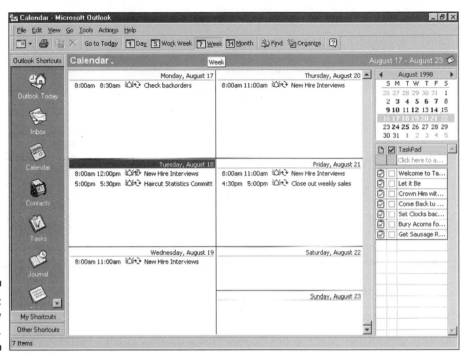

Figure 13-18:
The Weekly
view.

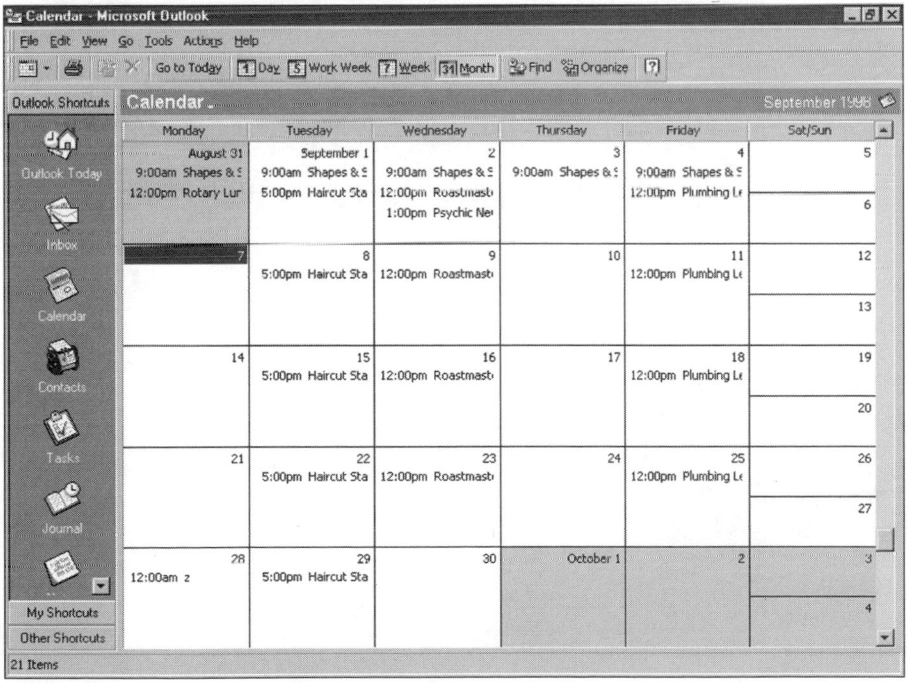

Figure 13-19:
The Monthly
view.

To view Active Appointments:

1. **Choose <u>V</u>iew⇨Current <u>V</u>iew.**

   The view menu appears.

2. **Choose Active Appointments.**

   You see a list of appointments yet to come.

In Active Appointments view (see Figure 13-20), you can see details of appointments that you have coming up in a list that's easy to read. You can also sort the view on any column, such as Location, Subject, or Start date by clicking the column's title.

The Active Appointments view is only one of a half-dozen preprogrammed views that come with Outlook. Pull down the menu and try each of the other choices: You've seen the Daily/Weekly/Monthly view, which lets you look at your schedule in the familiar calendar layout. Events view shows you items that last more than a day. Annual Events shows the list of items that last more than a day and return at the same time each year. Recurring is the view of appointments that you've set up to repeat themselves. By Category view groups your appointments according to the category you've assigned them.

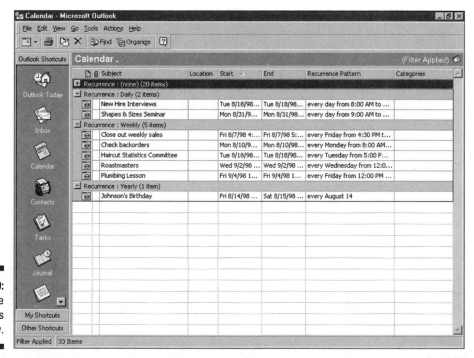

Figure 13-20: The Active Appointments view.

Printing Your Appointments

On plain old paper is still everybody's favorite way to read things. No matter how slick your computer organizer is, you may still need old-fashioned ink-on-paper to make it really useful. You use the same basic steps to print from any module in Outlook. Here's how to print your appointments:

1. **Click a date within the range of dates you want to print.**

   If you want to print a single day, click just one day (see Figure 13-21). If you want to print a range of dates, click the first date and then hold the Shift key and click the last date in the range. The whole range is then highlighted to show which dates you've selected.

2. **Choose File⇨Print (or press Ctrl+P).**

   The Print dialog box appears (see Figure 13-22).

3. **In the Print Style group, choose Daily, Weekly, Monthly, Trifold, Memo, or any other style you want that may be available in your Style box.**

   You can define your own print styles in Outlook, so you may eventually have quite a collection of choices here.

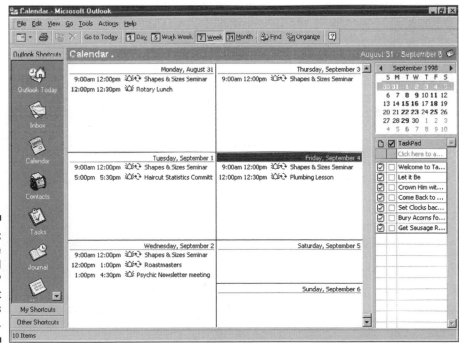

Figure 13-21: Click a single day and press Ctrl+P to print that day's appointments.

Figure 13-22:
The Print
dialog box.

4. In the Print Range box, set the range of dates you want to print.

Because you began by clicking on a date in that range, it should already be correct. If it's not correct, you can change the range in the Print dialog box to the print range you want.

5. Click OK.

Your dates are sent to the printer.

Clicking the Print icon on the toolbar is another handy way to start the print process. The icon looks like a tiny printer.

Scheduling your main events

You can enter more than just appointments in your calendar. You can also add events by clicking the All Day Event check box in the Appointment form, or you can begin by choosing Actions➪New All Day Event and follow the same steps you use to create an appointment (refer to "Meetings Galore: Scheduling Appointments," earlier in this chapter).

Events allow you to add things to your calendar, like business trips or conferences that last longer than an appointment, while still letting you quickly enter routine appointments that may take place at the event. For example, you can create an event called "1998 Auto Show" and then add appointments to see General Motors at 9 a.m., Chrysler at noon, and Ford at 3 p.m.

Chapter 14

A Sticky Subject: Using Notes

In This Chapter

▶ Composing a note

▶ Locating a note

▶ Opening and reading a note

▶ Deleting a note

▶ Resizing of a note

▶ Changing your colors

▶ Taking a look at your notes

▶ Putting your notes in categories

▶ Printing notes

▶ Changing your options for new notes

▶ Forwarding a note

*T*he simple, dopey features of a program are often my favorites — the features that I end up using all the time, like Outlook Notes. There's really nothing earth-shattering about Notes and certainly nothing difficult. This feature is just there when you need it, ready to allow you to type whatever strange, random thoughts are passing through your head while you're doing your work. (As you can tell from my writing, strange, random thoughts are a common occurrence for me. That's why I love using Notes.)

A note is the only type of item you can create in Outlook that doesn't use a normal dialog box with menus and toolbars. Notes are easier to use but somewhat trickier to explain than other Outlook items, because I can only describe the objects you're supposed to click and drag. No name appears on the Note icon and no name exists for the part of the note that you drag when you want to resize the note (see Figure 14-1).

Note

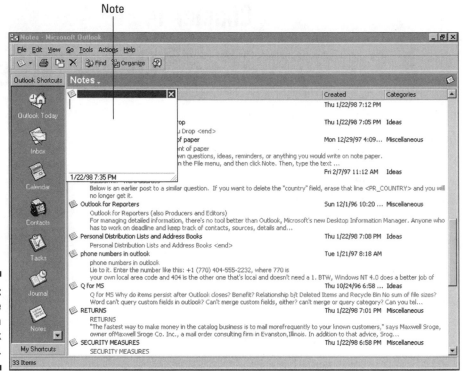

Figure 14-1:
Your note
begins as a
nearly blank
box.

Writing a Note

How did we ever live without those little yellow stick-on notes? They're everywhere! The funny thing about stick-on notes is that they came from an inventor's failure. A scientist was trying to invent a new formula for glue, and he came up with a kind of glue that didn't stick very well. Like the computer scientists who came later, he said, "That's not a bug; that's a feature!" Then he figured out how to make a fortune selling little notes that didn't stick too well. It's only natural that an invention like this would be adapted for computers.

Here's how to take notes while doing your work:

1. Click the Notes icon in the Outlook Bar.

The Notes list appears.

You don't actually have to go to the Notes module to create a new note; you can go right to Step 2. I suggest going to the Notes module first only so that you can see your note appear in the list of notes when you finish. Otherwise, your note seems to disappear into thin air, but it doesn't. Outlook automatically files your note in the Notes module unless you make a special effort to send it someplace else.

2. **Choose File▷New▷Note (or press Ctrl+N).**

   The blank Note box appears.

3. **Type what you want to say in your note (see Figure 14-2) and click the Note icon in the upper-left corner of the note.**

4. **Click Close (or press Alt+F4).**

An even quicker way to create a note is to press Ctrl+Shift+N in any Outlook module (except Notes). You don't see your note listed with all the other notes until you switch to the Notes module, but you can get that thought entered.

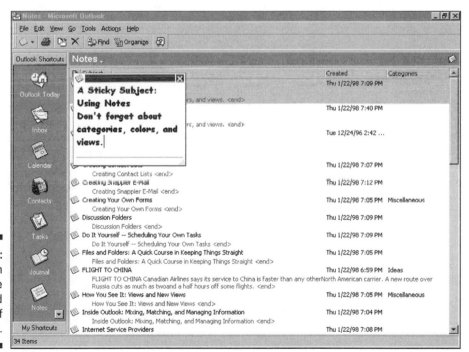

Figure 14-2:
You can write a note to remind yourself of something.

TIP

Tricks with Notes

Each time you start a program, the Windows 95 taskbar at the bottom of the screen adds an icon. That way, you know how many programs you are running. If you click an icon for a program in the taskbar, you switch to that program. If you start Word and Excel, for example, you see two icons in the taskbar. You can have two or more documents open in Word or Excel, but you see only one icon for each program.

When you choose File➪New to create a new item in Outlook, you see a second icon open in the taskbar for the item you're creating. The icon remains until you close and save the item.

It's like having two or more programs open in Windows 95 at the same time. The advantage of this arrangement is that you can leave something like a note open for a long time and keep switching to it to add comments. The disadvantage is that if you don't look at the taskbar to see how many notes you have open, you may be creating a clutter of notes when you may prefer just one.

Another advantage is that you can have two notes open at the same time, or a note and an e-mail message, and drag text from one to the other.

Finding a Note

Unlike paper stick-on notes, Outlook Notes always allow you to find the things you write — or at least your computer can find them. As a matter of fact, you can find any item you create in Outlook just by using the Find tool. (I wish I had a Find tool to help me round up all my lost galoshes and umbrellas.)

Here's how to find a misplaced note:

1. Click the Notes icon in the Outlook Bar.

Your list of notes appears.

2. Choose Tools➪Find Items (or click the Find button in the Toolbar).

The Find dialog box appears (see Figure 14-3). The Look For box contains a blinking bar, the insertion point, which shows you where the next thing you type will go.

3. In the Look For box, type the word or phrase you're looking for.

Don't worry about capitalization. Outlook doesn't worry about capitalization unless you click the words Advanced Find at the top-right corner of the Find window and mess around with the heavy-duty search tools. Most of the time, the Look For box can help you find what you want.

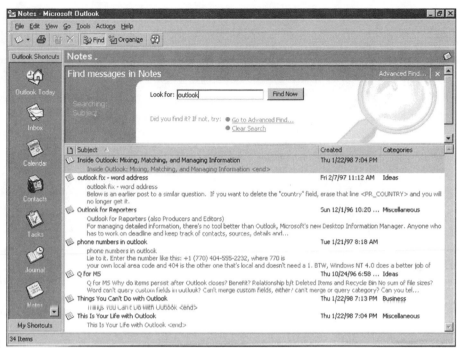

Figure 14-3:
The Find
dialog box.

4. **Click the Find Now button.**

   A list of notes that contain the text you typed appears at the bottom of the dialog box.

5. **If the note you're looking for turns up at the bottom of the dialog box, double-click the Note icon to read what the note says.**

6. **Close the Find dialog box by clicking the Find button in the Toolbar. The note stays on the screen so you can read it or change it.**

Reading a Note

When you write a note, no doubt you plan to read it sometime. Reading notes is even easier than writing them. To read a note:

1. **Click the Notes icon in the Outlook Bar.**

   Your list of notes appears.

2. **Double-click the title of the note that you want to open.**

   The note appears on your screen (see Figure 14-4). You can close the note when you're done by pressing Esc.

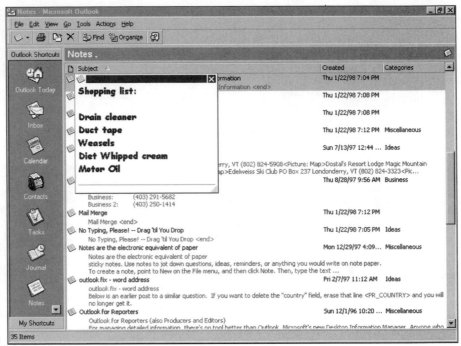

Figure 14-4:
Aha! The
missing
note is
found.

Funny how notes look the same when you're reading them as they do when you're writing them.

Deleting a Note

Notes don't have to be forever. You can write a note this morning and throw it out this afternoon. What could be easier?

Here's how to delete a note:

1. Click the Notes icon in the Outlook Bar.

Your list of notes appears.

2. Click the title of the note that you want to delete.

3. Choose Edit➪Delete (or press Delete).

You can also click the Delete button in the Outlook toolbar.

Taking your pick: Multiple selections

When you're sorting your notes or assigning them to categories, one way to work a little faster is to select several notes at the same time. If you want to select a group of notes that you can see one right after another in a list, click the first one and then hold down the Shift key while clicking the last one. That action selects both of the notes that you clicked and all the notes in between.

If you're selecting several items that aren't arranged next to one another, hold down the Ctrl key while clicking each item. The notes that you select are highlighted, and the others stay plain. Then you can open, move, delete, or categorize the entire group of notes that you've selected in a single stroke. To view several notes, right-click any notes you've selected and choose Open.

Changing the Size of a Note

You may be an old hand at moving and resizing boxes in Windows. Notes follow all the rules that other Windows boxes follow, so you'll be okay. If you're new to Windows and dialog boxes, don't worry — Notes are as easy to resize as they are to write and read.

To change the size of a note:

1. **Click the Notes icon in the Outlook Bar.**

   Your list of notes appears.

2. **Double-click the title of the note that you want to open.**

   The note pops up.

3. **Move your mouse pointer to the bottom-left corner of the note until the mouse pointer changes into a two-headed arrow pointed on a diagonal.**

   Use this arrow to drag the edges of the note to resize it. Don't be alarmed. Resizing boxes is much easier to do than to read about. After you resize one box, you'll have no trouble resizing another.

4. **Drag with your mouse until the note is the size you want it to be.**

   As you drag the mouse pointer around, a gray box appears, showing you what size the note will be when you release the mouse button (see Figure 14-5). Don't worry if the size doesn't come out right the first time; you can change the note size again by dragging the mouse again.

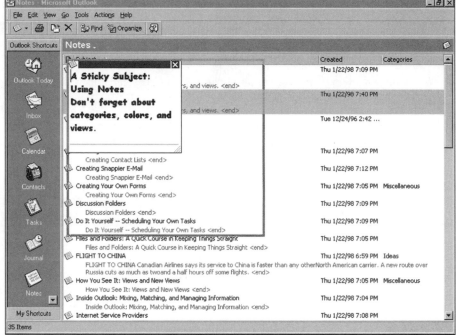

Changing Your Colors

Color may seem to be a trifling issue, but it can help you keep track of your notes. You can assign a color to a level of importance, for example, or to a specific task, so you can quickly see the note you want among the many notes in your list. Later in the chapter, I explain how you can sort your list of notes according to their color. Sorting is useful, so spending your entire day changing the colors of your notes isn't just aesthetic — it's also productive.

Here's how to change your note's color:

1. **Open the note and click the Note icon in the top-left corner of the note.**

   I wish there were a better way to describe this icon than "the little thingy up on the left," but that's what it is. The icon is easy to see; it's the only little thingy in the top-left corner of your note. Anyway, when you do click the thingy, the Note menu appears.

2. **Choose Color.**

   A menu of colors appears (see Figure 14-6). Currently, the only choices are Blue, Green, Pink, Yellow, and White. I hope you like pastels, because those are your only options at the moment. Perhaps Burgundy and Off-Mauve notes will be in next season for more color-conscious computer users.

Figure 14-6:
The Color
menu.

3. Pick a color.

You can also change the colors of notes when viewing a list of notes; just right-click the icon for a note and choose a color from the menu that appears.

Viewing Your Notes

Notes are handy enough to be able to stash tidbits of information any way you want, but what makes Notes really useful is what happens when you need to get the stuff back. You can open your notes one by one and see what's in them, but Outlook's Notes module offers even handier capabilities for arranging, sorting, and viewing your notes in a way that makes sense for you.

Icons view

Some folks like Icons view — just a bunch of notes scattered all over, just as they are on my desk. Because I can already see a mess of notes any time I look at my desk, I prefer organized lists for viewing my notes on my computer, but you may like the more free-form Icons view.

To use Icons view:

1. Click the Notes icon in the Outlook Bar.

The Notes list appears.

2. Choose View⇨Current View.

The Current View menu appears.

3. Choose Icons.

The screen fills with a bunch of icons and incredibly long titles for each icon (see Figure 14-7).

Outlook uses the entire text of your message as the title of the icon, so the screen gets cluttered fast. If you prefer creative clutter, this view is for you. If not, keep reading.

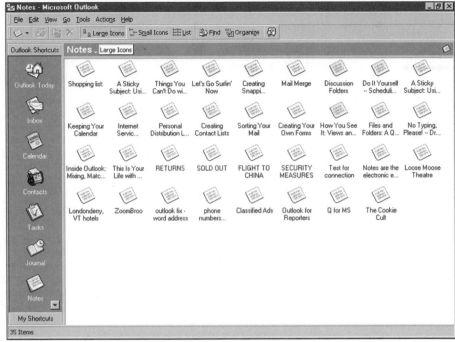

Figure 14-7:
The Icons
view — a
clutter of
notes.

Notes List view

The Notes list is as basic as basic gets. Just the facts, ma'am. The Notes list shows the subject and creation date of each note, as well as the first few lines of text.

To use Notes List view:

1. **Click the Notes icon in the Outlook Bar.**

   The Notes list appears.

2. **Choose View➪Current View.**

   The Current View menu appears.

3. **Choose Notes List.**

   A listing of your notes appears (see Figure 14-8).

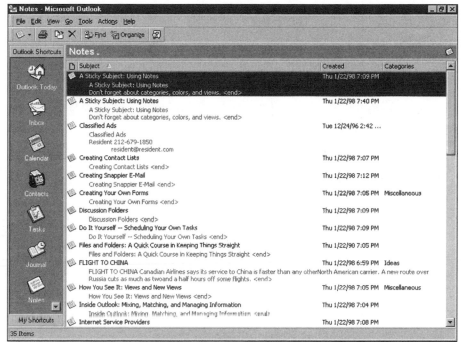

Figure 14-8:
Your notes
in Notes
List view.

I usually recommend Notes List view for opening, forwarding, reading, and otherwise dealing with notes because it's the most straightforward. Anything you can do to a note in Notes List view, you can do in the other Notes views as well. The difference is that the other views don't always let you see the note that you want to do things to.

Last Seven Days view

The notes that you dealt with in the last few days are most likely to be the notes that you'll need today. So, Outlook includes a special view of the notes that you've modified in the last seven days. You're more likely to quickly find what you're looking for in the seven-day view.

To see your notes for the last seven days:

1. Click the Notes icon in the Outlook Bar.

The Notes list appears.

   2. Choose <u>V</u>iew⇨Current <u>V</u>iew.

   The Current View menu appears.

   3. Choose Last Seven Days.

   You see seven days' worth of notes (see Figure 14-9).

If you haven't modified any notes in the past seven days, Last Seven Days view will be empty. If having an empty view bothers you, create a note. That'll tide you over for a week.

By Category view

Every item that you create in Outlook can be assigned to a category. You use the same category list for all items, and you can create your own categories. With categories, you have another useful way to organize your views of Outlook items. I explain how to assign categories to a note later in this chapter.

To see your notes arranged By Category:

   1. Click the Notes icon in the Outlook Bar.

   The Notes list appears.

   2. Choose <u>V</u>iew⇨Current <u>V</u>iew.

   The Current View menu appears.

   3. Choose By Category.

   Your notes are arranged by category (see Figure 14-10).

By Category view is a grouped view, meaning that the notes are collected in bunches, according to the categories that you've assigned. You can just look at the category of notes that you're interested in to organize the information that you've collected.

By Color

Color coordination means more than making sure your socks match. The fact that you can group notes by color means that you can create a system of organizing your notes that tells you something important about your notes at a glance. If sales representatives call, asking you to buy merchandise, you may want to create and color code a note for each request: green for requests that you're approving, yellow for requests that you're considering, and pink for requests that you're turning down.

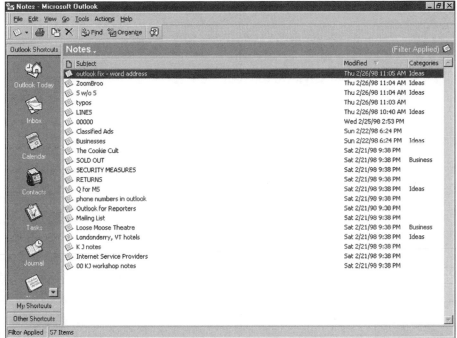

Figure 14-9:
Your notes for the past week, in all their glory.

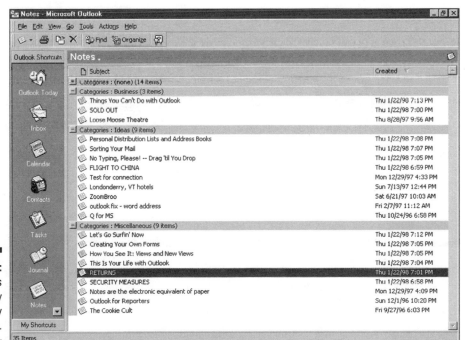

Figure 14-10:
Your notes in By Category view.

To view your notes By Color:

1. **Click the Notes icon in the Outlook Bar.**

   The Notes list appears.

2. **Choose View⇨Current View.**

   The Current View menu appears.

3. **Choose By Color.**

   You see a color-coded list of your notes (see Figure 14-11).

You can choose among only five colors for an Outlook note, so you can have only that many groups by color.

You can also right-click a note in By Color view and change the color for sorting.

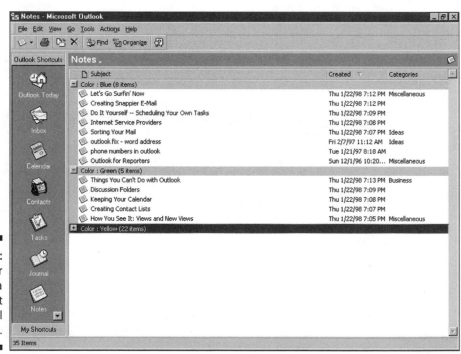

Figure 14-11:
By Color
view: not a
rainbow, but
colorful
nonetheless.

Assigning a Category to Your Notes

If you really want to get yourself organized, you can assign categories to all the items that you create in Outlook. That way, all your items can be sorted, grouped, searched, and even deleted according to the categories you've assigned them to.

To categorize your notes:

1. Click the Note icon in the upper-left corner of the Note.

The Note menu drops down (see Figure 14-12).

2. Choose Categories.

The Categories dialog box appears (see Figure 14-13).

3. Choose one of the existing categories, if one suits you, and then click OK.

You can also enter your own category in the Item(s) Belong to These Categories box.

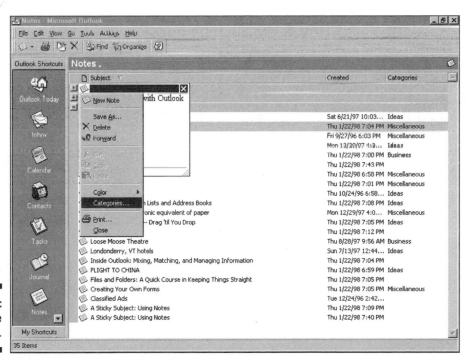

Figure 14-12:
The Note
menu.

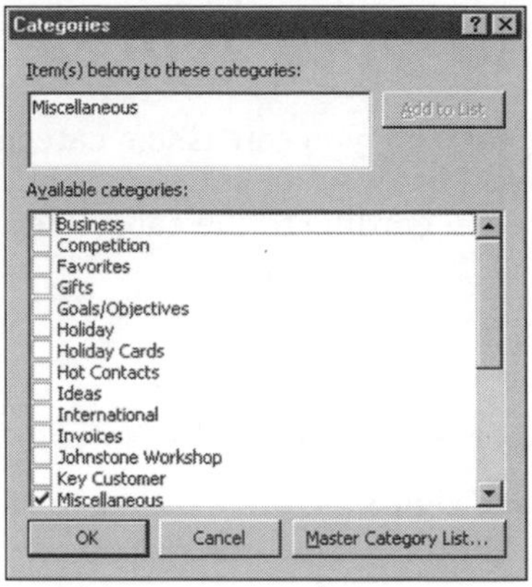

Figure 14-13:
The
Categories
dialog box
gives you
lots of
options.

4. **If none of the existing categories suits you, click <u>M</u>aster Category List.**

   From the Master Category List, you can add or delete categories (see Figure 14-14).

Figure 14-14:
The Master
Category
List.

5. **Type a category of your choice in the <u>N</u>ew Category box.**

   Be sure not to add too many new categories, or else finding things could get hard.

6. **Click <u>A</u>dd.**

   Your new category is part of the Categories list.

7. **Click OK.**

Whenever you see the Categories list, your new category will be among the categories that you can choose.

Printing Your Notes

You can organize and view your notes in so many clever ways that you'll also want to print what you can see, or at least the list of what you can see.

Printing a list of your notes

To print a list of your notes:

1. Click the Notes icon in the Outlook Bar.

The Notes list appears.

2. Choose File⇨Print (or press Ctrl+P).

The Print dialog box appears (see Figure 14-15).

3. In the Print Style box, choose Table Style.

If you choose Memo Style, you print the contents of a note rather than a list of notes.

4. Click OK.

If you want to print only a portion of your list of notes, click the first note that you want listed and then hold down the Shift key while clicking the last note that you want in your printout. When the Print dialog box appears, choose Only Selected Rows in the Print Range section.

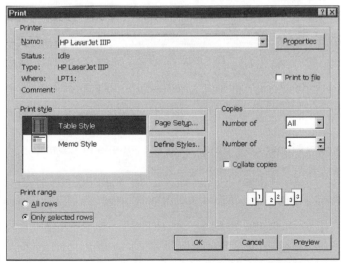

Figure 14-15:
The Print dialog box.

Printing the contents of a note

Computer screens are pretty, but there's still nothing like ink on paper. Of course you can print a note. Remember, though, that the pretty colors you've given your notes don't show on a black-and-white printer.

To print the contents of a note:

1. **Click the Notes icon in the Outlook Bar.**

   The Notes list appears.

2. **Click the title of the note that you want to print.**

3. **Choose File⇨Print (or press Ctrl+P).**

   The Print dialog box appears.

4. **In the Print Style box, choose Memo Style (see Figure 14-16).**

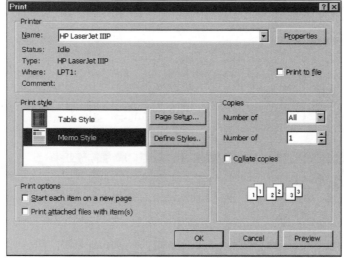

Figure 14-16:
The Print dialog box with Memo Style selected.

Choosing Memo Style prints the full contents of the note.

5. **Click OK.**

   Outlook prints the full contents of your note.

Changing Your Default Options for New Notes

Plain old notes are fine; you really don't need to change anything. But if you want to make some changes, the Options dialog box in the Tools menu gives you lots of . . . well . . . options. All the adjustments that you make in the Options dialog box change the size, color, and other qualities of your note when you first create the note. You can also change these qualities after you create the note.

Changing size and color

To change the color and size of your notes:

1. **Choose Tools➪Options.**

   The Options dialog box appears.

2. **Click the Note Options button.**

   The Note Options dialog box is where you change the options for the Notes module of Outlook.

3. **Click the triangle (scroll-down button) at the right end of the Color box.**

   A list of colors (Blue, Green, Pink, Yellow, White) drops down (see Figure 14-17). Choosing one of these options changes the color that all your notes will be when you create them.

Figure 14-17: Changing colors in the Note Options dialog box.

4. **Choose a color.**

5. **Click the scroll-down button (triangle) at the right end of the Size box.**

   The list reads Small, Medium, or Large. Choosing one of these options sets the size of your notes when you create them.

6. **Click OK.**

   Your notes are in the size and color to which you changed them.

Turning the date and time display on or off

At the bottom of each note, Outlook displays the date and time when you most recently changed the contents of the note. You may start to notice that you change a lot of notes on Mondays around 9:45 a.m. You may not want to notice that fact, so you can turn this handy little feature off.

To turn off the date and time display:

1. **Choose Tools⇨Options.**

   The Options dialog box appears.

2. **Click the Other tab.**

   I don't know why Microsoft called this the Other tab. Perhaps the programmers all kept arguing "Don't put that on MY tab! Put it on some OTHER tab!" Anyway, that's where you have to look. When you click the Other tab, the Other Options page appears.

3. **Click the Advanced Options button.**

   The Advanced Options dialog box appears (see Figure 14-18).

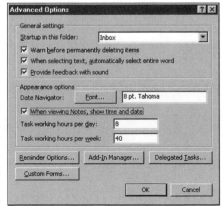

Figure 14-18: Time for some advanced options.

4. **Click the check box that says "When viewing Notes, show time and date."**

   A check mark appears in the check box if you click once, and then it disappears if you click a second time. If you want to turn off the time and date display, make sure that the box doesn't contain a check mark.

5. **Click OK.**

   The time and date will no longer show up on command, unless you follow the same steps you used in turning them off to turn the time and date on again.

Forwarding a Note

Forwarding a note really means sending an e-mail message with a note included as an attachment. It's helpful if the person to whom you're forwarding the note uses Outlook, too.

To forward a note:

1. **Click the Notes icon in the Outlook Bar.**

   The Notes list appears

2. **Click the title of the note that you want to forward.**

3. **Choose Actions⇨Forward (or press Ctrl+F).**

   The New Message form appears (see Figure 14-19).

4. **Click the To text box and type the e-mail address of the person to whom you're sending your note.**

   You can also click the To button to open the e-mail Address Book. Look up the name of the person to whom you want to forward your note, click To, and then click OK.

5. **Click the Cc text box and type the e-mail addresses of the people to whom you want to send a copy of your note.**

   If you're sending your note to several people, separate their addresses with a comma or a semicolon.

6. **Type the subject of the note in the Subject box.**

   The subject of your note will already be in the Subject box of the New Message form. You can leave it alone or type something else.

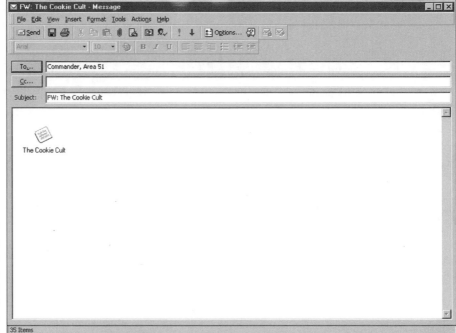

7. If you want, type the text of a message in the text box.

You don't really have to include a message. Your note may say all that you want to say, but you can also add regular e-mail message text.

8. Click the Send button.

Your message is off to its intended recipient.

If your note includes the address of a page on the World Wide Web, such as www.dummies.com, you can now just click the address to launch your Web browser as you can in all the other Outlook modules. Notes in Outlook 97 couldn't do that.

A Final Note

You can't take Outlook's Notes any more seriously than you take the little stick-on notes that you leave all over the fridge. They're just handy tools to help you save silly little scraps of information that you find you'll really need some day. After you've played with Notes a bit, you'll forget how you ever got along without them. When you remember again, make a note of it.

Chapter 15

Journaling

- -

In This Chapter

▶ Recording items in the Journal

▶ Checking out Journal entries for a contact

▶ Searching for a particular Journal entry

▶ Printing your Journal

▶ Changing your view of the Journal

▶ Setting up automatic Journal entries

- -

Stardate 1998: On *Star Trek,* the captain of the starship *Enterprise* faithfully makes daily entries in the star log. The captain records information about the planets the crew has explored, the aliens they've battled, and the bizarre phenomena they've observed out in deep space, where no man (or woman) has gone before!

Now it's your turn. Just like the captain of the *Enterprise,* you can record your daily interactions with strange beings in bizarre environments under stressful circumstances, even if the strange beings are all in your own office. The Outlook Journal is your star log.

No doubt the high muck-a-mucks of the galaxy use the captain's log for terribly important things, but your Journal serves you more directly. Sometimes, when you need to find a document or a record of a conversation, you don't remember what you called the document or where you stored it, but you do remember *when* you created or received the item. In this case, you can go to the Journal and check the date when you remember dealing with the item and find what you need to know.

To get good use from the Journal, you need to use it, though. You can set Outlook to make journal entries for nearly everything you do, or you can shut the Journal off entirely and make no entries to it. If you put nothing in the Journal, you get nothing out.

Don't Just Do Something — Stand There!

What's the easiest way to make entries in the Journal? Do nothing. The Journal automatically records any document you create, edit, or print in any Office 97 application. The Journal also automatically tracks e-mail messages, meeting requests and responses, and task requests and responses. In the future, programs other than the Microsoft Office suite may have the capability to make entries in the Journal, but right now, that feature is limited to Office 97 programs.

There's a catch: You have to tell Outlook that you want automatic Journal recording turned on (all right, so you do have to do something besides just standing there). Fortunately, if you haven't activated the Journal's automatic recording feature, Outlook 98 asks you whether you want to turn the feature on every time you click the Journal icon.

To turn on the Journal's automatic recording feature:

1. **Choose Tools➪Options.**

   The Options dialog box appears.

2. **Click the Journal Options button.**

   The Journal Options dialog box appears (see Figure 15-1) with check boxes for all the types of activities that you can record automatically and the names of all the people for whom you can automatically record transactions, such as e-mail.

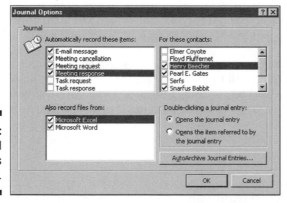

Figure 15-1:
The Journal
Options
dialog box.

3. **Click to place a check in the check box for those items and files you want to automatically record and for the contacts about whom you want the information recorded.**

The list of people in the For These Contacts box is the same as the list of people in your Contact list. You can manually create Journal entries for people who are not in your Contact list (see the section "Recording an Outlook item in the Journal manually").

When you add names to your Contact list in the Contacts module, those names aren't set for automatic recording in the Journal. You either need to check the name in the Journal Options dialog box or open the Contact record, click the Journal tab, and check Automatically Record Journal Entries for These Contacts.

4. Click OK.

The Journal automatically records those items and files you selected for the contacts you named.

Recording an Outlook item in the Journal manually

If you don't want to clutter your Journal by recording everything automatically, you can enter selected items manually — just drag them to the Journal icon. For example, you may not want to record every transaction with a prospective client until you're certain that you're doing business with that client. You can drag relevant e-mail messages to the Journal and retain a record of serious inquiries. When you actually start doing business with a new client, you can set up automatic recording.

To manually record items in the Journal:

1. Drag the item that you want to record (such as an e-mail message) to the Journal icon.

The Journal Entry form appears (see Figure 15-2). At the bottom of the form is an icon representing the item you're recording, along with the item's name.

2. Fill in the information that you want to record.

You don't have to record anything, though. The text box at the bottom of the screen gives you space for making a note to yourself, if you want to use it.

3. Click Save and Close.

The item that you recorded is entered in the Journal. You can see your new entry when you view your Journal, as I describe later in this chapter in the section "Viewing the Journal."

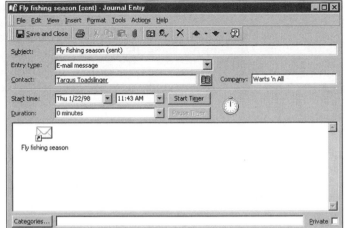

Figure 15-2:
A Journal entry with an e-mail message attached in the text box.

Recording a document in the Journal

If your favorite program, such as a drawing or desktop-publishing program, doesn't show up in the list of programs that can make automatic entries in the Journal, all is not lost — you can drag documents from Outlook's My Computer folder to the Journal folder to create Journal entries for those programs' files, too. Because the Journal can keep track of many types of information about a document other than date and time (such as client, subject, and some notes), you can use the Journal to keep track of files you create in programs that aren't part of Microsoft Office. If you've elected to let Outlook create Journal entries automatically for your Office 97 applications, you don't have to make entries for Office 97 documents.

To record a document in the Journal:

1. **Click the Other Shortcuts separator bar in the Outlook Bar.**

   The icons in the Other Shortcuts group appear, including the My Computer icon.

2. **Click the My Computer icon in the Outlook Bar.**

   Your list of drives appears (see Figure 15-3).

3. **Find the document that you want to record.**

   Double-click the drive that contains the document you want to record. Then double-click the folder in which you save your documents to find the document that you want to record. Highlight it.

4. **Click the Outlook Shortcuts separator bar in the Outlook Bar.**

   The icons in the Outlook Shortcuts group appear, including the Journal icon.

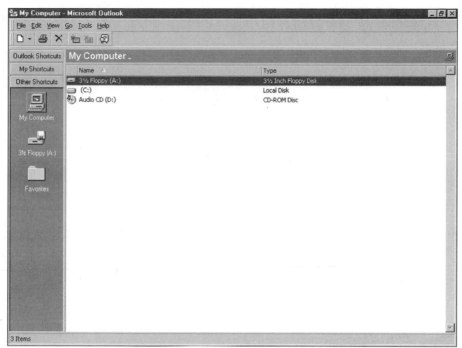

Figure 15-3:
The list of
drives in My
Computer.

5. Drag the document to the Journal icon.

The Journal Entry form appears, with an icon in the text box representing the file that you're recording.

6. Click Save and Close.

Your document is recorded in the Journal.

The big benefit of recording documents in the Journal is the fact that Journal entries are really shortcuts to the documents themselves. When you enter a document in the Journal, you have quick access to information you've saved about the document, and you're only one click away from the document itself. So if you use a non-Office 97 program that creates files that don't keep track of much information about themselves, the Journal is a great central location for keeping track of document information. For example, if you're saving pictures from a drawing program on your computer, you may want to save more information about each picture than just the filename. If you create Journal entries for each file, you can keep notes about each picture in the Journal. When you find the Journal entry for the picture you want, just double-click the icon for the picture. The program you use to see the picture opens.

Viewing Journal Entries for a Contact

My friend Vinnie in Brooklyn says, "You gotta know who you dealt wit' and when you dealt wit' 'em." You can use the Contact list together with the Journal to keep track of whom you dealt with when. Just look in the person's Contact record to see when you made Journal entries:

1. **Choose Go⇨Contacts.**

   The Contact list appears.

2. **Double-click the name of the contact that you want to view.**

   The Contact record opens.

3. **Click the Journal tab in the Contact form.**

   A list of every Journal entry you've made for that person appears (see Figure 15-4), including the automatic entries that Outlook made if you chose that option.

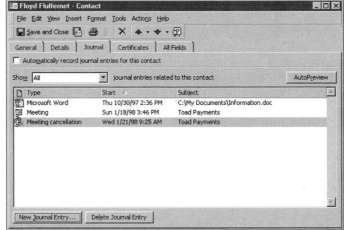

Figure 15-4:
Journal
entries for
Floyd
Fluffernet.

Finding a Journal Entry

When you don't remember exactly when you did something or dealt with somebody, you can look it up by searching for words in the Journal item.

To find a Journal entry when you don't know the *when:*

1. **Click the Journal icon in the Outlook Bar.**

   The list of Journal items appears.

2. **Choose Tools⇨Find.**

   The Find window appears (see Figure 15-5).

3. **Type a word or phrase that you can find in your Journal.**

   If you're looking for information about an upcoming meeting on the current Toad Inventory, type **toad**.

4. **Click the Find Now button.**

   A list of matching items appears below the Find window in your Journal list.

5. **Double-click the icon to the left of your item in the list at the bottom of the Find window.**

   The Journal item that you clicked appears. An icon in the text box at the bottom is a shortcut to any other Outlook item or document that the Journal entry represents. If you want to see the Calendar item that has details about the Toad Inventory meeting, double-click the icon at the bottom of the Journal entry. The Calendar item pops up.

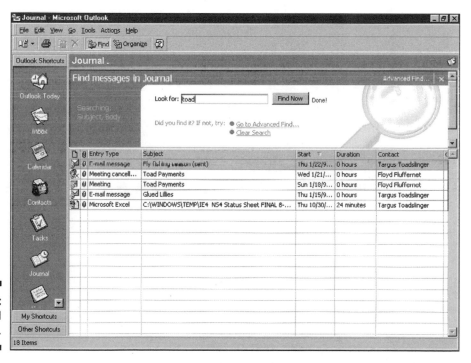

Figure 15-5:
The Find
window.

Printing Your Journal

I can't explain why, but I just don't get a complete picture from information on a screen. I still like to print out my work on paper to really see what I've done. Printing your Journal (or segments of it) allows you to see a printed list of recent or upcoming activities and stick it on the wall where you can look at it often.

To print your Journal:

1. Click the Journal icon in the Outlook Bar.

The list of Journal items appears.

2. Select the entries that you want to print.

If you select nothing, you print the entire list. Also, if you use one of the views I describe later in this chapter (or even create your own view by grouping, sorting, or filtering), what you see is what you print.

3. Choose File⇨Print (or press Ctrl+P).

The Print dialog box appears (see Figure 15-6).

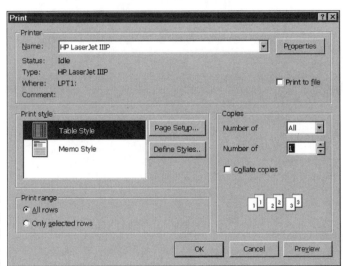

Figure 15-6:
The Print
dialog box.

4. Choose Table or Memo style.

Table style prints only a list of your Journal entries, not the contents of each entry. Memo style prints the contents of your Journal entries, with each item appearing as a separate memo.

5. Choose All Rows or Only Selected Rows.

If you want to print only certain rows, you have to select the rows that you want to print before you choose File⇨Print. Then click the Only Selected Rows button to limit what you print to those rows.

6. Click OK.

The list of Journal entries you selected prints.

The printed list won't go up on the wall for you, however, unless you put it there.

Viewing the Journal

As with other Outlook modules, the Journal comes with multiple views that show your entries in different ways, depending on what you need to see. You may just want to see your record of phone calls or a list organized by the names of the people you've dealt with. The Current View menu allows you to change from one view to the next quickly.

The Entry List

The Entry List is the whole tomato — all of your Journal entries, regardless of whom, what, or when. To call up the Entry List, simply choose View⇨ Current View⇨Entry List (see Figure 15-7).

You can click the heading at the top of any column to sort the list according to the information in that column. If you want to arrange your list of Journal entries by the type of entry, for example, click the header that says Entry Type. Your list is sorted alphabetically by type of entry, with conversations before e-mail before faxes and so on.

By Type

By Type view takes sorting one step further by grouping items according to their type. To view your entries by type, choose View⇨Current View⇨By Type. You can click the plus sign next to the name of the type to view your entire list of items of that type. Click the icon next to the name of the Entry Type again to close the list of that type. Then you can click to open another list of entries by type.

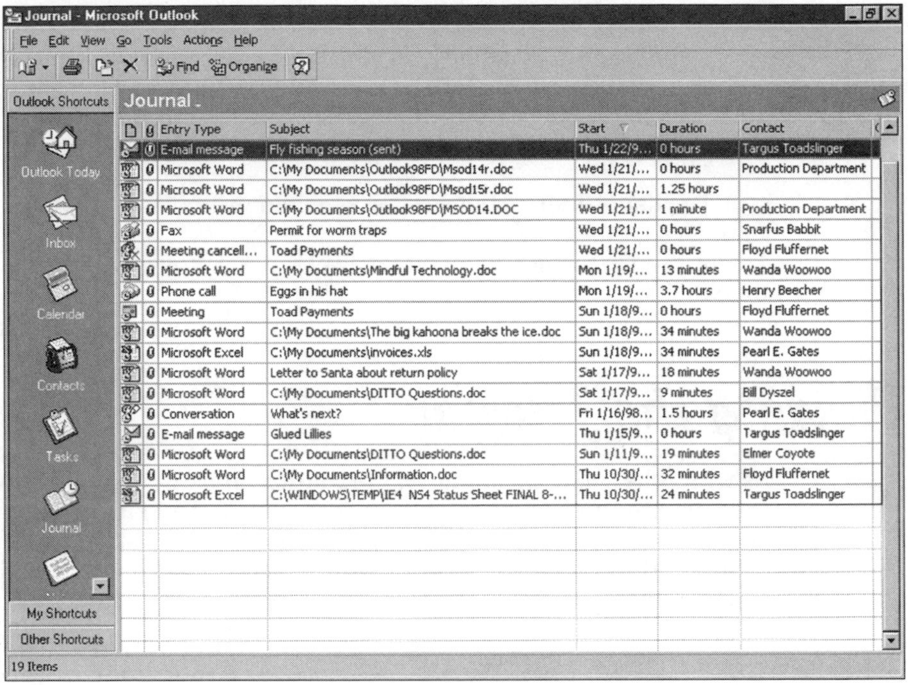

Figure 15-7:
Viewing the
Entry List —
everything
you've ever
entered.

By Contact

By Contact view shows your Journal items grouped by the name of the person associated with the item. To see your entries in By Contact view, choose View⇨Current View⇨By Contact (see Figure 15-8).

You can click the plus sign next to the name of the person whose entries you want to see. You can see entries for more than one person at a time.

By Category

If you've been assigning categories to your Journal items, By Category view collects all of your entries into bunches of items of the same category. To see your entries by category, choose View⇨Current View⇨By Category.

If you've assigned more than one category to an item, the item shows up under both categories you've assigned.

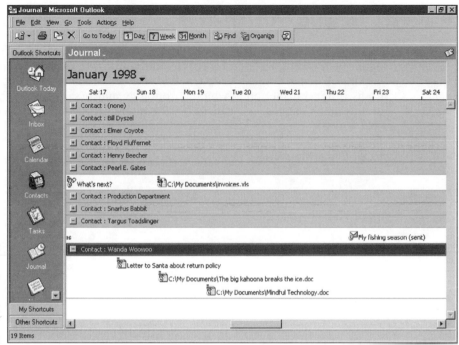

Figure 15-8:
Seeing your
entries in
By Contact
view.

Last Seven Days

The items that you're most likely to need first are the ones you used last.
Last Seven Days view is a quick way to see your most recent activities at a
glance. To see a week's worth of Journal entries, choose View➪Current View➪
Last Seven Days.

Documents that you've created, phone calls, e-mail messages — anything
you've done in the last seven days — you can see them all in Last Seven
Days view. This view shows anything you've worked on during the last week,
including documents you may have created a very long time ago; that's why
you may see some pretty old dates in this view.

Phone Calls

Because you can keep track of your phone calls in the Journal, the Journal
lets you see a list of the calls you've kept track of. Simply choose View➪
Current View➪Phone Calls.

To print a list of your phone calls, switch to Phone Calls view and press
Ctrl+P.

It's All in the Journal

The Journal can be enormously helpful whether you choose to use it regularly or rarely. You don't have to limit yourself to recording documents or Outlook items. You can keep track of conversations or customer inquiries or any other transaction in which chronology matters. If you set the Journal for automatic entries, you can ignore it completely until you need to see what was recorded. You can also play starship captain and record everything that you do — I haven't tried Outlook in outer space yet, but I know I would enjoy the views.

Chapter 16

Do It Yourself: Scheduling Your Own Tasks

In This Chapter

▶ Entering a new task

▶ Changing, copying, and deleting tasks

▶ Creating recurring and regenerating tasks

▶ Completing tasks

▶ Using views

You can store and manage more information about your daily tasks in Outlook than you may have wanted to know, but you'll certainly find that Outlook makes it easy to remember and monitor your daily work. Organizing your tasks doesn't have to be a task in itself.

Some people say that work expands to fill the available time, and chances are that your boss is one of those people. Who else would keep expanding your work all the time? One way of saving time is to keep a list of the tasks that are filling your time. That way, you can avoid getting too many more tasks to do.

I used to scrawl a to-do list on paper and hope I'd find the list in time to do the things I had written down. Now Outlook pops up and reminds me of the things I'm trying to forget to do just before I forget to do them. It also keeps track of when I'm supposed to have done my daily tasks and when I actually did them. That way, I can use all the things I was supposed to do yesterday as an excuse not to do the things I'm supposed to do today. (Outlook still won't do the stuff for me — it just tells me how far I'm falling behind. Be forewarned.)

Using the Outlook Tasks List

The Outlook Tasks list is easy to recognize as an electronic version of the good old plain-paper, scribbled to-do list. It's every bit as simple as it looks: a list of tasks and a list of dates for doing the tasks (see Figure 16-1).

The Tasks list actually turns up in more than one section of Outlook. Of course, it's in the Tasks module, but it also turns up in certain views of the Calendar. Seeing your Tasks list in Calendar view is very handy for figuring out when you need to do things, as well as what you need to do (see Figure 16-2).

Entering New Tasks

I don't mean for you to add work to your busy schedule; you already have plenty of that. But adding a task to your Tasks list in Outlook isn't such a task. Even though you can store gobs of information about your tasks in Outlook, you have both a quick way and a really quick way to enter a new task.

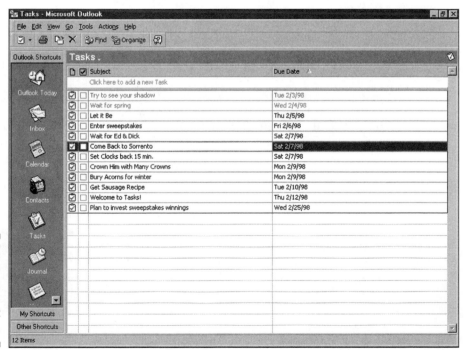

Figure 16-1:
Your Tasks list — more than you ever want to do.

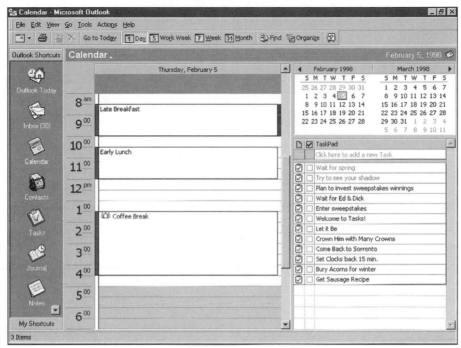

Figure 16-2:
A list of
your tasks
In Calendar
view.

The quick-and-dirty way to enter a task

If you're in one of the views that appear in Figure 16-1 and Figure 16-2, a little box at the top of the list says Click here to add a new Task. Do what the box says. (If you can't see the box, go on to the following section to discover the regular, slightly slower way to enter the task.)

To enter a task by using the quick-and-dirty way:

1. Click the text that says Click here to add a new Task.

The words disappear, and you see the Insertion Point (a blinking line).

2. Type the name of your task.

Your task appears in the block under the Subject line on the Tasks list. (See Figure 16-3.)

3. Press the Enter key.

Your new task moves down to the Tasks list with your other tasks.

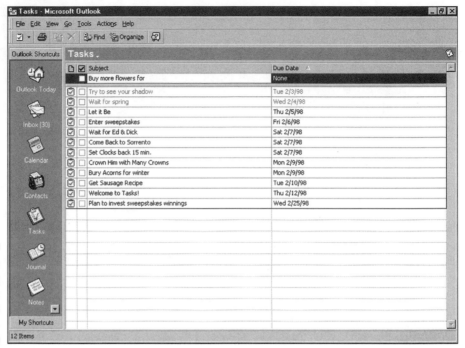

Figure 16-3:
Entering
your task in
the Tasks
list.

Isn't that easy? If only the tasks themselves were that easy to do. Maybe in the next version of Outlook, the tasks will get easier, too (in my dreams).

Of course, all you have is the name of the task — no due dates, reminders, or any of the cool stuff. If you want that information, you have to enter the task the regular way. (See the next section, "The regular way to enter a task.")

The regular way to enter a task

The regular way to enter a task is through the Task form, which looks like more work, but it's really not. As long as you enter a name for the task, you've done all that you really must. If you want to go hog-wild and enter all sorts of due dates or have Outlook remind you to actually *complete* the tasks that you've entered (heaven forbid!), you just need to put information in a few more boxes.

To add a task to your Tasks list, follow these steps:

1. Click the Tasks icon in the Outlook Bar.

Your Tasks list appears.

2. Choose File⇨New⇨Task.

The Task form appears (see Figure 16-4).

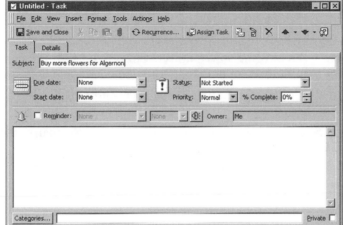

Figure 16-4:
You enter
your new
task in the
Task form.

3. Type the name of the task in the Subject box.

Use a subject that will help you remember what the task is. The main reason to create a task is to help you remember to do the task.

You can finish at this point by jumping to Step 22 (choose Save and Close or press Alt+S) if you want to add only the name of the task to your list. If you want to note a due date, start date, reminders, and so on, you have more to do. All the rest of the steps are optional; you can skip the ones that don't interest you.

4. (Optional) To assign a due date to the task, click the Due Date box.

5. (Optional) Enter the due date in the Due Date box.

You can enter a date in Outlook in several ways. You can type **7/4/97**, **the first Friday of July**, or **Three weeks from Friday**. You can also click the scroll-down button (triangle) at the right end of the Due Date text box and choose the date you want from the drop-down calendar.

6. (Optional) To assign a start date to the task, click the Start box and enter the start date.

If you haven't started the task, you can skip this step. You can use the same tricks to enter the start date that you use to enter the due date.

TIP

When you're entering information in a dialog box such as the Task form, you can press the Tab key to move from one text box to the next. You can use the mouse to click each text box before you type, but pressing the Tab key is a bit faster. I've written the directions in the order that you follow if you use the Tab key to move through the dialog box.

7. (Optional) Click the triangle at the right end of the Status box to choose the status of the task.

If you haven't begun, leave Status set to Not Started. You can also choose In Progress, Completed, Waiting on Someone Else, or Deferred.

8. (Optional) Click the triangle at the right end of the Priority box to choose the priority.

If you don't change anything, the priority stays Normal. You can also choose High or Low.

9. (Optional) Click the Reminder check box if you want to be reminded before the task is due.

If you'd rather forget the task, forget the reminder. But then, why enter the task at all?

10. (Optional) Click the date box next to the Reminder check box and enter the date when you want to be reminded.

If you entered a due date, Outlook has already entered that date in the Reminder box. You can enter any date you want (see Figure 16-5). If you choose a date in the past, Outlook lets you know that it won't be setting a reminder.

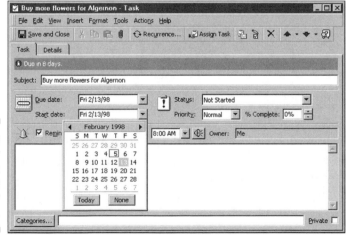

Figure 16-5:
A calendar drops down to show the date your task is due.

If you open the scroll-down menu by clicking the triangle on the right of the date box, a calendar appears. You can click the date you desire in the calendar.

11. **(Optional) Enter the time you want to activate the reminder in the time box.**

    The easiest way to set a time is to type the numbers for the time. You don't need colons or anything special. If you want to finish by 2:35 p.m., just type **235**. Outlook assumes that you're not a vampire, and it schedules your tasks and appointments during daylight hours unless you say otherwise. If you are a vampire, type **235a**; Outlook translates that to 2:35 a.m. If you simply *must* use correct punctuation, Outlook can handle that, too.

12. **(Optional) In the text box, enter miscellaneous notes and information about this task.**

    If you need to keep directions to the appointment, a list of supplies, or whatever, it all fits here.

13. **(Optional) Click the Categories button to assign a category to the appointment, if you want.**

    (Using the categories setting is another trick for finding things easily.) The Categories dialog box appears (see Figure 16-6).

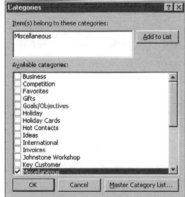

Figure 16-6:
The
Categories
dialog box.

14. **(Optional) Choose one of the existing categories, if one suits you, and then click OK.**

15. **(Optional) If none of the existing categories suits you, click _M_aster Category List.**

    The Master Category List dialog box appears (see Figure 16-7).

Figure 16-7:
The Master
Category
List.

16. **(Optional) Type a category of your choice in the New Category box.**

    Be sure not to add too many new categories; if you do, finding things could get hard.

17. **(Optional) Click Add.**

18. **(Optional) Click OK.**

19. **(Optional) Select the new category from the categories list.**

    You can choose more than one category at a time.

20. **(Optional) Click OK.**

21. **(Optional) Click the Private box, in the lower-right corner of the Task form, if you're on a network and you don't want other users to know about your tasks.**

22. **Click the Save and Close button to finish.**

    Your new task is now standing at the top of your task list, waiting to be done.

Adding an Internet link to a Task

If you type the name of a Web page, such as www.pcstudio.com, in the text box at the bottom of the Task form, Outlook changes the text color to blue and underlines the address, making it look just like the hypertext you click to jump between different pages on the World Wide Web. That makes it easy to save information about an exciting Web site; just type or copy the address into your task. To view the page you entered, just click the text to make your Web browser pop up and open the page.

Editing Your Tasks

No sooner do you enter a new task than it seems that you need to change it. Sometimes, I enter a task the quick-and-dirty way and change some of the particulars later — add a due date, a reminder, an added step, or whatever. Editing tasks is easy.

The quick-and-dirty way to change a task

For lazy people like me, Outlook offers a quick-and-dirty way to change a task, just as it has a quick-and-dirty way to enter a task. You are limited in the number of details you can change, but the process is fast.

If you can see the name of a task, and if you want to change something about the task you can see, follow the steps I describe in this section. If you can't see the task or the part that you want to change, use the regular method, which I describe in the next section of this chapter.

1. **Click the thing that you want to change.**

   You see a blinking line at the end of the text, a triangle at the right end of the box, or a menu with a list of choices.

2. **Select the old information.**

   The old text is highlighted to show you that it's selected (see Figure 16-8).

3. **Type the new information.**

   The new information replaces the old. If you click the Status box, a menu drops down and you can choose from the list.

4. **Press the Enter key.**

Isn't that easy? If all you want to change is the name, status, or due date, the quick-and-dirty way will get you there.

The regular way to change a task

If you don't want to be quick and dirty, or if the information that you want to change about a task isn't on the list you're looking at, you have to take a slightly longer route. The regular way is a little more work, but not much.

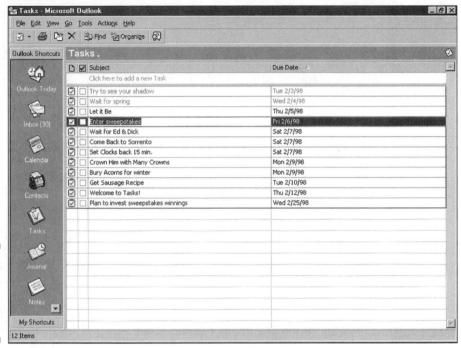

Figure 16-8:
A task
highlighted
in the Tasks
list.

To make changes to a task the clean-and-long way (also known as the regular way), follow these steps:

1. Click the Tasks icon in the Outlook Bar.

The Tasks module opens.

2. Choose View⇨Current View⇨Simple List.

You can choose a different Current View if you know that the view includes the task you want to change. The Simple List is the most basic view of your tasks; it's sure to include the task you're looking for.

3. Double-click the name of the task that you want to change.

The New Task form appears (see Figure 16-9). Now you can change anything you can see in the box. Just click the information you want to change, type the new information, and click Save and Close (or press Alt+S).

4. Change the name of the task.

The name is your choice. Remember to call the task something that helps you remember the task. There's nothing worse than a computer reminding you to do something that you can't understand.

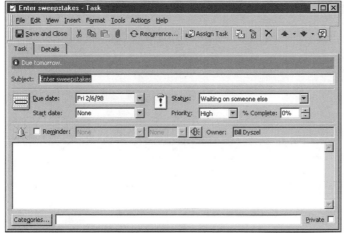

Figure 16-9:
The New
Task form.

5. **To change the due date, click the Due Date box.**

6. **Enter the new due date in the Due Date box.**

   Plenty of date styles work here — **7/4/97**, **the first Friday in July**, **Six weeks from now**, whatever. Unfortunately, **the 12th of Never** isn't an option. Sorry.

7. **Click the Start Date box and enter the new start date.**

   If you haven't started the task, you can skip this step. You don't absolutely need a start date; it's just for your own use.

8. **Click the scroll-down button (triangle) at the right end of the Status box to see a menu that lets you change the status of the task.**

   If you're using Outlook at work and you're hooked up to a network, the Status box entry is one way of keeping your boss informed of your progress. You'll need to check with your boss or system administrator if this is the case.

   If you're using Outlook at home, chances are that nobody else will care, but you may feel better if you know how well you're doing. You can't add your own choices to the Status box. I'd like to add "Waiting, hoping the task will go away." No such luck. Figure 16-10 shows the Task box with the Status line highlighted.

9. **Click the scroll-down button (triangle) at the right end of the Priority box to change the priority.**

   Switch the priority to High or Low, if the situation changes (see Figure 16-11).

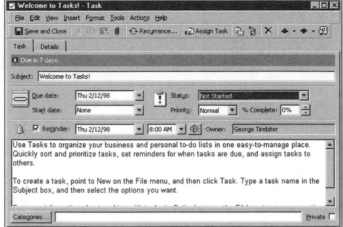

Figure 16-10:
This Task
form shows
a nonstarter
in the Status
box.

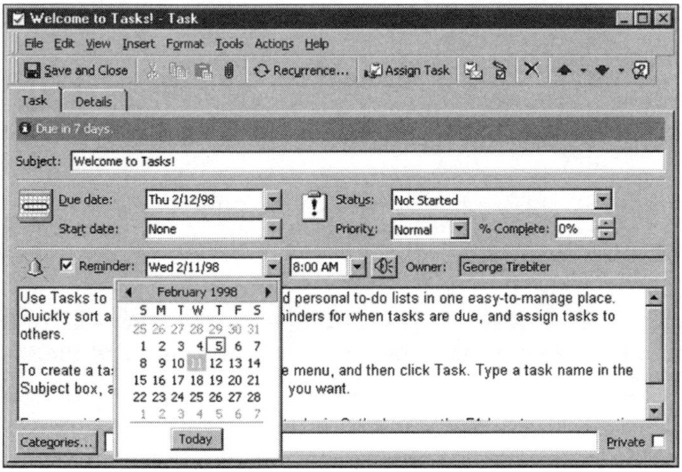

Figure 16-11:
Maybe this
nonstarter
should have
a lower
priority.

10. **Click the Reminder check box if you want to turn the reminder on or off.**

    Reminders are easy and harmless, so why not? If you didn't ask for one the first time, do it now.

11. **Click the date box next to the Reminder check box to enter or change the date when you want to be reminded.**

    You can enter any date you want. Your entry doesn't have to be the due date; it can be much earlier, reminding you to get started. You can even set a reminder after the task is due, which isn't very useful. You should make sure that the reminder is before the due date. The default date for a reminder is the date the task is due.

12. Change the time you want to activate the reminder in the time box.

When entering times, keep it simple. The entry **230** does the trick when you want to enter 2:30 p.m. If you make appointments at 2:30 a.m. (I'd rather not know what kind of appointments you make at that hour), you can type **230a**.

13. Click the text box to add or change miscellaneous notes and information about this task.

You can add detailed information here that doesn't really belong anywhere else in the Task form (see Figure 16-12). You see these details only when you open the Task form again; they don't normally show up in your Tasks list.

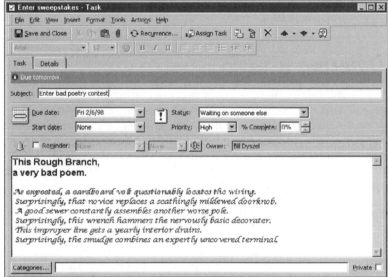

Figure 16-12: Details, details. Add 'em in the text box.

14. Click the Save and Close button to finish.

There! You've changed your task.

Copying a task

By now, you're probably saying, "I had so much fun setting up a task for myself; I'd like to set up another one." If it's the same task on a different day, the easiest approach is to copy the task.

To copy a task, follow these steps:

1. **Select the task that you want to copy.**

   The selected task is highlighted in blue (see Figure 16-13).

2. **Choose Edit⇨Copy (or press Ctrl+C).**

3. **Choose Edit⇨Paste (or press Ctrl+V).**

   A new, identical copy of your task appears just below the old one. The problem is that it's exactly the same task. You don't need Siamese-twin tasks, so you probably want to change the date of the new task. Double-click the new task and change the date.

For creating tasks that recur every day, copying the task is pretty laborious. That's why you can set up a task as a recurring task the way I describe in "Managing Recurring Tasks," later in this chapter.

Deleting a task

The really gratifying part about tasks is getting rid of them, preferably by completing the tasks you've entered. You may also delete a task you changed your mind about. Of course, nothing is stopping you from deleting tasks you just don't want to bother with; this version of Outlook can't really tell whether you've actually completed your tasks. Rumor has it that the next version of Outlook will know whether you've finished your tasks and report to Santa. Don't be naughty!

To delete a task, follow these steps:

1. **Select the task.**

2. **Choose Edit⇨Delete (or press Ctrl+D, or click the Delete button in the toolbar).**

   Poof! Your task is gone.

Managing Recurring Tasks

Lots of tasks crop up on a regular basis. You know how it goes — same stuff, new day. To save you the effort of entering a task like a monthly sales report or a quarterly tax payment over and over again, just set it up as a recurring task. Outlook can then remind you whenever it's that time again.

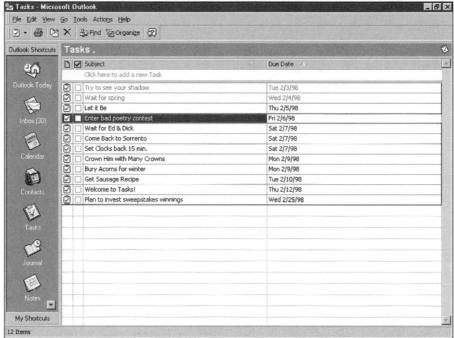

Figure 16-13:
Your
selected
task is
highlighted.

To create a recurring task, follow these steps:

1. Open the task by double-clicking it.

The Task form appears (see Figure 16-14).

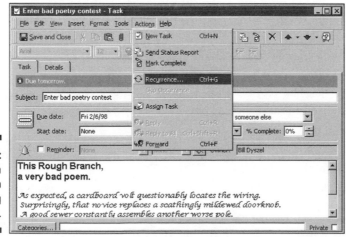

Figure 16-14:
Getting a
handle on
recurring
tasks.

2. **Click the Recurrence button in the Task Form toolbar (or press Ctrl+G).**

   The Task Recurrence dialog box appears (see Figure 16-15).

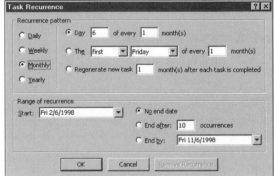

Figure 16-15:
How often
should this
task be
done?

3. **Choose the Daily, Weekly, Monthly, or Yearly option to specify how often the appointment occurs.**

   Each choice you make — Daily, Weekly, or Monthly — changes the types of exact choices available for when the task recurs. For example, a daily recurring task can be set to recur every day or every five days or whatever. A monthly recurring task can be set to recur on a certain day of the month, such as the 15th of each month, or on the second Friday of every month.

4. **In the next box to the right, specify how often the appointment occurs, such as every third day or the first Monday of each month.**

   If you choose to create a monthly task, for example, you can click the scroll-down buttons (triangles) to choose "First" then "Monday" to schedule a task on the first Monday of each month.

5. **In the Range of Recurrence box, enter the first occurrence in the Start box.**

6. **Choose when you want the appointments to stop (no end date, after a certain number of occurrences, or at a certain date).**

7. **Click OK.**

   A banner appears at the top of the Task form describing the recurrence pattern of the task.

8. **Click Save and Close.**

Your task appears in the list of tasks once, but it has a different type of icon than nonrecurring tasks so that you can tell at a glance that it's a recurring task.

Creating a regenerating task

A *regenerating task* is like a recurring task except that it only recurs when a certain amount of time passes after the last time you completed the task. Say that you mow the lawn every two weeks. If it rains for a week and one mowing happens a week late, you still want to wait two weeks for the next one. If you schedule your mowings in Outlook, you'd use the Regenerating Task feature to enter your lawn-mowing schedule.

To create a regenerating task:

1. Open the task by double-clicking it.

The Task form appears.

2. Click the Recurrence button in the toolbar in the Task form (or press Ctrl+G).

The Task Recurrence dialog box appears.

3. Click the Regenerate New Task button (see Figure 16-16).

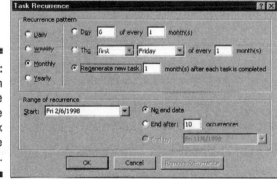

Figure 16-16:
You can regenerate a task in the Task Recurrence dialog box.

4. Enter the number of weeks between regenerating each task.

5. Click OK.

A banner appears in the Task form describing the regeneration pattern you've set for the task.

6. Click Save and Close.

Your task appears in the list of tasks once, but it has a different type of icon than nonrecurring tasks so that you can tell at a glance that it's a regenerating task.

Skipping a recurring task once

When you need to skip a single occurrence of a recurring task, you don't have to change the recurrence pattern of the task forever; just skip the occurrence you want to skip and leave the rest alone.

To skip a recurring task:

1. **Click the Tasks icon in the Outlook Bar.**

   Your list of tasks appears.

2. **Choose <u>V</u>iew⇨Current <u>V</u>iew⇨Simple List.**

   It doesn't matter which view you use, as long as you can see the name of the task that you want to skip. I suggest the Simple List because it's . . . well, simple.

3. **Double-click the name of the task that you want to change.**

   The Task form appears.

4. **Choose Actio<u>n</u>s⇨S<u>k</u>ip Occurrence.**

   The due date changes to the date of the next scheduled occurrence.

5. **Click <u>S</u>ave and Close.**

   Your task remains in the list with the new scheduled occurrence date showing.

Marking Tasks Complete

Marking off those completed tasks is even more fun than entering them, and it's much easier. If you can see the task that you want to mark complete in your Tasks list, just click the check box next to the name of the task. Nothing could be simpler.

To mark a task complete, follow these steps:

1. **Click the Tasks icon in the Outlook Bar.**

   The Tasks module opens.

2. **Choose <u>V</u>iew⇨Current <u>V</u>iew⇨Simple List.**

   Actually, you can choose any view you want, as long as the task that you're looking for shows up there. If the task that you want to mark complete isn't in the view you chose, try the Simple List, which contains everything.

3. **Click the box next to the name of the task that you want to mark complete.**

   The box in the second column from the left is the one that you want to check (see Figure 16-17).

   When you check the box, the name of the task changes color and gets a line through it. You're finished.

Marking several tasks complete

Perhaps you don't race to your computer every time you complete a task. Marking off your completed tasks in a bunch is faster than marking them one by one. Outlook allows you to do that by making a multiple selection.

To mark several tasks complete, follow these steps:

1. **Click the Tasks icon in the Outlook Bar.**

   The Tasks module opens.

2. **Choose View➪Current View➪Simple List.**

   Again, I'm just suggesting Simple List view because it's most likely to show you all your tasks. You can pick any view that allows you to see the tasks that you want to mark.

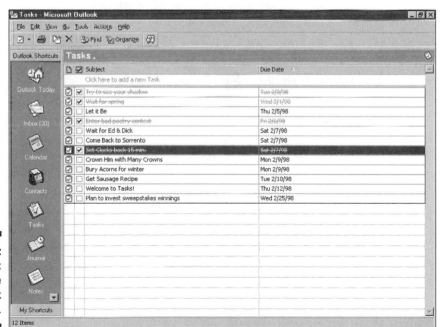

Figure 16-17:
A check marks the task complete.

3. **Click the first task that you want to mark.**

4. **Hold down the Ctrl key and click each of the other tasks that you want to mark.**

   All the tasks you clicked are highlighted, showing that you've selected them.

5. **Right-click one of the tasks that you've highlighted.**

   A menu appears (see Figure 16-18).

Figure 16-18:
A shortcut menu in the Tasks module.

6. **Choose Mark Complete.**

   The tasks you selected are marked complete.

Picking a color for completed or overdue tasks

When you complete a task or when it becomes overdue, Outlook changes the color of the text for the completed tasks to gray and the overdue tasks to red, which makes it easy for you to tell at a glance which tasks are done and which tasks remain to be done. If you don't like Outlook's color choices, you can pick different colors.

Here's how to change the color of completed and overdue tasks:

1. **Choose Tools⇨Options.**

   The Options dialog box appears.

2. **Click the Task Options button.**

   The Task Options page appears (see Figure 16-19).

Figure 16-19:
The Task
Options
page.

3. **Click the scroll-down button (triangle) at the right end of the Over-due Tasks box.**

   A list of colors drops down.

4. **Choose a color for overdue tasks.**

5. **Click the scroll-down button (triangle) at the right end of the Completed Tasks box.**

   A list of colors drops down.

6. **Choose a color for completed tasks.**

7. **Click OK.**

Your completed and overdue tasks will appear on your list in the colors you chose.

Viewing Your Tasks

Outlook comes with several ways to view your Tasks list and allows you to invent and save as many custom views as you like. The views that come with Outlook take you a long way when you know how to use them.

To change your view of your tasks, choose View⇨Current View, and then choose one of the following views from the menu:

- ✔ *Simple List* view is just the facts — the names you gave each task and the due date you assigned (if you assigned one). The Simple List view makes it easy to add new tasks and mark old ones complete. However, you won't see any extra information. If you want details . . .

- ✔ *Detailed List* view is a little more . . . uh, detailed than the Simple List view. It's really the same information, plus the status of the tasks, the percentage of each task complete, and whatever categories you may have assigned to your tasks.

- ✔ *Active List* view shows you only tasks that you haven't finished yet. After you mark a task complete, zap! Completed tasks vanish from the Active List view, which helps keep you focused on the tasks remaining to be done.

✔ *Next Seven Days* view is even more focused than the Active List view. The Next Seven Days view shows only uncompleted tasks scheduled to be done within the next seven days. It's just right for those people who like to live in the moment, or at least within the week.

✔ *Overdue Tasks* view means that you've been naughty. These are the tasks that needed doing yesterday but are still hanging around today.

✔ *By Category* view breaks up your tasks according to the category that you've assigned each task. You can open and close categories to focus on the type of tasks you're looking for. For example, you may assign a category of Sales to the sales-related tasks in your list. When you want to focus on sales, use the By Category view and click the Sales category.

✔ *Assignment* view lists your tasks in order of the name of the person upon whom you've dumped, er, I mean delegated, each task.

✔ *By Person Responsible* view contains the same information as the Assignment view, but the list is grouped to let you see the assignments of only one person at a time.

✔ *Completed Tasks* view shows (you guessed it) tasks you've marked complete. You don't need to deal with completed tasks anymore, but looking at the list gives you a warm, fuzzy feeling, doesn't it?

✔ *Task Timeline* view draws a picture of when each task is scheduled to start and end. Seeing a picture of your tasks gives you a better idea of how to fit work into your schedule sensibly.

Chapter 17

Outlook Express: Getting the Scoop on Newsgroups

In This Chapter

▶ Locating newsgroups

▶ Subscribing to a newsgroup

▶ Reading and replying to newsgroup messages

▶ Posting a message to a newsgroup

*M*icrosoft gave Outlook a cousin named Outlook Express. The two programs do many of the same jobs, but each has its own specialty. The most important difference between Outlook 98 and Outlook Express is that Outlook Express is free. Yep, you can get a copy of Outlook Express without spending a dime. The program is included with Internet Explorer 4.0 as well as with certain releases of Windows, so if you have Outlook 98, you also have Outlook Express.

The other difference between the two programs is that Outlook Express can read Internet newsgroups and Outlook 98 can't. Internet newsgroups are collections of messages that anyone can read. After you read the messages in a newsgroup, you can reply to any message you read or post a whole new message of your own. To participate in a newsgroup, you need a special type of program called a *newsreader* — Outlook Express is just the tool for the job.

Outlook Express can also send and receive e-mail just like Outlook 98, but only Outlook 98 can do all the fancy tricks with your tasks and calendar and contacts that I discuss throughout the rest of this book. If you only have Outlook Express but not Outlook 98, you have the basic tools you need for exchanging e-mail. After you've exchanged enough e-mail, you'll probably want to graduate from Outlook Express to full-strength Outlook to make your e-mail easier to handle.

The fact that Microsoft named both products Outlook causes plenty of confusion. What's even more confusing is that you can start Outlook Express from a menu in Outlook 98 — just choose Go⇨News. To further confuse the issue, the version of Outlook Express that appears when you choose Go⇨News from the Outlook 98 menu is different from the version that appears when you click the Outlook Express icon on your desktop.

The way I like to simplify the whole mess is by only opening Outlook Express from the Outlook 98 menu and only using Outlook Express for reading Internet newsgroups. Because you have this book, I'm assuming that you have Outlook 98, which means that you also have Outlook Express.

Finding Newsgroups

Newsgroups are out there on the Internet for anyone to see, so you may as well jump right in and explore what newsgroups have to offer. The first time you start up Outlook Express, you need to find a newsgroup to look at.

To view a newsgroup:

1. **Choose Go⇨News from the Outlook 98 menu.**

   The Outlook Express screen appears (see Figure 17-1).

2. **Click the News Groups button on the Outlook Express toolbar.**

   The Newsgroups dialog box opens (see Figure 17-2). The large window in the middle of the Newsgroups dialog box contains a list of all the newsgroups that are available for you to see. You can scroll down the list and find a newsgroup whose name looks interesting. But with tens of thousands of newsgroups on the Internet, scrolling through the whole list could take quite a long time, so I suggest a faster method in the following steps.

3. **Click in the text box that says *Display newsgroups which contain* and type a one-word name for a subject that interests you.**

   The list in the Newsgroups window changes to a list of newsgroups whose title includes the word you typed. For example, if you type the word *Outlook*, the newsgroups in which people post comments, questions, and answers about Outlook appear.

4. **Click the name of a newsgroup that interests you.**

   The name you click is highlighted to show that you've selected it.

5. **Click the Go To button at the bottom of the Newsgroups dialog box.**

   The Outlook Express main screen appears with a list of the most recent messages posted to the newsgroup you chose.

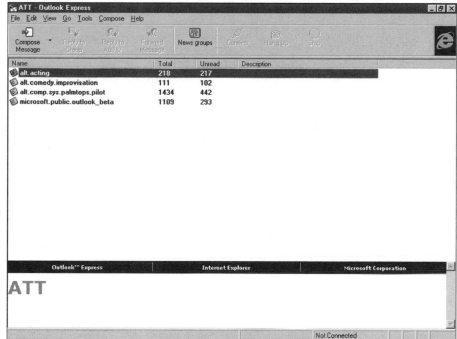

Figure 17-1:
Outlook
Express
looks
strangely
similar to
Outlook 98.

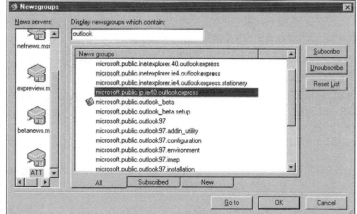

Figure 17-2:
Pick the
newsgroup
you want to
see in the
Newsgroups
dialog box.

Subscribing to Newsgroups

If you start hanging around in Internet newsgroups, you'll find that you spend a lot of time in a handful of groups, and you'll probably ignore the other tens of thousands of groups out there. Who has time to read 10,000 newsgroups anyway?

You can get into your favorite newsgroups more quickly if you subscribe. Subscribing to newsgroups is different from subscribing to a magazine. You don't pay a fee for subscribing to a newsgroup, and nobody needs to know you're reading a newsgroup unless you post messages to the group.

Don't post your e-mail address to an Internet newsgroup. People who send junk e-mail often gather e-mail addresses from newsgroups. After the junk e-mailers (or *spammers,* in Internet jargon) get your address, your Inbox may become stuffed with so many junk e-mail messages that you won't be able to find the messages you really want to see.

To subscribe to a newsgroup:

1. **Click the News Groups icon in the Outlook Express toolbar.**

   The Newsgroups dialog box appears.

2. **Click the name of a newsgroup to which you want to subscribe in the Newsgroups window.**

   The name of the group you selected is highlighted in blue to show that you've selected it.

3. **Click the Subscribe button on the right side of the Newsgroups dialog box.**

   A special icon appears next to the group you chose to show that you've subscribed.

From now on, whenever you start up Outlook Express by choosing Go⇨News from the Outlook 98 menu, the first thing you see is a list of the newsgroups to which you've subscribed. When you click the newsgroup you want to read, the latest messages in that newsgroup appear.

Reading Newsgroup Messages

The list of newsgroup messages is organized according to the subject of each message and the date when each message was posted to the newsgroup. You may see some messages with a little plus sign to the right of the subject (see Figure 17-3). The plus sign means that more than one message about that subject is posted to the list. You can see all the other messages by clicking the plus sign. The plus sign then turns into a minus sign, and all the other messages on that topic appear.

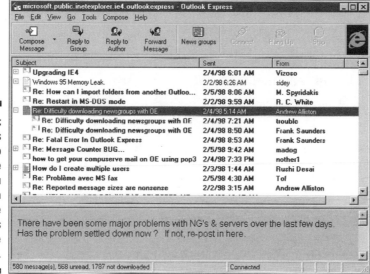

Figure 17-3:
The plus sign next to a message tells you that you can read more messages on the same subject.

If you want to read the text of a newsgroup message, click the title of the message once. That selects the message and makes the text of the message appear in the window below the list of message titles. To read the next message, just click the title of the next message in the list.

Replying to a Newsgroup Message

Reading messages in a newsgroup is only half the fun. It's only when you put your two cents in that things get really interesting.

Internet newsgroups can be time-consuming, emotionally draining, and habit-forming. No self-help group exists for newsgroup addicts yet, but I think it's only a matter of time. Remember, you don't know the other people on a newsgroup, so don't get your socks in a knot over what people say to you online. Not everybody in every Internet newsgroup is polite or considerate, but it pays for you to remain as civil as possible.

If you're *really* ready, here's how to reply to a newsgroup message:

1. **Double-click the message to which you want to reply.**

   The message you clicked opens in a new window.

2. **Choose <u>C</u>ompose⇨Reply to Newsgr<u>o</u>up (or press Ctrl+G).**

   A new message window appears (see Figure 17-4).

3. **Type your message.**

   Your message appears in the new message window.

4. **Click the Post button.**

   The new message window closes and your message is posted to the newsgroup.

Newsgroup messages don't appear instantly to the newsgroup. Thousands of servers are out there with millions of messages, so it can take anywhere from a few minutes to a day or so for your message to show up.

Figure 17-4: When you reply to a newsgroup message, the text of the message you're answering appears as part of your reply.

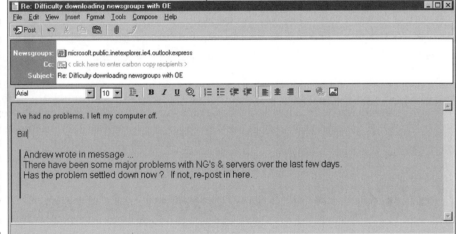

Posting a New Message

As your horoscope said one time (because everybody's has at least once), you have a creative streak and you need to express yourself. A newsgroup is the cheapest place to publish your latest stroke of literary genius. On the other hand, an Internet newsgroup is probably not the best place to reveal your most private thoughts. Remember, anybody on earth can read this stuff. Before you post anything too original to the Internet, read your high school yearbook, see what you said then, and decide whether you want to make that kind of mistake again.

If you still can't restrain yourself, here's how to post an original message to a newsgroup:

1. **View the newsgroup to which you want to post your new message.**

   The list of messages in the newsgroup that you selected appears.

2. **Choose Compose⇨New Message (or press Ctrl+N).**

   A new message window appears.

3. **Type a new subject on the Subject line.**

   You're better off making your subject short, snappy, and relevant. You'll find plenty of newsgroup messages with titles that are neither snappy nor relevant. The poor souls who wrote those messages haven't read this book. Have pity on them, but set a good example, okay?

4. **Type your message in the message text box.**

   The text of your message appears in the message text box.

5. **When your message is complete, choose File⇨Send Message.**

   The message window closes.

There's one thing I can't overemphasize (but I'll try): Anybody on earth can read what you've posted to an Internet newsgroup. If you plan to post a statement that could cause you problems with your job, your relationships, or the law, you should assume that the wrong people will see what you post. Be careful.

Chapter 18

Mail Merge from Outlook to Microsoft Word

In This Chapter

▶ Creating mailing labels

▶ Addressing envelopes

▶ Compiling form letters

▶ Merging from selected contacts

*O*utlook and Word 97 were made to work as a team. Word adds its services as your e-mail editor in Outlook, and the Contact list in Outlook is on-call for mail-merge duty. Any information in the Address Book can be plugged into Word so that you can create a *Mail Merge* — a repetitive letter that's printed many times with the same contents, but each letter is addressed to a different person. You typically use Mail Merge to plug addresses into a form letter, but you can include other information as well.

If you already use the Mail Merge feature in Word, you'll enjoy how Outlook manages your address lists and makes using your address lists simple. If you're new to Word or the Mail Merge feature, take a look at *Word 97 For Windows For Dummies* by Dan Gookin (published by IDG Books Worldwide, Inc.).

Creating Mailing Labels

You can create a set of mailing labels for everyone in your Address Book lickety-split. The Outlook Contact list turns up right in Word's mail-merge dialog boxes, so you don't have to mess around with exporting files and figuring out where they went when you want to merge to them. All you have to do is pick Outlook as the source of your addresses.

To create a set of mailing labels in Word 97:

1. **Choose Tools➪Mail Merge.**

   The Mail Merge Helper appears.

2. **Click Create.**

   A drop-down list appears (see Figure 18-1).

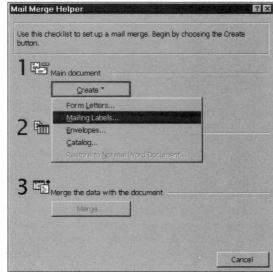

Figure 18-1:
The Mail
Merge
Helper with
the Create
drop-down
list
showing.

3. **Choose Mailing Labels.**

   A dialog box appears, asking whether you want to turn the active document window into your mail-merge document or create a new document.

4. **Click the Active Window button.**

   If your active document window contains text that you don't want to use in the mail merge, click the New Main Document button instead. When the dialog box disappears, the choice you make appears in the Mail Merge Helper dialog box.

5. **Click the Get Data button in the Mail Merge Helper.**

   A drop-down menu appears, giving you a choice about where to get the data for your labels.

6. **Choose Use Address Book.**

   A dialog box appears (see Figure 18-2), offering you another choice about which address book to use for your label data.

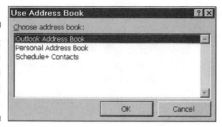

Figure 18-2:
The Use
Address
Book dialog
box.

7. **Choose the Outlook Address Book.**

   If you have more than one folder designated as your Outlook Address Book, another dialog box appears, asking you to choose which Address Book to use. If in doubt, choose the default by clicking OK; otherwise, pick the one that you know is right.

8. **Click OK.**

   A dialog box appears. It has only one button, which says Set Up Main Document.

9. **Click the <u>S</u>et Up Main Document button.**

   The Label Options dialog box appears (see Figure 18-3).

10. **Choose the label type you want; then click OK to return to the Mail Merge Helper.**

    Check the stock number on your label and make sure it's the same as the one you're choosing. If the stock number isn't available, you can look at the label dimensions in the Label Information section of the Label Options dialog box.

11. **In the Mail Merge Helper, click Insert Merge Field.**

    A list of field names appears. The collection of names in the list bears a striking resemblance to the kinds of data that you can enter in the Outlook Contact list. Funny, huh?

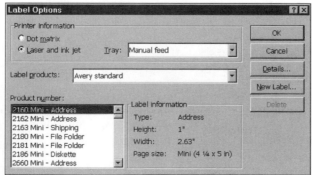

Figure 18-3:
The Label
Options
dialog box.

12. **Click each piece of data that you want to include in your label.**

    For example, on a typical address label, you click Insert Merge Field, select First_Name, press the spacebar, click Insert Merge Field, select Last_Name, press Enter, click Insert Merge Field, and select Postal_Address. You don't have to mess with City, State, and Zip, because Outlook deals with the entire mailing address as a single unit.

13. **Click OK.**

    The Mail Merge Helper reappears.

14. **Click the Merge button.**

    The Mail Merge dialog box opens.

15. **Click Merge again.**

    Again? Yes, there are two Merge buttons. The first button was the Mail Merge Helper; the second one is the actual Merge command.

I like to test a Mail Merge in mailing-label format before doing an actual merge, just to be sure that everything works out. You can print labels on regular paper to see what they look like. If you make a mistake setting up the merge, it's faster to find out by printing ten pages of messed-up "labels" on plain paper than by printing 300 messed-up letters.

Printing Envelopes

You don't have to print to labels at all if you're planning a mass mailing; you can print directly onto the envelopes that you're sending. Make sure that your printer has an envelope feeder. Feeding envelopes one at a time gets old fast.

To print addresses directly onto your envelopes in Word 97:

1. **Choose Tools⇨Mail Merge.**

    The Mail Merge Helper appears.

2. **Click Create.**

    A drop-down list appears.

3. **Choose Envelopes.**

    A dialog box appears (see Figure 18-4), giving you a choice between adding the envelope to the document that you currently have open on the screen (Active Window) or creating a new main document for the envelope.

Figure 18-4:
Does your
document
need an
envelope?

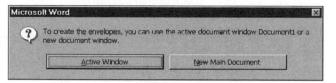

4. **Click the New Main Document button.**

   A new document is created as your main mail-merge document, and
   you return to the Mail Merge Helper.

5. **Click the Get Data button in the Mail Merge Helper.**

   A menu drops down, giving you a choice of where to get the names and
   addresses.

6. **Choose Use Address Book.**

   Another menu appears, listing several Address Books, including the
   Outlook Address Book.

7. **Double-click the Outlook Address Book.**

   If you have more than one Outlook Address Book available, a dialog box
   appears, asking you to choose the Address Book you want to use.

8. **Click OK to return to the Mail Merge Helper.**

9. **Click the Set Up Main Document button.**

   The Envelope Options dialog box appears, with a choice of envelope
   sizes (see Figure 18-5).

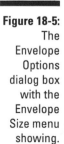

Figure 18-5:
The
Envelope
Options
dialog box
with the
Envelope
Size menu
showing.

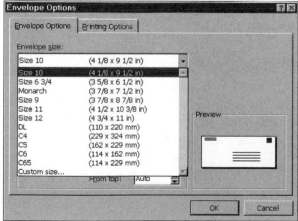

10. Choose the size and type you want to use; then click OK to open the Envelope Address form.

Normal business envelopes are number 10. Pull down the menu to choose a different size.

11. Click Insert Merge Field on the Envelope Address form.

The list of fields from the Outlook Contact list drops down (see Figure 18-6).

12. Click each piece of data that you want to include in your envelope.

The simplest entry is to click Insert Merge Field, choose Company, press Enter, click Insert Merge Field, and choose Postal_Address. You can add as many fields as will fit on the envelope.

13. Click OK.

14. Click the Merge button.

The Merge dialog box appears.

15. Click Merge again.

The merge begins.

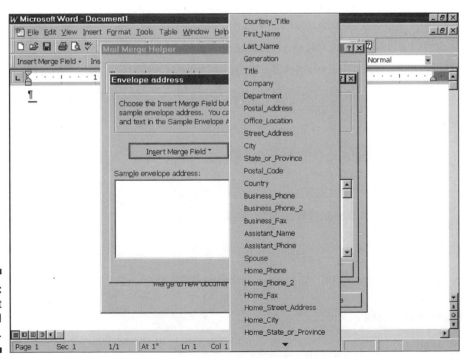

Figure 18-6:
The Insert
Merge Field
list.

If you've never printed multiple envelopes on your printer before, start small. Try printing four or five, just to make sure that your printer feeds envelopes properly. Word and Outlook happily send your printer a command to print hundreds of envelopes in a flash. If your printer chokes on the fourth envelope, however, fixing the problem can take a long time.

Creating a Form Letter from the Contact List

Today I received a personalized invitation to enter a $250,000 sweepstakes that had my name plastered all over the front of the envelope. How thoughtful and personal! Whenever you get a sweepstakes letter with your name already entered, you're getting a form letter. A form letter is a letter with standard text that's printed over and over but with a different name and address printed on each copy. You can send form letters, too, even if you're not holding a sweepstakes. An annual newsletter to family and friends is one form letter you may want to create.

To create a form letter in Word 97:

1. Choose Tools⇨Mail Merge.

The Mail Merge Helper appears.

2. Click Create.

A drop-down list appears.

3. Choose Form Letters.

A dialog box appears.

4. Click the Active Window button in the dialog box.

You return to the Mail Merge Helper.

5. Click the Get Data button.

A drop-down menu appears, giving you a choice about where to get the data for your labels (see Figure 18-7).

6. Choose Use Address Book.

Another menu appears, with choices including the Outlook Address Book.

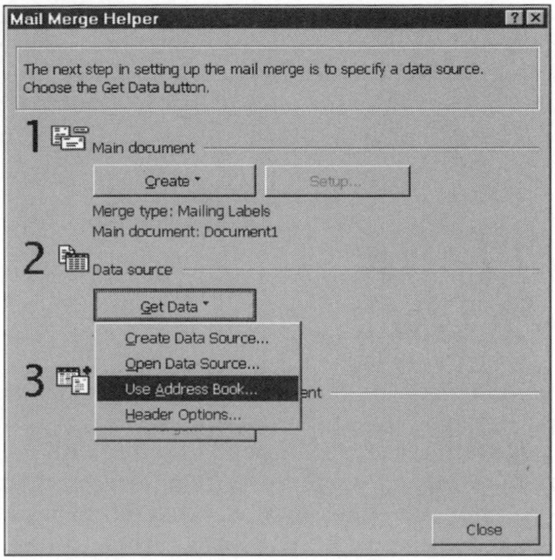

Figure 18-7:
Getting data
for your
mail merge.

7. **Double-click the Outlook Address Book.**

If you have more than one Address Book running in Outlook, a dialog box asks you to choose just one as the source of names and addresses for your letters.

8. **Click OK.**

A dialog box appears, offering you only one choice: Edit Main Document. Go figure.

9. **Click the Edit Main Document button.**

You return to the Microsoft Word main editing screen, which now has one more toolbar. The new toolbar includes buttons that say Insert Merge Field and Insert Word Field.

10. **Type your form letter, clicking the Insert Merge Field button to insert merge fields everywhere you want data from your Outlook Address Book to appear in your form letter (see Figure 18-8).**

Now you don't have to settle for sending impersonal, annoying form letters to dozens of people; you can send a *personal,* annoying form letter to hundreds of people. If you're planning to send an annoying form letter to me, my address is 1600 Pennsylvania Avenue, Washington, D.C.

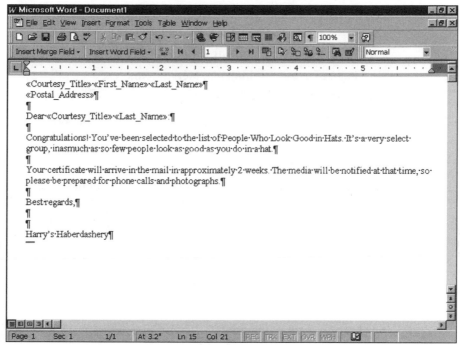

Figure 18-8:
Adding
merge
fields to
your letter.

Merging Selected Records

You can assemble a large Contact list in Outlook. Chances are that you don't want to send a merge letter to everybody in a 5,000-name Contact list every day. You really should have a way to select a few records in an Outlook Contact list and send a letter to those people.

But you don't — at least, not in Outlook.

In this section, I spell out Microsoft's prescribed way of dealing with a selective merge from Outlook, but I think it's a lame method. So if the process doesn't seem to make sense, it's because it doesn't make sense. Sorry. But I'll try my best to make some sense of it for you.

I start with the bottom line. You can merge only an entire Outlook Contact list to Word. You can have more than one Contact list, however, and you can copy names from one list to another. So here's what you do:

1. Click the Contact icon.

The Contact list appears.

2. **Choose File⇨Folder⇨New Folder (or press Ctrl+Shift+E).**

   The Create New Folder dialog box appears (see Figure 18-9).

3. **Type a name for your new folder.**

   I like to use something like Merge Items.

4. **Click OK.**

   The Add Shortcut to Outlook Bar dialog box appears.

5. **Click Yes.**

   The new folder appears in the Outlook Bar.

6. **While holding down the Ctrl key, drag the contact items that you want to use in your Mail Merge to the new icon in the Outlook Bar.**

   You now have a new Contact list to use as a merge file.

When you create your main merge document, as I describe earlier in this chapter, you need to specify Merge Items (or whatever you named the new folder) when Word asks for the name of the Address Book you want to use.

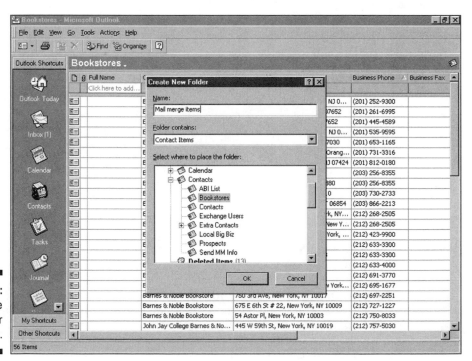

Figure 18-9:
The Create
New Folder
dialog box.

Several things can go wrong when you're merging from a list made of copies of contacts:

- ✔ If you fail to hold down the Ctrl key when you're dragging the contacts, the contacts will be moved, but *not* copied, so you have to make sure to move the contacts back when you're done by dragging them with your mouse again.

- ✔ If you have two copies of each contact in your merge list, it's easy to change the wrong one accidentally. The "real" contact and the "temporary" contact don't synchronize automatically. If a contact's phone number or other information has changed, you could easily change the wrong set of information, so don't keep more than one copy of each of your contacts hanging around for too long.

I wish I could find a more sensible way to merge from selected records in Outlook. You have a couple of other ways to get around the problem, such as exporting a file (which defeats the purpose of merging from Outlook) or using some of the advanced features in Word, but those methods are limited. I'm sure that a better selective merge method will be developed in the future, but for now, this is what Microsoft recommends.

Chapter 19

The Net Effect: Sharing Information with Net Folders

- -

In This Chapter

▶ Using Net Folders

▶ Sharing a folder with another person

▶ Adding shared items to a folder

▶ Delivering your shared items

- -

*A*lthough some information is most valuable if you keep it to yourself, other information is more useful when you share it. The Outlook 98 feature called Net Folders lets you share any information with any other Outlook 98 user with whom you can exchange e-mail.

Setting the Net

If you collaborate with other people, you need to keep a mutual record of what things you're doing, when you're doing things, and whom you're doing things with. The most obvious things you may want to share are your contacts, tasks, and calendar items. Although you can simply write an e-mail message covering every move you make and send it to everyone concerned, Net Folders simplify collaboration by automatically creating the e-mail messages to the associates you designate and placing copies of all the items you create in the Outlook folder where each item belongs.

Installing Net Folders

Unfortunately, Net Folders don't automatically set themselves up when you install Outlook. You have to make a point of adding them to Outlook. Here's how:

1. **Insert the Outlook CD in your CD-ROM drive.**

   The Outlook CD install screen appears.

2. **Click the words *Install Outlook 98 Add-On Components*.**

   Internet Explorer opens, revealing a page called Microsoft Outlook 98 Component Install.

3. **Click the Net Folders check box.**

   A check mark appears next to the words *Net Folders* (see Figure 19-1).

4. **Click Next.**

   The Component Confirmation and Installation screen appears.

5. **Click Install Now.**

   The Net Folders component is installed, and then the Install Complete dialog box appears.

6. **Click OK.**

The only change you see in Outlook after installing Net Folders is a new choice in the File menu named Share. You must install the Net Folders option whether you want to share someone else's folders or allow someone else to share yours.

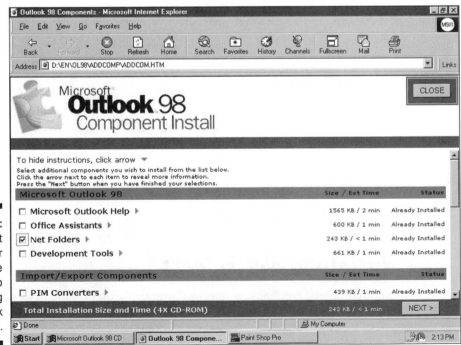

Figure 19-1: Internet Explorer holds the secret to installing Outlook options.

Allowing another person to share your folders

If you want to let someone share one of your folders, you need to add that person to the list of people who are allowed to share. You must repeat this process for each folder you want to share and for each person with whom you want to share the folder. The Net Folder Wizard takes you through the whole process step-by-step, like this:

1. **Choose File➪Share.**

   A menu appears, saying Calendar, Tasks, Contacts, or This Folder (see Figure 19-2).

2. **Choose the name of the folder you want to share.**

   The Net Folder Wizard appears.

3. **Click Next.**

   The next Net Folder Wizard dialog box appears. The top line of the dialog box says `Create the list of people with whom you will share this folder.`

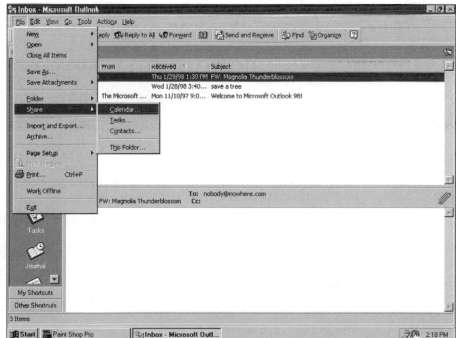

Figure 19-2:
Calendar,
Tasks, and
Contacts
folders are
easy to
share.

4. Click <u>A</u>dd.

The Add Entries to Subscriber Database dialog box appears. This dialog box looks strikingly similar to your Address Book because it's the same thing. As you can probably guess, you can only assign names to your subscriber list if you've entered those names in the Address Book first.

5. Double-click the name of each person you want to add to your Subscriber Database.

Each name you double-click appears in the To box on the right side of the dialog box.

6. Click OK when you've added all the names you want to add to your Subscriber Database.

The first screen of the Net Folder Wizard appears again with the names you chose in the Member List. The word `Reviewer` appears next to each name you've just added (see Figure 19-3).

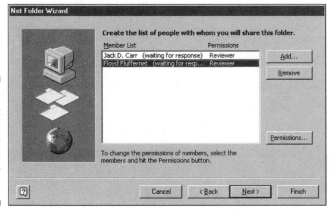

Figure 19-3:
You can let several other people share your folders.

7. (Optional) Click the <u>P</u>ermissions button if you want to allow your newly added members to do more than read the items to which you've subscribed them.

The Net Folder Sharing Permissions dialog box appears, listing the permissions you can grant each subscriber in increasing order of power. The dialog box tells you what each permission level means.

8. (Optional) Click the button next to the permission level you want to grant.

The button next to the permission level you click appears blackened (see Figure 19-4).

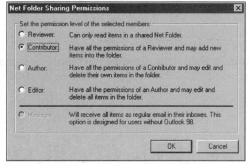

Figure 19-4:
You can
give some
subscribers
more
permission
than others.

9. (Optional) Click OK.

The main Net Folder Wizard dialog box reappears.

10. Click Next.

The next Net Folder Wizard dialog box appears. The sentence Please describe this folder for the members of your shared folder appears at the top of the dialog box.

11. (Optional) Type a description of the folder.

Your subscribers will receive an e-mail message inviting them to subscribe to your folder, so this is a good time to tell them what you're doing.

12. Click Next.

The final screen of the Net Folder Wizard appears, telling you that you're finished. You already knew that.

13. Click Finish.

A progress bar appears briefly, followed by a dialog box saying Invitations for your Net Folder have been sent successfully. (That's not entirely true; if you're not on a network, the invitations just went to your Outbox. You have to press F5 to get the invitations out of your Outbox and on to your recipients, just like any other piece of e-mail.)

14. Click OK.

You've completed your end of the process of sharing your folder, but there's still more. The people you've invited to share your folder each get a special e-mail message inviting them to subscribe to your folder. If they use Outlook for their e-mail and they also have Net Folders installed, the e-mail messages they get have buttons on the bottom of the message saying _Accept_ or _Decline_. If they click Accept, a message goes back to you confirming their subscription and Outlook starts sharing folder items automatically. If they decline . . . too bad, they miss out.

Adding Shared Items to a Folder

After you give someone a subscription to one of your folders, every item you add to that folder automatically gets sent to each subscriber so that they can see the contents of the folder. You don't have to do anything special.

Dealing with Shared Items in Net Folders

Your Net Folders only update themselves when you exchange e-mail. If you're on a corporate network, all your e-mail goes out as soon as you click Send, so sharing items with Net Folders seems to happen instantly. If you send your e-mail over a telephone line, you have to choose Tools⇨Send to deliver your shared items to the subscribers of your folder.

Part IV
The Part of Tens

The 5th Wave — By Rich Tennant

"WHOA, HOLD THE PHONE! IT SAYS, 'THE ELECTRICITY COMING OUT OF A SURGE PROTECTOR IS GENERALLY CLEANER AND SAFER THAN THAT GOING INTO ONE, UNLESS—UN-LESSS— YOU ARE STANDING IN A BUCKET OF WATER.'"

In this part . . .

Top Ten lists are everybody's favorite. They're short. They're easy to read. And they're a perfect spot for writers like me to toss in useful stuff that doesn't easily fit into the main chapters of the book. Flip through my top ten lists for tips you'll want to use, including a time-saving look at things you can't do with Outlook, so you won't waste your time trying.

Chapter 20

Ten (Plus One) Office 97 Tricks for Creating Snappier E-Mail

In This Chapter

▶ Animated text

▶ New table tools

▶ Office Art

▶ Hyperlinks

▶ Document Map

▶ Versions

▶ Browsing

▶ Automatic grammar checking

▶ Excel conditional formatting

▶ Merged Excel cells

▶ Angled Excel text

*O*utlook can use Word 97 as an e-mail editor, which means that you can create extremely cool e-mail like you've never seen before — graphics, special effects, you name it. E-mail was never this much fun.

If you're an old hand at Microsoft Office and feel confident that you know what you need to know to get around Office 97, you're probably right. Everything that you knew from before still works; Outlook is the only new part of Microsoft Office. If you're not familiar with Microsoft Office, pick up a copy of *Microsoft Office 97 For Windows For Dummies* (written by Wallace Wang and Roger C. Parker) from IDG Books Worldwide, Inc. (Okay, another plug, but have I steered you wrong so far?) The other parts of Office have acquired some really cool new features that can help you create attractive, impressive documents to send by e-mail. This chapter describes some of my favorites.

Tricks That Work in Word

When you want to dream up snazzy-looking e-mail text, Word is your tool. These tricks help customize your e-mail text to give it punch and pizzazz.

Animated text

Now you can put your message in blinking lights (in your e-mail, anyway). Blinking, flashing, or sparkling text is easy to create. Just follow these steps:

1. **Select the text that you want to animate.**

2. **Choose Format⇨Font (or right-click the selected text and choose Font).**

   The Font dialog box appears.

3. **Click the Animation tab.**

   The Animations page of the Font dialog box appears, including a list of animation effects (see Figure 20-1).

4. **Choose an animation effect, such as Sparkle Text.**

   A sample of the animation effect appears at the bottom of the dialog box.

5. **Click OK.**

Figure 20-1: The Animations page.

Animated text, of course, is not useful for a document that you plan to print or for e-mail that goes to someone who is not set up to read animated text, but it's great for calling attention to text in your interoffice e-mail.

Table tools

The new Table tools are wild! Just grab a pencil tool and start drawing boxes; then draw lines in the boxes and erase some of the lines. You just have to try these tools. Tables will never be the same.

To use the Table tools:

1. **Choose Table⇨Draw Table.**

   A special Table toolbar appears.

2. **Click the Draw Table button in the Table toolbar.**

   This button is the little pencil at the left end of the toolbar.

3. **Drag a diagonal line to draw a box where you want the table to be.**

   You've got to see this to appreciate it (see Figure 20-2).

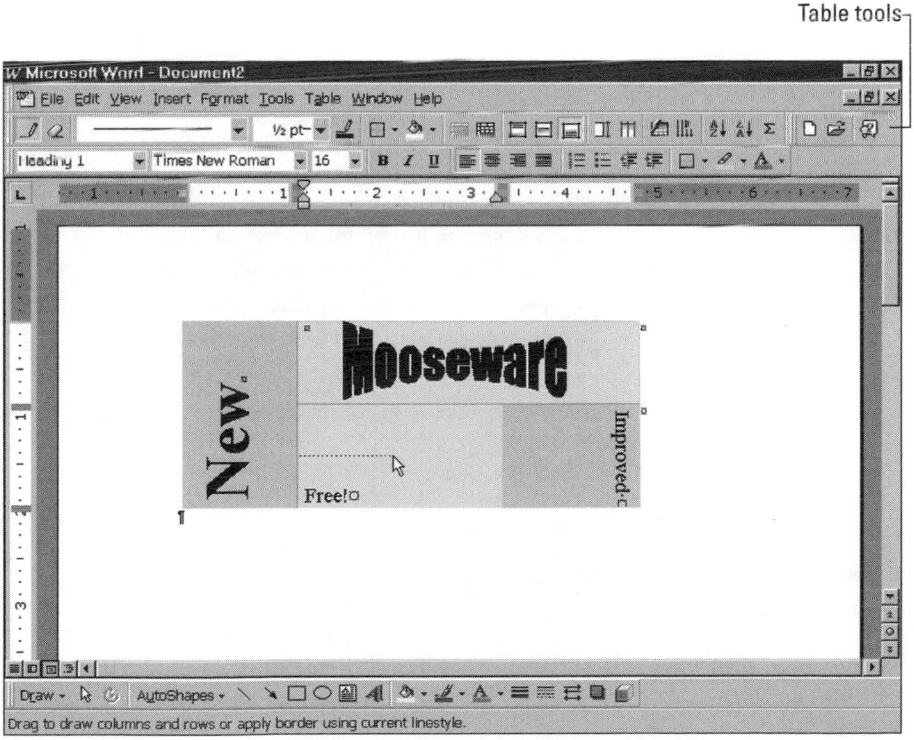

Table tools

Figure 20-2:
Use these neat tools to create a table.

4. Draw lines where you want to divide the table.

You can create the strangest tables you ever imagined just by dragging that pencil around. Creating tables in Word 97 is as much fun as creating strange drawings in the Paint accessory that comes with Windows. (If you haven't tried making strange drawings with Paint, give it a try. There's no better way to get comfortable with using a mouse.)

Office Art

Office Art is so cool that I could easily write an entire chapter — if not an entire book — on it. I think Office Art is nearly as cool as Outlook. (Nearly, I said.) Here's how to use Office Art:

1. Click the Drawing button in the toolbar.

The Drawing toolbar appears.

2. Click one of the drawing buttons to create drawn objects in your document.

The toolbar includes a great collection of predefined shapes, as well as tools for rotating, aligning, and editing the graphics that you've drawn (see Figure 20-3).

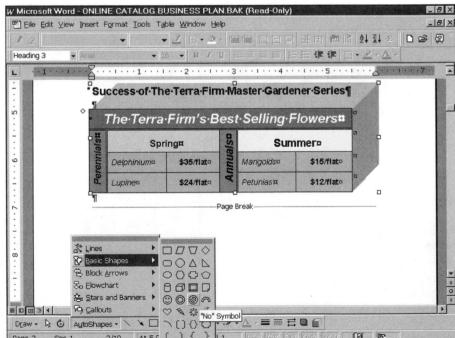

Figure 20-3:
The Drawing toolbar.

3. Click any text to return to text-entry mode.

You can also place graphics on top of your text or wrap text around a drawing.

Hyperlinks

The Internet-hyperlink mania has struck Office 97 like a tidal wave. You can create links from any Office document to a Web page as well as to another Office document. Linking is a method of letting you move from one document to another by using your mouse to click on a picture or specially formatted text (usually underlined blue text) that makes the document you're looking at disappear and another document appear. You create your own web of links between Office documents that acts like the World Wide Web, but better; it's quicker and more versatile, and you can create it yourself.

To create a hyperlink:

1. Click the Insert Hyperlink button in the toolbar.

The Insert Hyperlink dialog box appears (see Figure 20-4).

2. Enter the Internet address (URL) of the Web page or the filename of the Office document that you want to link to.

You can also click the Browse button and select the file that you want to link.

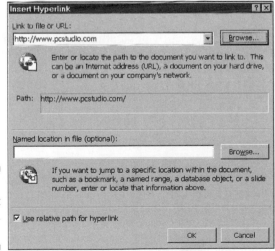

Figure 20-4:
The Insert Hyperlink dialog box.

3. If you're creating a link to another Office document, enter the cell address (for an Excel spreadsheet) or the bookmark name (for a Word document) in the Named Location in File box.

Including a link in an e-mail message is a handy way to refer to information without creating an enormous message. To call your reader's attention to a file on the Internet or on your local network (as long as you're both on the same network), just include a link in your document to the file that you want your reader to see.

4. Click OK.

Your link appears in the document in blue underlined text, just like it would on the World Wide Web.

Document Map

To get where you're going quickly, use a map. Word 97 can show you a map of your document right alongside the document itself. The Document Map is an outline of your document that sits to the left of the free-text version on-screen. You can move between widely separated sections of your document with a single click of the heading.

To use a Document Map:

1. Choose View⇨Document Map.

Any text to which you've assigned a Heading style appears in the Document Map, becoming the mileposts of your Document Map (see Figure 20-5).

2. Click the name of the heading of the text that you'd like to read.

Clicking among the headings and swiftly navigating your document is easy, just like having a table of contents alongside it. I find the Document Map especially handy when creating long documents, such as chapters for this book. I can jump back and forth between headings to get a quick look at different parts of my document without having to scroll up and down.

Versions

I confess: I'm a compulsive reviser. I revise documents over and over. I revise some things so much that I can't remember what they were supposed to be about in the first place. I'll get help; I promise. But first, I've got to show you the repeat reviser's dream: Versions. You can keep a separate version of each revision of a document that you make. Then you can go back to an earlier version after you've revised the first version beyond recognition. You can also revise someone else's revisions and not lose either set of revisions.

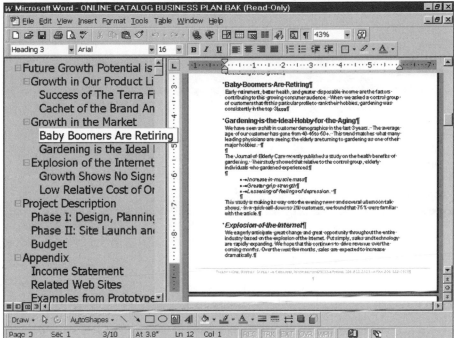

Figure 20-5:
Traverse
your
document
with a
Document
Map.

Here's how to keep different versions:

1. Choose File⇨Versions.

The Versions dialog box appears (see Figure 20-6).

2. Click the Save Now button.

The Comments dialog box appears. You can enter a brief description of the current version and say what you think of it.

3. Type your comments, if any, about the version that you're currently saving.

The comments you type appear in the Comments dialog box.

4. Click OK.

Remember that other people can see your comments, so entering a comment like "A great improvement on the boss's illiterate version" is not advisable. The boss might suggest that you use the Version feature to create a new version of your résumé.

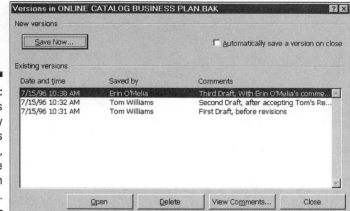

Figure 20-6:
Have as many versions as you want, complete with comments.

Browsing

There's more to Word than just words; you can find tables, fields, graphics, and good old-fashioned pages in a Word 97 document. You can use the Object browser to skip from one table to the next or to move from field to field, or even from edit to edit.

To use the Object browser:

1. **Click the Select Browse object in the scroll bar.**

   The Browse Object shortcut menu shows you the tools you can use for browsing (see Figure 20-7).

2. **Choose the type of object that you'd like to browse on.**

   A nice, round, dozen choices should suffice. A ToolTip tells you the function of each object.

3. **Click the Next button to move to the following object of the type that you selected or click Previous to move to the preceding object of that type.**

I particularly like the tool that moves you from one edit to the next; it works only on edits for the current session of Word, but even that's a big help. A reviseaholic like me needs to know where the next revision is.

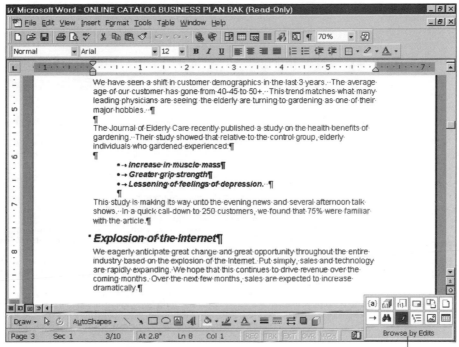

Figure 20-7:
Ready to
browse?

Browser Object shortcut menu

Check grammar as you type

I have another confession: I slept through the classes where they taught
sentence diagramming. I'm never sure when who is what to whom,
grammaticallywise. You may have seen the wavy red underlines that Word
puts below misspelled words; now there's a wavy green line that Word uses
to show that your grammar ain't what it ought to be. As you can tell from
this paragraph, you can turn off automatic grammar checking.

To use the grammar checker:

1. **Right-click text that has a green underline.**

   A little shortcut menu appears (see Figure 20-8), displaying a list of
   suggested revisions and a little grammar lecture (just what I wanted).

2. **Choose the option that you prefer.**

   Throwing a spitball is no longer a choice (not that you could ever get
   away with it in grammar school).

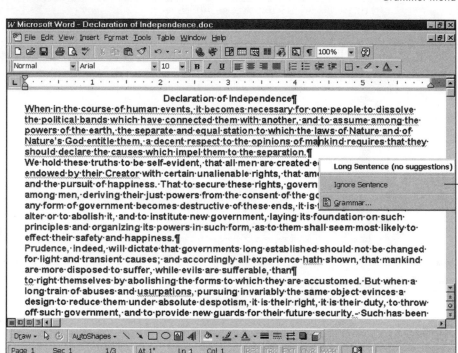

Figure 20-8:
Click on the
wavy green
lines to
see the
Grammar
menu.

3. Click OK.

Now you ain't got no more excuse for no bad grammar.

Tricks You Can Do in Excel

You can send Excel spreadsheets by e-mail or include portions of spreadsheets in the Word documents that make up your e-mail messages. So if you
want to create impressive e-mail, the new features of Excel should be part of
your palette.

Apply conditional formatting

Spreadsheets full of numbers don't have much visual pizzazz. Excel has a
new way to make a list of numbers mean something at first glance; it's called
conditional formatting.

Imagine a chart of average daily temperatures for a year. You could create conditional formatting that would make any cell that contains a temperature below 32 degrees chilly blue and any cell with a temperature above 72 degrees hot red. That way, you can tell the warmer days from the cooler ones at first glance, without having to study the numbers and without making a chart.

To apply conditional formatting:

1. **Select the range of cells to which you want to apply conditional formatting.**

2. **Choose F̲ormat⇨Conditional Formatting.**

   The Conditional Formatting dialog box appears (see Figure 20-9).

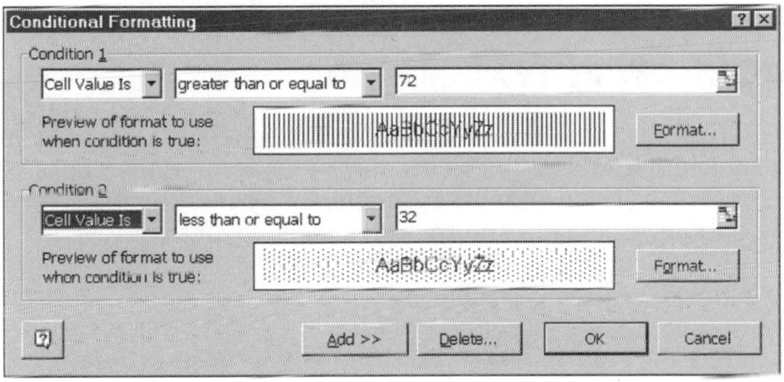

Figure 20-9:
The
Conditional
Formatting
dialog box.

3. **Set rules for formatting, such as** `If Value Is Greater Than 50.`

   Choose the conditions from the Condition box.

4. **Set formatting that will apply if the condition is met.**

   You can set more than one condition. In my high-low temperature example, you need to set two conditions. Set one condition for temperatures below 32 degrees; then click the Add button and add a second condition for temperatures above 72 degrees.

5. **Click OK.**

After you create conditional formatting, it stays there until you remove it, even if the formatting isn't showing. In the example, temperatures between 32 degrees and 72 degrees have conditional formatting, but the formatting doesn't show unless the temperature listed in the cell crosses the threshold for conditional formatting (in this case, below 32 or above 72). If you enter a number below 32 or above 72, the cell changes to blue or red.

Merge Excel cells

Spreadsheets used to be nothing but rows and columns. Now you can merge cells vertically and horizontally to your heart's content.

To merge cells in Excel:

1. Select the cells that you want to merge.

2. Click the Merge Cells button in the toolbar.

All the cells that you highlighted are now one cell (see Figure 20-10).

If you still worry about things like cell names, the new one takes the name of the upper-leftmost cell that you selected. You can put a formula, a number, or plain text in the merged cell.

Angle Excel text

Those true-blue, pencil-necked number crunchers don't need cute text effects like rotated text, but to the rest of us, rotated text looks better. That's enough for me. The capability to angle text by rotating it also gives you some options for creating more professional layouts.

Here's how to reorient your boring old cells:

1. Select the cells that contain the text you want to rotate.

2. Choose Format⇨Cells (or press Ctrl+1).

The Format Cells dialog box appears (see Figure 20-11).

3. Click the Alignment tab.

The Orientation box shows the current angle of the selected text.

4. Drag the angle indicator to the angle that you desire.

You can also set the angle by typing a number in the Degrees box.

5. Click OK.

The cells that you selected resize to accommodate the angled text.

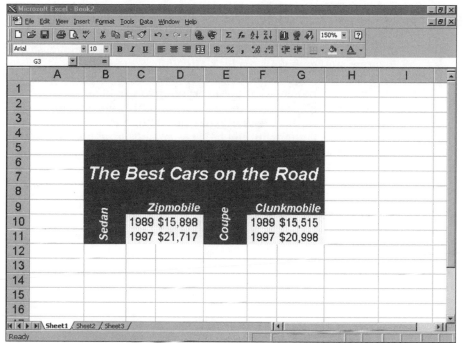

Figure 20-10:
Excel has completed a merger.

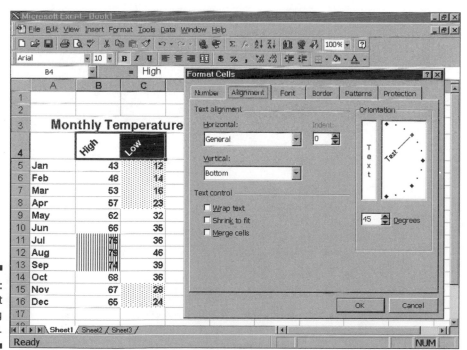

Figure 20-11:
The Format Cells dialog box.

Now for This Message

Use the creative tools in Office 97 to make your e-mail messages jump off the screen and grab your reader's attention.

 Be aware, however, that not everybody to whom you can send e-mail can get the special effects you create. Many Internet e-mail recipients still get by on plain text, so your creativity may be lost on them until everybody in the world uses nothing but the latest Microsoft products (that sounds a little scary to me).

But when you're creating messages for people who have what you have, such as people in your own office, go ahead and knock 'em dead with your snazzy e-mail tricks.

Chapter 21

Ten Shortcuts Worth Taking

In This Chapter

▶ Using the New Item tool
▶ Sending a file to an e-mail recipient
▶ Sending a file from an Office 97 application
▶ Clicking open the Folder List
▶ Keeping the Folder List open
▶ Undo-ing
▶ Using the Go To Date command
▶ Adding items to list views
▶ Keeping a note open
▶ Navigating with browser buttons

*E*ven though computers are supposed to save you time, some days this just doesn't seem to be the case. Juggling menus, keys, and buttons can seem to take all day. Here are some shortcuts that can really save you time and tension as you work.

Using the New Item Tool

To create a new item in whatever module you're in, just click the New Item tool at the far left end of the toolbar. The icon changes when you change modules, so it becomes a New Task icon in the Tasks module, a New Contact icon in the Contacts module, and so on. You can also click the arrow next to the New Item tool to pull down the New Item menu (see Figure 21-1).

When you choose an item from the New Item menu, you can create a new item in an Outlook module other than the one you're in without changing modules. If you're answering e-mail, for example, and you want to create a note, pull down the New Item menu, choose Note, create your note, and then go on working with your e-mail.

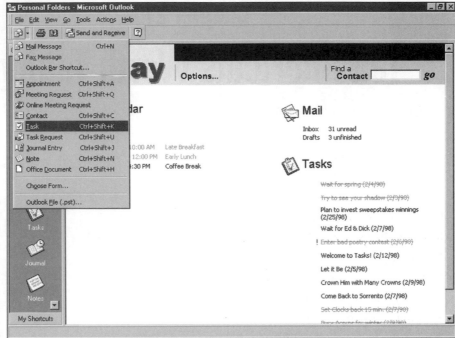

Figure 21-1:
The New
Item tool
with the
New Item
menu pulled
down.

Sending a File to an E-Mail Recipient

You can send a file by Outlook E-Mail with only a few mouse clicks, even if Outlook isn't running. When you're viewing files in the Windows Explorer, you can mark any file to be sent to any e-mail recipient. Here's how:

1. **Right-click the file that you want to send after finding the file with the Windows Explorer.**

   A menu appears.

2. **Choose Send To.**

   Another menu appears.

3. **Choose Mail Recipient.**

   A New Message form appears. An icon representing the attached file is in the text box.

4. **Type the subject of the file and the name of the person to whom you're sending the file.**

   If you want to add comments to your message, type them in the text box, where the icon for the file is.

5. Click Send.

Your message goes to the Outbox. Then press F5 to send it on its way. If you send your files by modem, you also have to press F5 to dial your e-mail service.

Sending a File from an Office 97 Application

You can e-mail any Office 97 document from the Office application itself, without using Outlook's e-mail module. Here's how:

1. Open an Office 97 document that you want to send in the application that created it.

2. Choose File⇨Send To⇨Mail Recipient.

A New Message form appears, displaying an icon for the file in the text box to indicate that the file is attached to the message.

3. Type the subject of the file and the name of the person to whom you're sending the file.

If you want to add comments to your message, type them in the text box where the icon for the file is.

4. Click Send.

Your message goes to the Outbox. If you send your files by modem, you also have to switch to Outlook and press F5 to dial your e-mail service.

Clicking Open the Folder List

If you need to open the Folder List for only a second to open a folder, just click the name of the Outlook module that you're using (Calendar, Tasks, and so on) where it appears in large type just above the Information Viewer. A small triangle next to the name of the module indicates that you can click there to drop down the Folder List for one operation. The Folder List drops down until you click it or something else; then the Folder List disappears.

Keeping the Folder List Open

After you open the Folder List, you see a little figure that looks like a thumb-tack in the upper-right corner of the Folder List window. If you click that thumbtack with your mouse, the thumbtack turns into a black X and the Folder List stays open until you click the black X.

Undo-ing Your Mistakes

If you don't know about the Undo command, it's time that you heard the good news. When you make a mistake, you can undo it by pressing Ctrl+Z or choosing Edit➪Undo. So feel free to experiment; the worst that you'll have to do is undo! (Of course, you must undo what you've done right away, before you do too many things to undo at one time.)

Using the Go To Date Command

You can use the Go To Date command in all Calendar and Timeline views (see Figure 21-2). If you're looking at the Calendar, for example, and you want to skip ahead 60 days, press Ctrl+G and type **60 days from now**. The Calendar advances 60 days from the current date.

Adding Items to List Views

Many Outlook lists have a blank line at the top where you can type an entry and create a new item for that list. When you see the words Click here to add a new task, that's exactly what they mean. Just click in that line and type your new item.

Keeping a Note Open

If you like to keep random notes throughout the day, open a note and leave it open. When a note is open, an icon appears in the Windows 95 taskbar at the bottom of the screen. To edit today's note, click the note's icon at the bottom of the screen; the note pops up again. When you see a note, you can click in it and edit what you see. Click any part of any other application screen that you can see and you return to that application. If you want to close the note, right-click the note's icon on the taskbar and choose Close.

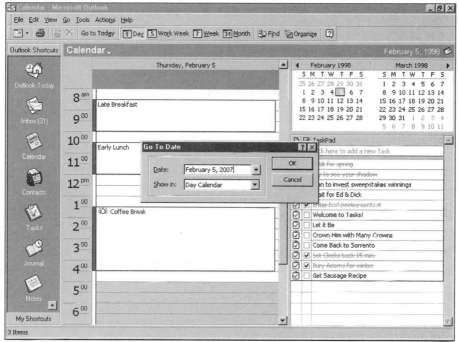

Figure 21-2:
The Go To
Date dialog
box.

Navigating with Browser Buttons

The Go menu has two buttons with blue arrows that point left and right.
These buttons serve as *browser buttons*. When you change from one Outlook
module to another and then want to change back, click the button with the
arrow that points to the left. To change to the second module again, click
the button with the arrow that points to the right.

If you're accustomed to using Web browsers such as Netscape or Microsoft
Internet Explorer, you'll find that the Outlook browser buttons work exactly
the same way as the navigation buttons in your Web browser.

Chapter 22

Let's Go Surfin' Now: Ten Ways to Use Outlook with the Internet

In This Chapter

▶ Using the Favorites folder

▶ Storing a contact's Web pages

▶ Sending Internet e-mail

▶ Receiving Internet e-mail

▶ Including Internet hot links in e-mail messages

▶ Saving Internet e-mail addresses in your Address Book

▶ Dragging scraps of text and graphics from a Web page to an Outlook item

▶ Downloading Outlook stationery from the Internet

▶ Getting help on the Web

*E*veryone wants to surf the Net or pull the strands on the Web these days. Outlook and the Internet work together just fine. Here are just some of the ways Outlook and the Internet can interact.

Using the Favorites Folder

When you install Outlook, one optional feature is Integrated File Management. If you install Integrated File Management, the Favorites folder automatically turns up in the Other Shortcuts group in the Outlook Bar. The Favorites folder is full of shortcuts to all the Web pages that you added to your favorite places section of Microsoft Internet Explorer.

To see a Web page that's listed in your Favorites folder (assuming you've entered some favorites there), all you have to do is double-click the name of the page. Your Web browser automatically opens, dials, and finds that page. If you run across any other pages that you want to keep track of while you're surfing the Web, choose Favorites➪Add to Favorites in Internet Explorer.

Storing a Contact's Web Pages

Every Contact record has a field in which you can store the address of the person's Web page, along with all other vital information about that person. That way, you don't have to remember that Jack's Web page is called `www.wherever.net/wiseguys/jackwalters.htm`.

Just look up Jack in your Contact list and choose Actions⇨Explore Web Page.

Sending Internet E-Mail

To send e-mail to someone on the Internet, just type that person's Internet e-mail address in the To box of your message. If the person is already entered in your Contact list, just drag his or her Address Card to the Inbox icon.

Receiving Internet E-Mail

You don't have to do anything to receive Internet e-mail; it comes to you. If you use an online service such as CompuServe or The Microsoft Network for your e-mail, you need to check for mail periodically by pressing the F5 key.

Including Internet Hot Links in E-Mail Messages

You can use Word 97 as your e-mail editor. If you do, you can create links between one Word document and any other Office 97 document by clicking the Insert Hyperlink button in the toolbar and filling in the Insert Hyperlink dialog box. If you want to create a link to a particular bookmark in a Word document, choose the name of the bookmark in the Insert Hyperlink dialog box.

Including Internet Hot Links in Any Outlook Item

As soon as you type **http://**, any Office 97 application — including Outlook — recognizes that text as the beginning of an address for a Web page. If you type the address of a Web page in the text box of any Outlook item, the address immediately changes to blue underlined text. If you click that text, your Web browser launches and shows you the corresponding page.

Saving Internet E-Mail Addresses in Your Address Book

A great deal of mail is flying around the Internet, some of it useful and lots of it junk. You'll want to ignore the junk, but now and then, you'll want to save an address for future use. The easiest way to save an address is to drag the message to the Contacts icon and have Outlook create a new contact.

Sometimes, though, you don't want to clutter your Contact list with addresses that you got from Internet junk mail. If you open the message and right-click the From line, a menu appears. To save just the address, choose Enter in Personal Address Book. That way, the address of the person who sent you the message is saved without adding anything to your Contact list.

Dragging Scraps of Text from a Web Page

I often cull through hundreds of pages of junk on the Web, only to find a single sentence that I want to save. I don't want to save the entire page, and I surely don't want to try to surf my way back to the same place in the same page again; I probably won't remember how I got there in the first place.

I like to save small scraps of text from the Web by selecting the text with my mouse and then dragging the text to the Notes icon in Outlook. I end up saving exactly the text that I want — and nothing more.

Downloading Outlook Stationery from the Internet

Microsoft has many extra goodies for Office 97 applications available on the World Wide Web. All you have to do is choose Help⇨Microsoft on the Web⇨ Free Stuff and cruise around until you find what you want.

Getting Help on the Web

You can also find a great deal of free support for all Office 97 applications on the Web. Just choose Help⇨Microsoft on the Web⇨Online Support.

Chapter 23

Ten Things You Can't Do with Outlook

In This Chapter

▶ Using Outlook categories in a Word 97 mail merge

▶ Running Outlook 98 without installing Internet Explorer 4.0

▶ Backing up your Outlook files to a floppy disk

▶ Making Outlook start other programs

▶ Displaying two parts of Outlook in one view

▶ Saving the Folder List in a custom view

▶ Embedding pictures in notes

▶ Making the Journal automatically record everything for all contacts

▶ Using Journal Phone Call entries to calculate expenses

▶ Cross-referencing items to jump to different modules

Maybe I sound crabby listing the things that Outlook can't do, considering all the things that it *can* do. But it takes only a few minutes to find out something that a program can do, and you can spend all day trying to figure out something that a program can't do. I could easily list *more* than ten things that Outlook can't do; this chapter lists just the first big ones that I've run into.

The Top Ten List

Bear in mind that Outlook can't do these ten things when you first get it. Because Outlook can be reprogrammed with the Visual Basic programming language, however, a clever programmer could make Outlook do many of these things.

Using Outlook categories in a Word 97 Mail Merge

When you do a mail merge in Word 97, you can use any of several dozen of the fields from your Outlook Contacts module, but not the Categories field — a very unfortunate oversight. If you have a 1,500-name Contact list, and you want to send different mailings to different groups of a few hundred people each, you have to copy the Contact records to separate folders and tell Word to merge from them, rather than use the Word Query feature to address different mailings to people in different categories. You also can't use any custom fields that you create in Outlook in a mail merge in Word. I've been praying to Our Lady of the Painfully Obvious in the hope that Microsoft will correct this silly omission. She's still working on it.

Running Outlook 98 without installing Internet Explorer 4.0

Outlook 97 ran just fine with no matter what other software was installed on your system. But for some reason, Outlook 98 can't seem to function unless Microsoft's Web browser, Internet Explorer 4.0, is also installed. Funny about that. Even though the U.S. Government wants to stop Microsoft from ramming Internet Explorer down everyone's throat, we're stuck with this entirely unnecessary arrangement in Outlook 98. In my opinion, it's pretty stinky (and transparent).

Backing up your Outlook files to a floppy disk

The most frequent question I get from readers is "How do I save all my Outlook data to a floppy disk?" You can't. Floppies aren't big enough to handle the enormous data file that Outlook creates if you've used Outlook for more than a few days. If you want to make your data safe, you really need to back up your whole system. If you're looking to use the same collection of Outlook data on a laptop and a desktop computer, you need to use a product like Laplink to connect the two computers and copy one set of Outlook data back and forth. It's pretty hairy.

Making Outlook start other programs

I wish that I could make Outlook start my checkbook program once a month to remind me to pay the bills or balance the checkbook or automatically open the Excel spreadsheet that I use every day. Sorry — no can do.

Displaying parts of different modules in the same view

I'm glad that I can see the Calendar and the Tasks list at the same time, but sometimes, I'd like to see the Calendar and the Phone Book side by side and save that as a view. No such luck.

Saving the Folder List in a custom view

Sometimes the Folder List is essential, such as when you're using Outlook to move or copy files. Sometimes the Folder List is useless, such as when you're viewing the Calendar. I wish that I could save certain views that include the Folder List and save other views that exclude it. I'll have to keep waiting.

Embedding pictures in notes

You can copy and paste a picture, file, or other item into the text box at the bottom of any item when you open the item's form. You can paste a photo of a person in the text box of the person's Contact record, for example. But those little, yellow stick-on notes don't let you do that; they accept only text.

Automatically recording all contact stuff in the Journal

You can open the Options dialog box and check off all the names of contacts you want to record, but you can't click a single button that checks 'em all. When you add new contacts, you have to be sure to check the Journal page box titled Automatically Record Journal Entries for This Contact. Otherwise, that contact's transactions won't be recorded.

Calculating expenses with Journal Phone Call entries

You can keep track of how much time you spend talking to any person, but you can't calculate the total call time or total call cost for billing purposes.

Cross-referencing items to jump to different modules

You can include a Contact record in a Journal Entry, for example, but when you double-click the icon for the record in the Journal, Outlook only opens that person's record; it doesn't jump to the Contacts module. If someone from XYX Company calls, and you want to look at the names of your other contacts from that company, you have to switch from the Journal module to the Contacts module and search for the names you want.

Ten More Things Outlook Can't Do for You

Outlook is also deficient in some other ways, though you may prefer to do these things for yourself anyway.

Outlook can't

- Do the Locomotion.
- Play "Misty" for you.
- Pierce any body parts.
- Catch the Energizer Bunny.
- Stop tooth decay.
- Take the *Jeopardy!* Challenge.
- Refresh your breath while you scream.
- Fight City Hall.
- Predict the Lottery.
- Find Mr. Right (unless you send e-mail to me!).

Oh, well. At least you can save time and work more smoothly with all the things Outlook *can* do for you.

Chapter 24

Ten Things You Can Do After You're Comfy

In This Chapter

▶ Adding a group to the Outlook Bar

▶ Renaming a group in the Outlook Bar

▶ Deleting a group from the Outlook Bar

▶ Renaming an icon in the Outlook Bar

▶ Selecting merge records by Outlook fields

▶ Selecting dates as a group

▶ Turning on the Advanced Toolbar

▶ Customizing the Toolbar

▶ Creating your own type of Outlook field

▶ Setting up fax service

I show you only the tip of the iceberg in this book in terms of the things you can do with Outlook. It's hard to say how much more you'll be able to do with Outlook, Internet Explorer, and all the other powerful technology that will be associated with Outlook as time goes by.

You can't do much to really mess up Outlook, so feel free to experiment. Add new fields, new views, new icons — go wild. This chapter describes a few things to try.

Adding a Group to the Outlook Bar

The Outlook Bar starts with three groups, but it doesn't have to stay that way. You can add groups, rename groups, or delete the existing groups.

To add a group to the Outlook Bar, follow these steps:

1. **Right-click any of the group dividers.**

   A menu appears.

2. **Choose Add New Group.**

   A New Group divider appears at the bottom of the Outlook Bar. The name (New Group) is highlighted.

3. **Type a new name for the group.**

   You can leave the name New Group, if you want. You can even have several groups of the same name in the Outlook Bar.

Renaming a Group in the Outlook Bar

You can name Outlook groups anything you want. You can change the names at the drop of a hat (well, actually at the click of a mouse).

To rename a group:

1. **Right-click the divider of the group that you want to rename.**

   A menu appears.

2. **Choose Rename Group.**

   The text in the divider you right-clicked is highlighted.

3. **Type the new name.**

   The name you type appears in the divider bar.

4. **Press Enter.**

   Your group has a new name.

Deleting a Group from the Outlook Bar

Enough is enough, already! I think that the three groups that the Outlook Bar starts with are enough. You can delete any extra groups in a snap. Or is that a click?

To delete a group from the Outlook Bar:

1. **Right-click the divider of the group that you want to delete.**

   A menu appears.

2. **Choose Remove Group.**

   A dialog box appears, asking whether you're sure that you want to delete this group.

3. **Click Yes.**

   Your excess group is gone for good. You can't undo this one.

Renaming an Icon in the Outlook Bar

The names of the icons in the Outlook Bar are descriptive, but not personal. If you want to name the icons after movie stars or chemical elements, Outlook does nothing to stop you. I suggest that you leave the names of the original icons alone, however, to make running the program easy. But when you add icons, anything goes.

To rename an icon:

1. **Right-click the icon that you want to rename.**

   A menu appears.

2. **Choose Rename Shortcut.**

   The name of the icon is highlighted. (By the way, *shortcut* is not a politically correct name. The term *vertically challenged cut* is more palatable, but harder to spell.)

3. **Type a new name.**

4. **Press Enter.**

   Now your icon has a new stage name. Name your folder Norma Jean, but name the icon Marilyn.

Using Outlook Fields to Create Special Mailings

Suppose that you want to mail invitations to a party. If your Contact list includes people who live in another part of the country, you probably don't want to invite them, and they probably don't want to come (unless they're *very* good friends). To prevent hurt feelings, you may want to mail invitations only to the people who live in your state.

To select only those records you want from a merge list:

1. **Choose Tools⇨Mail Merge after you set up your document in Word 97.**

   The Mail Merge Helper appears. Follow the Wizard's on-screen instructions for setting up your Mail Merge document, as I detail in Chapter 18.

2. **Choose Query Options.**

   The Query Options dialog box appears.

3. **Click the first field box and choose the field Home_State from the menu.**

   The Home_State field appears in the field box, and the words `Equal to` appear in the Comparison box.

4. **Type the abbreviation for your state in the Compare To box.**

   You've now told Word to address invitations only to people in your state.

5. **Click OK.**

Now when you click the Merge button, the only names that appear in your form letter are those of people in your state. None of the other names will appear in this document. Each time you want to create a new Mail Merge document, you need to reset any query options you want.

Selecting Dates as a Group

When you're viewing a range of dates, you don't have to limit yourself to fixed days, weeks, or months. Suppose that you need to look at a range of dates from September 25 to October 5. Click September 25; then hold down the Shift key and click October 5. All the dates in between are selected, and the dates appear in the Information Viewer.

Turning On the Advanced Toolbar

Outlook 97 had only one toolbar, so it was the most advanced Outlook toolbar you could use. For some reason, the folks at Microsoft decided that the old toolbar just did too many things, so they chopped a bunch of tools off the old toolbar and called the new reduced toolbar the Standard toolbar.

For those users who were accustomed to the old Outlook toolbar, it's still around — now it's called the Advanced toolbar. The Standard toolbar is visible when you first install Outlook. You can only see the Advanced toolbar if you turn it on by choosing View⇨Toolbars⇨Advanced.

Customizing the Toolbar

You can customize either Outlook 98 toolbar to display a button for nearly any task you use Outlook 98 to do repeatedly. You also may want to make the Standard toolbar a little more advanced by adding one or two of your favorite tools from the Advanced toolbar. Customizing the toolbar is as easy as drag-and-drop, if you know where to start dragging. Here's what you need to do:

1. **Choose View⇨Toolbars⇨Customize.**

   The Customize dialog box appears.

2. **Click the Commands tab.**

   A list of command categories appears on the left side of the dialog box and the commands in each category appear on the right.

3. **Click the name of the category of the command you want to add from the category column.**

   The commands in the selected category appear on the right.

4. **Select the command you want to add from the list on the right by clicking it once.**

   A heavy black border appears around the command you select.

5. **Drag the selected command to the toolbar.**

   The command that you dragged appears in the toolbar.

6. **Click Close.**

   Your command is now part of your toolbar.

When the Customize dialog box is open, you can drag tools and menu commands to and from the Outlook toolbars and menus. Messing up Outlook's controls this way is amazingly easy, so be careful. If you do make a mess of things, choose View⇨Toolbars⇨Customize; then click the Reset button to set everything right.

Creating Your Own Type of Outlook Field

You can create your own fields in any Outlook module, form, or view. You can even define what type the field will be and how it will look.

To create your own type of Outlook field:

1. **Right-click the heading of any column.**

   A menu appears

2. **Choose Field Chooser.**

   The Field Chooser appears.

3. **Click New.**

   The New Field dialog box appears.

4. **Type the name of your new field in the Name box.**

5. **In the Type box, choose the type of field from which you want to make your new field.**

   The Type box allows you to choose which kind of information will go in the field — text, time, or percentage. Feel free to experiment; changing the type later by using the Format➪Fields command is easy.

6. **In the Format list, choose the format of the information that you want to put in the field.**

   Some types of information have several possible formats. Dates, for example, could have the format 7/4/98, July 4, 1998, or Sat 7/4/98. Some types of information, such as plain text, have only one format.

7. **Click OK.**

   Your new field appears in the Field Chooser.

8. **Drag your new field to the position where you want it to appear.**

You have so many different ways to customize and use Outlook; I've only begun to scratch the surface. Feel free to experiment; you really can't break anything, and most features of Outlook are easiest to understand when you see them in action.

Setting Up Fax Service

Microsoft has always had a fax program that you could bolt on to Outlook and make sending and receiving faxes possible. Unfortunately, that program was finicky to install and a pain in the neck to use. With Outlook 98, Microsoft is including a program called Winfax (written by a different company) to handle fax chores. Good move! As I write this book, it's not yet clear how Outlook 98 and Winfax will be packaged together, but I've always found Winfax easy to set up and use. The version of Winfax that you'll get for free with Outlook won't be as powerful as the version of Winfax you buy in the store, but it'll be a real time-saver. If you send and receive very many faxes, Winfax will be a big help.

Chapter 25

Top Ten Accessories for Outlook

In This Chapter

▶ PalmPilot

▶ Microsoft Office 97

▶ Desktop to Go

▶ Winfax Pro

▶ A business card scanner

▶ Laplink

▶ A high-capacity, removable disk drive

▶ A tape backup system

▶ Microsoft Exchange Server

▶ Keyview

*O*utlook 98 can do plenty for you without any outside help, but a few well-considered accessories can make your life even easier. Some of my favorite accessories make up for things Outlook ought to have but doesn't. Some of my other favorite accessories help me to use my Outlook data anywhere, anytime.

PalmPilot

The PalmPilot handheld computer is far and away my favorite accessory for Outlook. While I can enter and manage data in a snap with Outlook, I can carry my most important Outlook info in my pocket on my PalmPilot. I can even read my e-mail on the subway using the PalmPilot, something I wouldn't try with a laptop. Microsoft doesn't make the PalmPilot, and Bill Gates is known to have plans for a product to compete with PalmPilot, so we'll see how popular the PalmPilot is in a year or so. On the other hand, Mr. Gates often "announces" products years before he gets them to work right, so all I can say is that the PalmPilot is here now and works like a champ.

Microsoft Office 97

When Outlook was first released, it was a part of the Microsoft Office 97 suite. Now that you can buy Outlook as a stand-alone product (or in a package with Internet Explorer), you may not have the benefits of using Microsoft Office and Outlook 98 in concert. Office lets you do all sorts of tricks with outgoing e-mail and graphics, while Outlook makes it a snap to exchange the work you've created in Office via e-mail. I recommend using both, if possible.

Desktop to Go

Outlook still doesn't do a good job of talking to other devices on its own — even other devices that are running Outlook. To make your Outlook data useful on something like the PalmPilot, you need a program such as Desktop to Go, from a company called Dataviz, to help you move the data back and forth. You can find out more about Desktop to Go from the manufacturer's Web site at www.dataviz.com. Another popular tool for synchronizing Outlook with other devices is called Intellisynch by Puma Technology (www.pumatech.com). With either of these products, you can move your most important data from Outlook to your PalmPilot by pressing one button. Pretty slick.

Winfax Pro

Microsoft is including a baby version of Winfax with Outlook 98 to allow you to send and receive faxes while using Outlook to keep track of all the faxes you exchange. The baby version is nice, but if your business depends on healthy fax traffic, you need grownup Winfax to do the job.

A Business Card Scanner

You can use several brands of business card scanners to copy contact information into Outlook from the business cards you collect at conferences and trade shows. Of course, you can enter all the info manually, but if you collect more than a few dozen cards per week, a business card scanner can save you lots of work.

Laplink

One of the most common questions I get from readers is "How do I share Outlook information between my desktop and laptop computers?" Outlook doesn't provide a practical method for synchronizing information between two computers, so you're better off using a tool like Laplink to copy the Outlook data file (its filename ends in the letters .PST) between the two computers. Be careful, though — Laplink has a synchronization tool that can make a mess of your Outlook data. Your best bet is to use Laplink to copy the whole file from one computer to another.

A Large, Removable Disk Drive

The second most common question I hear is "How do I back up my Outlook data for safekeeping?" Again, because the Outlook data file is much too big to save on a floppy disk, you may want a large-capacity device for storing your data. The Iomega Zip drive and the Syquest Sparq drive both cost between one and two hundred dollars, hook up to your printer port, and give you lots of space. The Zip drive is more popular, while the Sparq drive is cheaper and larger.

A Tape Backup

If you use your computer for business, your Outlook data probably isn't the only data that's crucial to your work. The cheapest way to keep your business data safe is to get a tape backup system and run the system every night. Depending on the size of your computer's hard disk, you can get tape backup units for around $200 and tapes run about $20 each — a bargain compared to the cost of losing your data.

Microsoft Exchange

Many of the Outlook features that Microsoft trumpets most require a network product called Microsoft Exchange Server. You need to have a network running Windows NT Server in order to run Exchange Server, so this accessory isn't cheap, and it's not so simple to set up. If you have a small business, a product called Microsoft Small Business Server has everything you need to set up a network with Exchange Server. You'll still spend several thousand dollars to get this arrangement going, but you'll be able to share schedules, tasks, and calendars, and exchange interoffice e-mail. So you get a lot for what you spend.

Keyview

Windows comes with a file viewing program called Quickview that lets you look at the contents of a file without actually opening the file — a real time-saver if you send and receive lots of attachments. Keyview is a competitor to Quickview.

I prefer Keyview because it's smart enough to figure out what kind of file it's looking at, regardless of what the file is named. Quickview won't view a file if the last three letters of the filename don't accurately reflect what type of file it is. For example, I get lots of incoming faxes — some end with the extension .TIF and others end with the extension .FXD. Except for the names, the files are alike. Keyview knows that those two types of files are the same thing and reads either; Quickview only reads the file if the extension is .TIF. I hate messing with that stuff, so I stick with Keyview.

Index

• A •

accessories for Outlook 98
business card scanners, 338
Desktop to Go program, 338
Keyview file viewing program, 340
Laplink, 339
Microsoft Exchange Server, 339–340
Microsoft Office 97, 338
PalmPilot handheld computer, 337
tape backup system, 339
Winfax Pro, 338
Zip drive or Sparq drive, 339
Act!, 27, 184
Actions menu commands
Actions⇨Call Contact, 20
Actions⇨Explore Web Page, 322
Actions⇨Flag for Followup, 121
Actions⇨Forward as vCard, 175
Actions⇨New All Day Event, 216
Actions⇨New Mail Message using
Stationery, 124
Active Appointments view of Calendar
module, 204
Active List view of tasks, 271
Address Book dialog box, 179, 183
Address Books (Corporate version of
Outlook 98)
creating a Personal Distribution List, 179–181
editing a Personal Distribution List, 183–184
importing an Address Book from Schedule+
and other applications, 184–185
types of, 178–179
using a Personal Distribution List, 181–182
Address Cards view, 73
addresses, e-mail
figuring out contact's address using
AutoName feature, 105
figuring out what your e-mail address is, 103
saving Internet, 323
storing a contact's, 160
addressing envelopes, 284–287
Advanced toolbar, 38, 332–333

alphabetical order, putting lists in, 80
America Online (AOL), 188–189
animated text, 302–303
Animations page, Font dialog box, 302
Annual Events view of Calendar, 214
Appointment form, 200–201
pull-down Calender in, 206
appointments
Active Appointments view of Calendar, 214
assigning a category to an appointment,
202–203
changing an appointment, 205–207
clicking the New tool icon to create, 209
creating new, 200–204
Daily view of, 212
Date Navigator as a tool for making, 198–199
Day/Week/Month view of, 73–74
deleting appointments, 207–208
entering appointments in Calendar, 15–16
entering times (AM or PM), 207
Monthly view of, 213
printing, 215–216
recurring, 208–211
reminders delivered by Office Assistant,
203–204
reminders for, 201–202
scheduling, 200–204
scheduling events, 216
sending e-mail about, 46–47
time-saver shortcut for creating, 200
views of, 212–214
Weekly view of, 213
Art, Office, 304–305
assigning a category to appointment, 202–203
assigning a category to contact, 161–162
Assignment view of tasks, 272
Assistant, Office
appointment reminders from, 203–204
choosing the Clipit character, the Genius,
or Power Pup for your assistant, 41
clicking Reminder box to schedule
reminders from Office Assistant, 201–202
getting help from, 41–42

AT&T WorldNet Service, national ISP, 189
attachments, e-mail
  defined, 47
  sending, 127–128
Author view, By, 62–63
AutoDialer, 19–21
automatic recording feature, Journal's,
    240–241
AutoName feature, 103, 105
AutoPreview mode
  choosing, 138
  reading e-mail in, 12–13
  using Preview Pane instead of, 146

• B •

backing up files
  to floppy disks (no can do), 326
  to removable disk drives, 339
  to tapes, 339
Balloon Party Invitation stationery, 135
Boardwatch magazine, 190
bold command shortcut (Ctrl+B), 6
breaking dates on Calendar, 207–208
browser, Object, 308–309
browser buttons, 319
browsing in Information Viewer, 35–37
browsing Word 97 documents, 308–309
business card scanners, 338
business cards, sending electronic, 175–176
By Author view, 62–63
By Category view
  of appointments, 214
  of Contact lists, 169–170
  of Journal entries, 248
  of tasks, 272
By Company view of Contact lists, 84,
    168–169
By Contact view of Journal entries, 248, 249
By Conversation Topic view of e-mail,
    141–142
By Follow Up Flag view of e-mail, 139
By Person Responsible view of tasks, 272
By Sender view of e-mail Inbox, 142–143
By Type view of Journal entries, 247

• C •

Calendar, Outlook 98, 197
  Active Appointments view of, 214
  changing an appointment, 205–207
  Daily view of, 212
  Date Navigator, 198–199
  Day/Week/Month view of, 73–74
  deleting appointments, 207–208
  entering appointments in, 15–16
  Monthly view of, 213
  printing your appointments, 215–216
  recurring dates in, 208–211
  scheduling appointments, 200–204
  scheduling events, 216
  Weekly view of, 213
Calendar icon, 15
calendars in Information Viewer, 35–37
Call Status dialog box, 20–21
Card views for Contacts module, 73
Categories dialog box, 202–203
changing an appointment
  to a date you can't see on Calendar,
    206–207
  lengthening an appointment, 207–208
  shortening an appointment, 207
  using drag-and-drop, 205–206
changing color of a note, 224–225
changing size of a note, 223–224
Check Address dialog box, 158–159
Check Full Name dialog box, 157
Check Names button in toolbar, 182
Christmas, 171
chronological order, viewing files in, 64–65
Clipit character, Office Assistant, 41
close button, dialog box, 5
Color menu for notes, 224–225
colors of completed or overdue tasks,
    270–271
columns in Table view, 74
  adding, 75
  as fields, 77
  formatting, 77–78
  moving, 75–76
  removing, 78–79
  widening or shrinking, 78–79

completed tasks in Tasks list
  changing the color of, 270–271
  marking a task complete, 268–269
  marking several tasks complete, 269–270
Completed Tasks view, 272
composing a note, 218–219
CompuServe, 188–189
computers, functions taken over by, 25
Concentric Network, National ISP, 189
conditional formatting in Excel 97, 310–311
Contact form, 14–15
Contact lists, creating, 155
  assigning a category to a contact, 161–162
  formatting Contact text box, 160–161
  setting Journaling Preferences, 163
  storing an address, 158–159
  storing an e-mail address, 160
  storing a name, 156–158
  storing phone numbers, 158–159
  storing a URL address for contact's Web
    page, 160
Contact lists, viewing
  Address Card view, 19–20, 165
  By Category view, 169–170
  By Company view, 168–169
  changing the view, 164–165
  in Contacts module, 156
  grouped views, 168–170
  rearranging views, 166–167
  sorting a view, 165–166
Contact⇨Explore Web Page, 160
contacts
  adding a flag to a contact, 170–172
  assigning a category to a contact, 161–162
  creating contacts from e-mail, 50–51
  finding contacts by last name, 173
  finding contacts using Find Items tool,
    174–175
  storing an address, 158–159
  storing an e-mail address, 160
  storing a name, 156–158
  storing phone numbers, 158–159
  storing a URL address for contact's Web
    page, 160
  storing Web pages of a contact, 322
  viewing, 164–170
Contacts Address Book, 178

Contacts module
  Address Cards view of, 19–20, 73
  finding contacts in, 173–175
  Phone List view of, 165–166
  storing a name in, 156–163
control buttons, dialog box, 5
copying a task, 263–264
corporate network users, 23, 187
Corporate version, Outlook 98
  description of, 26
  features that exist only in, 177
  figuring out whether you have Internet
    Outlook or Corporate version, 177–178
Corporate version Address Books
  bottom line on, 185
  creating Personal Distribution List in
    Personal Address Book, 179–181
  editing Personal Distribution List, 183–184
  importing address books from Schedule+
    and other applications, 184–185
  Personal Address Book, 178, 179
  Personal Distribution List, defined, 177
  types of, 178–179
  using Personal Distribution List, 181–182
Create New Folder dialog box, 290
creating Contact lists, 155
  assigning a category to a contact, 161–162
  formatting Contact text box, 160–161
  setting Journaling Preferences, 163
  storing an address, 158–159
  storing an e-mail address, 160
  storing a name, 156–158
  storing phone numbers, 158–159
  storing a URL address for contact's Web
    page, 160
creating contacts from e-mail, 14–15
  in four steps, 50–51
  time-saver tip for, 51
creating e-mail messages, 44
  from an appointment, 46–47
  from a name in Address Book, 45–46
creating Journal entry for a contact,
    51–52, 163
creating tasks on Tasks list, 16–17
cross-referencing items to jump to different
    modules (no can do), 328
Current View menu, 70
customizing e-mail stationery, 134–136

customizing forms, 87–88
  adding a standard field to a form, 88–93
  adding a user-defined field to a form, 93–94
customizing Outlook 98, 31
customizing the toolbar, 333

• *D* •

Date Navigator, 198–199
dates, viewing a range of, 332
Day/Week/Month view, Calendar's, 73–74
Define Views dialog box, 85
Deleted Items folder, 52
deleting
  appointments, 207–208
  e-mail messages, 115–116
  a group from Outlook Bar, 330–331
  items using drag and drop, 52
  notes, 222
  tasks, 264
Desktop to Go program, 338
Detailed List view of tasks, 271
Details view, 61–62
dialog boxes, 5–6, 256
directory services, setting up, 192–193
disk drives
  list of your, 54–55
  removable, 339
displaying parts of different modules in the
  same view (no can do), 327
Distribution Lists, Personal (for users with
  Corporate version of Outlook 98)
  creating, 179–181
  defined, 177
  editing, 183–184
  using, 181–182
Document Map, 306–307
Document Timeline view, 64–65
documents
  creating hyperlinks in, 305–306
  keeping different versions of, 306–308
  traversing a document with Document
    Map, 306–307
Documents folder, My, 21, 56
DOS For Dummies, Windows 95 Edition
    (Gookin), 53
downloading stationery from the Internet, 324

Drafts folder, 116–117
drag-and-drop method
  defined, 43–44
  deleting items using, 52
  grouping views with, 81–82
dragging appointments to another time,
    205–206
dragging column headings in Table view,
    75–76
dragging Contact listing to Journal icon,
    51–52
dragging items to Journal icon, 241–242
dragging scraps of text from Web pages, 323
Drawing toolbar, Office Art, 304–305
drives, seeing a list of your, 54–55

• *E* •

Earthlink Network, national ISP, 189
Ecco, importing files from, 184
Edit menu
  Edit⇨Copy (or Ctrl+C), 264
  Edit⇨Delete (or Ctrl+D), 116, 264
  Edit⇨Paste (or Ctrl+V), 264
  Edit⇨Undo (or Ctrl+Z), 318
editing a Personal Distribution List (for
    Outlook 98 Corporate version users),
    183–184
editing recurring appointments, 211
editing tasks
  quick way to change a task, 259
  regular way to change a task, 259–263
e-mail, 3–4. *See also* Office 97 tricks for
    snappier e-mail; sorting e-mail; viewing
    e-mail
  adding an Internet link to, 108
  addresses, 103
  attachments, 127–128
  automatically adding your name to
    message replies, 124–125
  changing appearance of, 125–126
  creating a contact, 14–15
  creating messages, 102–104
  creating messages using drag-and-drop,
    44–47
  deleting, 115–116
  etiquette, 115

flagging, 120–123
forwarding, 113–115
front-end and back-end service, 101–102
junk, 150–151, 276
opening and reading, 109
in Outlook Express, 273
previewing message text, 110–111
reading, 12–14
replying to, 111–113
saving e-mail messages as files, 116–118
saving e-mail to Sent Messages folder,
    123–124
saving incomplete messages in Drafts
    folder, 116
sending a file by, 21–22, 47–49
setting options for appearance of, 125–126
setting priority of messages, 104–107
setting sensitivity of messages, 107–108
setting up an e-mail account in Internet
    Mail Only version of Outlook 98, 190–192
signatures, 128–130
special features for, 119
e-mail addresses
  figuring out contact's address using
    AutoName feature, 105
  figuring out what your address is, 103
  saving Internet, 323
  storing a contact's, 160
E-mail Options dialog box
  automatically adding your name to message
    replies, 124–125
  saving outgoing mail to Sent Messages
    folder, 123–124
  setting options, 125–126
embedding pictures in notes (no can do), 327
Entry List view of Journal entries, 247, 248
Envelope Options dialog box, 285
envelopes, addressing, 284–287
etiquette, e-mail, 115
events, scheduling, 216
Events view of Calendar, 214
Excel, Office 97
  conditional formatting in, 310–311
  merging cells in, 312, 313
  rotating text in, 312–313

Exchange program, Microsoft Office 95,
    28, 119
Explorer, Windows
  managing files with Outlook instead of, 23,
    59, 67
  sending a file to an e-mail recipient when
    you're in, 316–317
extensions, file, 58–59

● *F* ●

F1 key, to summon Office Assistant, 41
Favorites folder, 321
fax service, setting up, 335
Field Chooser, finding fields to add to forms
    with, 91–92
Field Chooser dialog box, 75–76
fields
  adding merge fields to form letters,
    288–289
  adding standard fields to forms, 88–93
  adding user-defined fields to forms, 93–94
  creating your own type of, 334
  Mail Merge, 283–284, 286
  in Table View, 77
file compression programs, 49
file extensions, 58–59
file management. *See also* Net Folders
  backing up files, 326, 339
  By Author view of files, 62–63
  By File Type view of files, 63–64
  creating a new folder, 56–57
  defined, 54
  Details view of files, 61–62
  Document Timeline view of files, 64–65
  Icons view of files, 60–61
  installing file management tools, 53, 67–68
  moving and copying files, 56
  My Documents folder, 21, 56
  Programs view of files, 66–67
  renaming files, 58–59
  renaming folders, 57–58
  selecting files, 56
  sharing folders, 293, 295–297
  sorting files in a folder, 60
  viewing list of files, 54–55

File menu commands
File⇨Close, 110
File⇨Import and Export, 185
File⇨New, 87, 96
File⇨New⇨Contact, 156
File⇨New⇨Folder, 57, 132
File⇨New⇨Note, 219
File⇨New⇨Task, 255
File⇨Print (Ctrl+P), 215
File⇨Save (Ctrl+S), 116
File⇨Save As (F12), 117
File⇨Send To⇨Mail Recipient, 49, 317
files, backing up
to floppy disks (no can do), 326
to removable disk drives, 339
to tapes, 339
files, importing Address Book, 184–185
files, sending, 21–22
attachments, defined, 47
and file size, 49
nine steps for, 47–49
filing e-mail messages in folders
creating a folder for new mail, 132–133
moving messages to another folder, 133
filtering junk e-mail, 150–151
Find dialog box, 220–221
finding contacts
by last name, 173
using Find Items tool, 174–175
finding Journal entries, 244–245
finding misplaced notes, 220–221
Flag for Follow Up dialog box, 171–172
Flagged for Next Seven Days view of e-mail
Inbox, 140–141
Flagged view of e-mail Inbox, 139
flagging a contact's name, 170–172
flagging e-mail, 120–123
floppy disk, backing up Outlook files to, 326
Fluffernet, Floyd, 244
folder, My Documents, 21, 56
renaming, 57
viewing files in, 54–55
Folder List
on main screen, 29
navigating with, 37
shortcut for opening, 317–318
using, 38
viewing, 40–41

folders
creating new, 56–57
default forms for, 96–97
filing e-mail messages in, 132–133
renaming, 57–58
folders, sharing, 293
adding shared items to a folder, 298
allowing another person to share your
folders, 295–297
installing Net Folders feature, 293–294
form letters
creating, 287–289
defined, 287
formatting a column in Table view, 77–78
forms
adding standard fields to, 88–93
adding user-defined fields to, 93–94
default forms for folders, 96–97
understanding, 87–88
using, 95
Forward screen, 114
forwarding e-mail, 113–115
forwarding notes, 237–238
free stationery, downloading, 324

• G •

Gates, Bill, 337
Genius assistant, 41
Global Address List, 178
Go, changing modules by clicking, 30
Go To Date command (Ctrl+G), 199, 318–319
Go menu commands
Go⇨Calendar, 36
Go⇨Contacts, 156
Go⇨Go To Today, 199
Go⇨Inbox, 109
Go⇨News, 274
Go⇨Outbox, 102
Go⇨Outlook Today, 34
Gookin, Dan, 53, 104, 281
grammar checker, 309–310
graphics
creating drawings with Office Art, 304–305
embedding pictures in notes (no can do), 327
Group By dialog box, 82–83
grouped views of Contact list
By Category view, 169–170
By Company view, 168–169

grouping
  defined, 81
  with drag-and-drop, 81–82
  with Group By dialog box, 82–83
  versus sorting, 81
  viewing grouped items, 84
groups
  adding a group to Outlook Bar, 33, 329–330
  defined, 31–32
  deleting a group from Outlook Bar, 330–331
  reason for having, 34
  renaming a group in Outlook Bar, 330
GTE Internet Solutions, 190

• *H* •

hard drives, 54
help from Office Assistant
  appointment reminders, 203–204
  choosing the Clipit character, the Genius,
    or Power Pup for your assistant, 41
  clicking Reminder box to schedule
    reminders from Office Assistant, 201–202
  pressing F1 and asking questions, 41–42
Help menu commands
  Help⇨About Microsoft Outlook, 178
  Help⇨Microsoft on the Web⇨
    Free Stuff, 324
  Help⇨Microsoft on the Web⇨
    Online Support, 324
holidays, reminders involving, 171
hot links
  in any Outlook Item, 323
  in e-mail messages, 322
  in tasks, 258
hyperlinks, creating, 305–306
hypertext, 35

• *I* •

IBM Internet Connection Service, 190
icons, renaming Outlook Bar, 331
icons used in this book, 7
Icons view
  for viewing file folders, 60–61
  for viewing notes, 70–72
IDT Internet Services, 190
Import and Export Wizard, 185
importing files from Schedule+, 184–185
Inbox, e-mail, 109

Inbox icon, 12–13
  numbers next to, 109
Information Viewer, 35–37
  on main screen, 29
Insert File dialog box, 127
Insert Hyperlink dialog box, 305, 322
installing file management tools, 67–68
installing Net Folders, 293–294
installing Outlook 98, 23
Integrated File Management tools, 53
  Favorites Folder, 321
  installing, 67–68
Intellisynch, for synchronizing Outlook with
    other devices, 338
Internet, difference between intranet
    and, 193
Internet e-mail
  receiving, 112, 322
  sending, 322
Internet e-mail addresses, saving, 323
Internet Explorer 4.0, 27
  Outlook Express included with, 273
  for running Outlook 98, 326
Internet hot links
  in any Outlook item, 323
  in e-mail, 322
  in tasks, 258
Internet icon used in this book, 7
Internet links
  in e-mail messages, 108, 113, 322
  in tasks, 258
Internet Mail Only version of Outlook 98
  biggest differences between Corporate
    version and, 187
  description of, 26
  figuring out if you have, 177–178
  online services to use with, 188–189
  picking an ISP for, 189–190
  setting up directory services, 192–193
  setting up e-mail account in, 190–192
Internet newsgroups
  addicts of, 277
  defined, 273
  finding, 274–275
  messages with plus signs, 276–277
  Outlook Express as a newsreader
    program, 273
  posting messages to, 279
  reading newsgroup messages, 276–277
  replying to newsgroup messages, 277–278
  subscribing to, 276

Internet Service Providers (ISPs)
  defined, 187–188
  national, 189–190
  online services that function as, 188–189
intranets, defined, 193
ISPs (Internet Service Providers)
  defined, 187–188
  national, 189–190
  online services that function as, 188–189

• J •

Journal, 4
  automatic recording feature of, 240–241
  automatically recording all contact stuff
    in, 327
  By Category view of, 248
  By Contact view of, 248, 249
  By Type view of, 247
  as a captain's log, 239
  creating a Journal entry for a contact,
    51–52
  dragging items to Journal icon, 241–242
  Entry List view of, 247, 248
  finding a Journal entry, 244–245
  as a helpful tool, 250
  for keeping track of document
    information, 243
  Last Seven Days view of, 249
  Phone Call view of, 249
  printing entries, 246–247
  recording a document in, 242–243
  recording phone conversations in, 17–18
  setting Journaling Preferences when you're
    first entering a contact, 163
  viewing journal entries for a contact, 244
  views, 247–249
Journal icon, 17
  dragging a Contact listing to, 51–52
  dragging an item to, 241–242
Journal Options dialog box, 240
Journal tab in Contact form, 163, 244
junk e-mail
  filtering, 150–151
  warning about Internet newsgroups
    and, 276

• K •

keyboard shortcuts, 6
  for creating an appointment
    (Ctrl+Shift+A), 200
  for creating a new item (Ctrl+N), 200
  for deleting an appointment (Ctrl+D), 208
  for Go To Date dialog box (Ctrl+G), 199,
    318–319
  for making text bold (Ctrl+B), 6
  for opening the Edit menu (Alt+E), 6
  for opening the File menu (Alt+F), 6
  for opening the Help menu (Alt+H), 6
  for printing appointments or Journal
    (Ctrl+P), 215
  for Recurrence dialog box (Ctrl+G), 210
  for taking notes (Ctrl+N), 219
  for taking notes in any Outlook module
    except Notes (Ctrl+Shift+N), 219
Keyview file viewing program, 340

• L •

Label Options dialog box, 283
labels, mailing, 281–284
Laplink, 339
laptop, checking e-mail from a, 152–154
Last Seven Days view
  of e-mail, 140
  of Journal, 249
limitations of Outlook 98 (things Outlook 98
    can't do), 325
  automatically recording all contact stuff in
    the Journal, 327
  backing up files to a floppy disk, 326
  calculating expenses with Journal Phone
    Call entries, 328
  cross-referencing items to jump to different
    modules, 328
  displaying parts of different modules in the
    same view, 327
  embedding pictures in notes, 327
  making Outlook start other programs, 327
  running Outlook 98 without installing
    Internet Explorer 4.0, 326
  saving the Folder List in a custom view, 327
  using categories in a Word 97 mail
    merge, 326

links, Outlook, 6
links in e-mail messages, 108, 113
Lotus Organizer, 27
  importing files from, 184

• M •

Mac version of Outlook, 26
Mail Merge feature, Word 97
  creating form letters in Word 97, 287–289
  creating mailing labels with, 281–284
  merging selected records from Outlook 98, 289–291
  printing addresses directly onto envelopes, 284–287
  selecting only those records you want from a merge list, 331–332
  using Outlook categories in a Word 97 mail merge (you can't), 326
Mail Merge Helper, 282, 284
making appointments
  assigning a category to an appointment, 202–203
  changing an appointment, 205–207
  Date Navigator as a tool for, 198–199
  entering appointments in Calendar, 15–16
  entering times (AM or PM), 207
  for events, 216
  New Tool icon as tool for, 209
  for recurring meetings, 208–211
  with reminders, 201–202
  reminders delivered by Office Assistant, 203–204
  steps for, 200–204
  time-saver shortcut for, 200
managing files
  By Author view of files, 62–63
  By File Type view of files, 63–64
  creating a new folder, 56–57
  defined, 54
  Details view of files, 61–62
  Document Timeline view of files, 64–65
  Icons view of files, 60–61
  installing file management tools, 67–68
  moving and copying files, 56
  My Documents folder, 21, 56
  Programs view of files, 66–67

renaming files, 58–59
renaming folders, 57–58
selecting files, 56
sharing files. *See* Net Folders
sorting files in a folder, 60
viewing list of files, 54–55
Master Category List dialog box, 202–203
MCI Internet, 190
Meeting form, 15
menu, pulling down, 6
menu commands, 6. *See also* keyboard shortcuts
merging cells in Excel 97, 312, 313
merging selected records, 289–291, 331–332
Message Options dialog box
  setting priority of messages, 104–106
  setting sensitivity of messages, 107–108
Message Timeline view of e-mail, 146, 147
Messages view of your e-mail Inbox, 137
Microsoft Exchange Server, 27, 119
  as an accessory for Outlook 98, 339–340
Microsoft Network (MSN), 102
  addresses, 103
  comparing AOL, CompuServe, and, 188
  phone number for, 189
Microsoft Office 95, 27
  personal information management programs, 28
Microsoft Office 97, 26–27, 338
Microsoft Office 97 For Windows For Dummies, (Wang & Parker), 2, 301
Microsoft Outlook 98. *See also* Microsoft Outlook 98 Corporate version; Microsoft Outlook 98 Internet Mail Only version; things you can't do with Outlook
  accessories for, 337–340
  browser buttons, 319
  comparing a car's dashboard to, 119
  Corporate version, 26, 177–178
  customizing, 31
  Folder List, 37–38
  general information about, 1, 11–12
  Help system, 41–42
  Information Viewer, 35–37
  Internet Explorer 4.0 needed for, 326
  Internet Mail Only version, 26, 177–178
  modules, 30–31

(continued)

Microsoft Outlook 98 *(continued)*
  Office Assistant, 41–42
  Outlook Bar, 31–34
  versus Outlook Express, 273–274
  Outlook Today page, 34–35
  programs linked with, 26–27
  screen, 28–29, 40–41
  toolbars, 38–40
  versions of, 26, 177–178
  views, 69–74
Microsoft Outlook 98 Corporate version, 26
  features that exist only in, 177
  figuring out if you have, 177–178
Microsoft Outlook 98 Internet Mail Only
    version, 26
  biggest differences between Corporate
    version and, 187
  figuring out if you have, 177–178
  online services to use with, 188–189
  picking an ISP for, 189–190
  setting up directory services, 192–193
  setting up e-mail account in, 190–192
Microsoft Small Business Server, 339–340
MindSpring, national ISP, 190
minimize button, dialog box, 5
misplaced notes, finding, 220–221
mistakes, undoing, 318
modules
  defined, 30–31
  displaying parts of different modules in the
    same view (no can do), 327
  using New Item tool to create a new item in
    whatever module you're in, 315–316
  using New tool to avoid switching to
    another module, 39–40
Move to Folder button, 133
moving columns in Table view, 75–76
moving e-mail messages to another
    folder, 133
moving files, 56
My Computer icon, 21–22
  list of drives found in, 57, 242–243
My Documents folder, 21, 56
  renaming, 57
  viewing files in, 54–55

• *N* •

names in To line of e-mail messages, 105, 182
navigating with browser buttons, 319
Net Folders
  adding shared items to a folder, 298
  installing, 293–294
  sharing a folder, 295–297
Netcom, national ISP, 190
Network icon used in this book, 7
networks, 54
New Call dialog box, 19–21
New Contact form, 156–157
New Item menu, 18, 315–316
New Item tool, 315–316
New Message form, 102–103
New tool, 39–40
  creating new appointments with, 209
Newsgroups dialog box, 274–275
newsgroups, Internet
  addicts, 277
  defined, 273
  finding, 274–275
  messages with plus signs, 276–277
  Outlook Express as a newsreader
    program, 273
  posting messages to, 279
  reading newsgroup messages, 276–277
  replying to newsgroup messages, 277–278
  subscribing to, 276
Next Seven Days view
  of flagged e-mail, 140–141
  of tasks, 272
Note icon
  clicking icon to see Notes list, 218–219
  clicking icon to change note's color,
    224–225
  dragging scraps of text from Web pages
    to, 323
  no name on, 217
Notes, Outlook
  By Category view, 228–229
  By Color view, 228, 230
  categorizing notes, 231–232
  changing color of a note, 224–225
  changing default options in, 235–237
  changing size of a note, 223–224
  creating a note, 218–219

deleting a note, 222

embedding pictures in notes (no can do), 327

finding a misplaced note, 220–221

forwarding a note, 237–238

as a handy tool, 238

Icons view, 225–226

keeping a note open, 318

Last Seven Days view, 227–228, 229

Notes List view, 226–227

printing contents of a note, 234

printing list of your notes, 233

reading a note, 221–222

selecting a group of notes, 223

taking notes while doing your work, 18–19, 218–219

time-saver shortcut for creating a note, 219

tricks, 220

viewing your notes, 225–230

• *O* •

Object Browser, 308–309

Office 97, Microsoft, 26–27, 98, 338

Office 97 tricks for snappier e-mail, 301

animated text, 302–303

Document Map, 306–307

Excel's conditional formatting, 310–311

Excel's Merge Cells button, 312, 313

Excel's rotated text, 312–313

grammar checker, 309–310

hyperlinks, 305–306

Object browser, 308–309

Office Art, 304–305

and reminder about e-mail recipients, 314

Table tools, 303–304

Version feature, 306–308

Office Art, 304–305

Office Assistant

appointment reminders from, 203–204

choosing the Clipit character, the Genius, or Power Pup for your assistant, 41

clicking Reminder box to schedule reminders from Office Assistant, 201–202

getting help from, 41–42

online services

America Online (AOL), 188–189

CompuServe, 188–189

Microsoft Network, 102, 103, 188–189

outgoing mail, saving, 123–124

Outlook 98. *See also* Outlook 98 Corporate version; Outlook 98 Internet Mail Only version; things you can't do with Outlook

accessories for, 337–340

browser buttons, 319

comparing a car's dashboard to, 119

Corporate version, 26, 177–178

customizing, 31

Folder List, 37–38

general information about, 1, 11–12

Help system, 41–42

Information Viewer, 35–37

Internet Explorer 4.0 needed for, 326

Internet Mail Only version, 26, 177–178

modules, 30–31

Office Assistant, 41–42

Outlook Bar, 31–34

with Outlook Express, 26, 273–274

Outlook Today page, 34–35

programs linked with, 26–27

screen, 28–29, 40–41

toolbars, 38–40

versions of, 26, 177–178

views, 69–74

Outlook 98 Corporate version, 26

features that exist only in, 177

figuring out if you have, 177–178

Outlook 98 Corporate version Address Books bottom line on, 185

creating Personal Distribution List in Personal Address Book, 179–181

editing Personal Distribution List, 183–184

importing address books from Schedule+ and other applications, 184–185

Personal Address Book, 178, 179

Personal Distribution List, defined, 177

types of, 178–179

using Personal Distribution List, 181–182

Outlook 98 Internet Mail Only version, 26

biggest differences between Corporate version and, 187

figuring out if you have, 177–178

online services to use with, 188–189

picking an ISP for, 189–190

setting up directory services, 192–193

setting up e-mail account in, 190–192

Outlook Bar, 29
  adding groups to, 33, 329–330
  adding items to, 32–33
  deleting a group from, 330–331
  groups, 31–34
  renaming a group in, 330
  renaming an icon in, 331
Outlook Express, 26, 27
  difference between Outlook 98 and, 273–274
  finding newsgroups with, 274–275
  as a newsreader program, 273
  posting a new message to a newsgroup, 279
  reading newsgroup messages, 276–277
  replying to a newsgroup message, 277–278
  screen, 274–275
  subscribing to newsgroups with, 276
Outlook Today page, 34–35
Outlook Web View, 26
overdue tasks, changing color of, 270–271
Overdue Tasks view, 272

● *P* ●

Paint accessory, Windows, 304
PalmPilot handheld computer, 337
parts of this book, 3–5
Personal Address Book, 178
Personal Distribution Lists (feature found in
    Corporate version of Outlook 98)
  creating, 179–181
  defined, 177
  editing, 183–184
  using, 181–182
Personal Information Managers (PIMs),
    27–28
  of the past, 28
phone calls
  calculating expense of (no can do), 328
  recording conversations as Journal entries,
    17–18
  returning, 19–21
Phone Calls view of Journal, 249
Phone List view of Contacts module, 165–166
phone number types for contacts, 159
phone numbers
  for national Internet Service Providers,
    189–190
  for online services, 189

PKZIP file compression program, 49
plus signs
  in grouped views, 84
  Internet newsgroup messages with,
    276–277
Pocket Outlook, 26
posting a message to a newsgroup, 278–279
Power Pup assistant, 41
Preview Pane, 146–147
previewing e-mail message text
  with AutoPreview, 110–111
  Internet e-mail gobbledygook, 112
  with Preview Pane, 146–147
Print icon, 216
printing appointments, 215–216
printing envelopes, 284–287
printing Journal entries, 246–247
printing mailing labels, 281–284
printing notes, 233–234
printing Outlook Today page, 35
priority of e-mail messages, 104–107
Private box
  in New Appointment form, 203
  in New Contact form, 163
Programs view of files, 66–67
publishing, defined, 93

● *Q* ●

Quickview file viewing program, 340

● *R* ●

Rathbone, Andy, 2
reading e-mail, 12–14
reading newsgroup messages, 276–277
reading notes, 221–222
recommended reading
  DOS For Dummies, Windows 95 Edition,
    (Gookin), 53
  *Microsoft Office 97 For Windows For
    Dummies,* (Wang & Parker), 2, 301
  Windows 95 For Dummies, 2nd ed.,
    (Rathbone), 2
  Word 97 For Windows For Dummies
    (Gookin), 104, 281
recording phone conversations as Journal
  entries, 17–18

Recurrence dialog box, 210
Recurring Appointment dialog box, 211
recurring appointments
   creating, 208–210
   editing, 211
recurring tasks
   creating, 264–266
   skipping a recurring task once, 268
regenerating tasks
   creating, 267
   defined, 267
Remember icon used in this book, 7
Reminder box
   flagging a contact using, 171
   making appointments using, 16, 201
Reminder dialog box's Snooze button, 172
Reminder Sound dialog box, 201–202
reminders, creating
   flagging a contact's name, 170–172
   flagging e-mail, 120–123
   reminding yourself with notes, 218–219
Remote Connection Wizard, 152–154
Remote Mail feature, 152–154
Rename dialog box, 57–58
renaming files, 58–59
renaming folders, 57–58
renaming an icon in Outlook Bar, 331
Reply screen, 112
replying to e-mail, 111–113
   automatically adding your name when,
      124–125
replying to newsgroup messages, 277–278
resizing a note, 223–224
returning a phone call with AutoDialer,
   19–21
revising documents, 306–308
Rules Wizard, for sorting e-mail, 146, 148–150

• S •

Save As dialog box, 117–118
saving e-mail messages
   in Drafts folder, 116
   as files, 116–118
saving Internet e-mail addresses, 323
saving Outlook 98 data
   to floppy disks (no can do), 326
   to removable disk drives, 339
   to tapes, 339

saving views, 85
Schedule+ program
   importing an Address Book from, 184–185
   from Microsoft Office 95, 28
scheduling appointments, 200–204
   Active Appointments view of Calendar, 214
   assigning a category to appointment,
      202–203
   changing an appointment, 205–207
   Daily view of Calendar, 212
   Date Navigator, 198–199
   Day/Week/Month view of Calendar, 73–74
   deleting appointments, 207–208
   entering appointments in Calendar, 15–16
   for events, 216
   Monthly view of Calendar, 213
   printing your appointments, 215–216
   for recurring dates, 208–211
   with reminders, 201–202
   selecting a new appointment, 200
   time-saver shortcut for, 200
   Weekly view of Calendar, 213
scheduling tasks, 251
   adding task to Tasks list, 16–17, 252–258
   changing the color of completed and
      overdue
      tasks, 270–271
   copying a task, 263–264
   creating a recurring task, 264–266
   creating a regenerating task, 267
   deleting a task, 264
   editing tasks, 259–263
   Internet links added to a task, 258
   marking a task complete, 268–269
   marking several tasks complete, 269–270
   quick way to add to Tasks list, 253–254
   quick way to change a task, 259
   regular way to add to Tasks list, 254–258
   regular way to change a task, 259–263
   skipping a recurring task once, 268
   viewing your tasks, 271–272
screen
   main, 28–29
   turning parts of screen on and off, 40–41
searching for a misplaced note, 220–221
searching for contacts in Contacts module
   by last name, 173
   using Find Items tool, 174–175

Select a Stationery dialog box, 134
Select Names dialog box, 135–136
selecting files, 56
selecting items, 44
Send button (Alt+S), 16, 22
sending e-mail replies, 111–113
sending files by e-mail, 21–22
  attachments, defined, 47
  from an Office 97 application, 317
  sending attachments, 127–128
  shortcut for, 316–317
sending Internet e-mail, 322
sensitivity of e-mail messages, 107–108
Sent Items folder, 145
Sent To view of e-mail, 144–145
separator bars, 29, 31–32
Seven Day view of Calendar, 198
sharing information with Net folders
  adding shared items to a folder, 298
  installing Net Folders, 293–294
  sharing a folder, 295–297
shortcuts worth taking
  adding items to list views, 318
  clicking open Folder List, 317–318
  keeping a note open, 318
  keyboard, 6. *See also* keyboard shortcuts
  navigating with browser buttons, 319
  sending a file by e-mail, 316–317
  sending a file from an Office 97
    application, 317
  undoing mistakes with Ctrl+Z, 318
  using Go To Date command, 318, 319
  using New Item tool, 315–316
SideKick, 27, 184
Signature Picker dialog box, 129
signatures, e-mail, 128–130
Simple List view of tasks, 271
size button, dialog box, 5
size-to-fit, for columns, 78
skipping a recurring task once, 268
snappier e-mail with Office 97 tricks, 301
  animated text, 302–303
  Document Map, 306–307
  Excel's conditional formatting, 310–311
  Excel's Merge Cells button, 312, 313
  Excel's rotated text, 312–313
  grammar checker, 309–310
  hyperlinks, 305–306

Object browser, 308–309
Office Art, 304–305
and reminder about e-mail recipients, 314
Table tools, 303–304
Version feature, 306–308
Snooze button, 172
Social Interface system, Office Assistant's, 42
Sort dialog box, 80
sorting
  defined, 79
  versus grouping, 81
  from Table view, 80
  two or more columns, 80
sorting e-mail, 132. *See also* viewing e-mail
  creating a folder for new e-mail, 132–133
  moving messages to another folder, 133
  using Remote Mail feature when traveling,
    152–154
  using Rules Wizard for, 146, 148–150
sorting files in a folder, 60
sorting view of contacts, 165–166
sounds, as appointment reminders, 201–202
spammers, 276
Sparkle Text animation effect, 302
Sparq drive, Syquest, 339
spreadsheets, Excel 97
  conditional formatting in, 310–311
  creating impressive e-mail with, 310
  merging cells in, 312, 313
  rotating text in, 312–313
SpryNet, national ISP, 190
Standard toolbar, 38
Star Trek, 239
stationery
  Balloon Party Invitation, 135
  downloading free Internet stationery, 324
  using electronic, 134–136
stick-on notes. *See also* Notes, Outlook
  disadvantages of, 4
  invention of, 218
  Outlook, 18–19.
subject lines, e-mail message, 104, 141–142
subscribing to newsgroups, 276
suite, Office. *See also* Office 97 tricks for
    snappier e-mail
  defined, 26
  Microsoft's Office 97 as an accessory for
    Outlook 98, 338

• T •

Tab key, moving through dialog boxes with, 256
Table view
  adding a column, 75–76
  in all modules, 70
  columns and fields, 77
  creating custom Table views, 85
  defined, 70
  formatting a column, 77–78
  moving a column, 75–76
  names, 70
  playing with columns, 74
  removing a column, 78–79
  sorting from, 80
  Tasks module in, 70–71
  widening or shrinking columns, 78
tables, creating Word 97, 303–304
tabs, dialog box, 5
taking notes, 218–219
  categorizing notes, 231–232
  changing color of a note, 224–225
  changing default options in Notes, 235–237
  changing size of a note, 223–224
  deleting a note, 222
  doing your work while, 18–19, 218–219
  embedding pictures in notes (no can do), 327
  finding a misplaced note, 220–221
  forwarding a note, 237–238
  printing contents of a note, 234
  printing list of your notes, 233
  reading a note, 221–222
  selecting a group of notes, 223
  time-saver shortcut for, 219
  tricks for, 220
  viewing your notes, 225–230
tape backups of Outlook data, 339
Task Options page, 270–271
Task Recurrence dialog box, 266–267
Task Timeline view, 72, 272
Tasks icon, 16
Tasks list
  adding task to, 16–17, 252–258
  changing the color of completed and overdue tasks, 270–271
  copying a task, 263–264
  creating a recurring task, 264–266
  creating a regenerating task, 267
  deleting a task, 264
  editing tasks in, 259–263
  marking a task complete, 268–269
  marking several tasks complete, 269–270
  quick way to add task to, 253–254
  quick way to change a task, 259
  regular way to add a task to, 254–258
  regular way to change a task, 259–263
  skipping a recurring task once, 268
  as a to-do list, 251
  typing Web page name in Task form, 258
  viewing your tasks, 72, 271–272
Tawdry French Clichés, 207
Technical Stuff icon used in this book, 7
telephone calls
  calculating expense of, 328
  recording conversations as Journal entries, 17–18
  returning, 19–21
text
  animated, 302–302
  bold, 6
text box, Contact, 160–161
text boxes, dialog box, 5
things you *can't* do with Outlook 98, 325–328
  automatically recording all contact stuff in the Journal, 327
  backing up files to a floppy disk, 326
  calculating expenses with Journal Phone Call entries, 328
  cross-referencing items to jump to different modules, 328
  displaying parts of different modules in the same view, 327
  embedding pictures in notes, 327
  making Outlook start other programs, 327
  running Outlook 98 without installing Internet Explorer 4.0, 326
  saving the Folder List in a custom view, 327
  using categories in a Word 97 mail merge, 326
threads, defined, 142
time box, activating reminders in, 257
Time Saver icon used in this book, 7

Timeline view, 72
Tip icon used in this book, 7
title bar, 5
Today page, Outlook, 34–35
toolbars
  customizing, 333
  defined, 38
  turning on Advanced toolbar, 332–333
  using the New tool, 39–40
  viewing ToolTips, 38–39
tools, defined, 38
Tools menu commands
  Tools⇨Accounts, 190
  Tools⇨Address Book, 179
  Tools⇨Check for New Mail, 136
  Tools⇨Empty Deleted Items Folder, 116
  Tools⇨Find, 174
  Tools⇨Find Items, 220
  Tools⇨Forms⇨Design This Form, 90
  Tools⇨Mail Merge, 282, 284, 332
  Tools⇨Options, 123, 240
  Tools⇨Organize, 150–151
  Tools⇨Publish Form As, 93
  Tools⇨Remote Mail⇨Connect, 152
  Tools⇨Rules Wizard, 148
ToolTips, viewing, 38–39
traveling, checking e-mail while, 152–154
triangles
  in headings of sorted lists, 79–80
  tools with down-pointing, 39

• *U* •

Undo command (Ctrl+Z), 318
Uniform Resource Locator (URL), 160
Unread Messages view of e-mail, 143–144
URL (Uniform Resource Locator), 160
Use Address Book dialog box, 282–283

• *V* •

Valentine's Day, 171
vCards, sending, 175–176
versions, Outlook 98, 26
  figuring out which version you have,
    177–178

Versions feature, keeping different versions
    of a document with, 306–308
View menu commands
  View⇨Current View, 70
  View⇨Current View⇨By Author, 62
  View⇨Current View⇨By File Type, 63
  View⇨Current View⇨Define Views, 85
  View⇨Current View⇨Details, 62
  View⇨Current View⇨Document
    Timeline, 65
  View⇨Current View⇨Icons, 61
  View⇨Current View⇨Programs, 66
  View⇨Folder List, 37, 40
  View⇨Preview Pane, 146
  View⇨Toolbars⇨Advanced, 333
  View⇨Toolbars⇨Customize, 333
  View⇨Toolbars⇨Formatting, 161
viewing Calendar
  in Active Appointments view, 214
  in Daily view, 212
  with Date Navigator, 198–199
  in Day/Week/Month view, 73–74
  in Monthly view, 213
  in Weekly view, 213
viewing contacts
  in Address Cards view, 73
  changing view of Contact list, 164–165
  rearranging views, 166–167
  sorting a view, 165–166
  using grouped views, 168–170
viewing dates as a group, 332
viewing e-mail. *See also* sorting e-mail
  AutoPreview view, 110–111, 138
  By Conversation Topic view, 141–142
  By Sender view, 142–143
  Flagged for Next Seven Days view, 140–141
  Flagged view, 139
  Last Seven Days view, 140
  menu method for changing views, 136
  Message Timeline view, 146, 147
  Messages view of your Inbox, 137
  with Preview Pane, 146, 147
  Sent To view, 144–145
  Unread Messages view, 143–144
viewing information, 69–70
  Address Cards view in Contacts module, 73
  in Icons view, 70–72

in Table view, 70–71
in Timeline view, 72
using Information Viewer, 35–37, 70
viewing Journal entries
in By Category view, 248
in By Contact view, 248, 249
in By Type view, 247
in Entry List view, 247, 248
in Last Seven Days view, 249
in Phone Calls view, 249
viewing lists of files, 59
By Author view, 62–63
in chronological order, 64–65
By File Type view, 63–64
Details view, 61–62
Document Timeline view, 64–65
Icons view, 60–61
in lists, 54–55
Programs view, 66–67
viewing notes
by category, 228, 229
by color, 228, 230
as icons, 225–226
from the last seven days, 227–228, 229
in Notes List view, 226–227
viewing parts of different modules in the
same view, 327
viewing Tasks list, 271–272
in Timeline view, 72
viewing ToolTips, 38–39
views, Outlook 98
Card views for Contacts module, 73
Day/Week/Month view for Calendar, 73–74
defined, 69
for every module, 70
Icons view, 70–72
Table view, 70–71
Timeline view, 72
Visual Basic programming language, 2, 325

Wang, Wally, 2, 301
Warning icon used in this book, 7
Web pages
dragging scraps of text from, 323
storing a contact's, 322

Whole Earth Networks, 190
Windows 95
filenames and file extensions in, 59, 67
folders, 37, 53
Help system, 41–42
helpful books on using, 2
Microsoft Network icon, 102
taskbar, 220
Windows 95 For Dummies, 2nd ed.,
(Rathbone), 2
Windows 98, 27
Windows Explorer
managing files with Outlook instead of, 23,
59, 67
sending a file to an e-mail recipient when
you're in, 316–317
Winfax program, 335, 338
WinZip compression program, 49
Wizards
defined, 185
Import and Export Wizard, 185
Remote Connection Wizard, 152–154
Rules Wizard for sorting e-mail, 146,
148–150
Word 97 For Windows For Dummies
(Gookin), 104, 281
Word 97 Mail Merge feature
creating form letters in Word 97, 287–289
creating mailing labels with, 281–284
merging selected records from Outlook 98,
289–291
Outlook 98 and Word 97 as a team, 281
printing addresses directly onto envelopes,
284–287
Word 97 tricks for snappier e-mail
animated text, 302–303
Document Map, 306–307
as an e-mail editor, 301
grammar checker, 309–310
Object browser, 308–309
Office Art, 304–305
Table tools, 303–304
Versions feature, 306–308
World Wide Web
downloading free stationery from, 324
getting free online support for all Office 97
applications from, 324

writing a note with Outlook Notes, 218–219
  categorizing notes, 231–232
  changing color of a note, 224–225
  changing default options in Notes, 235–237
  changing size of a note, 223–224
  deleting a note, 222
  doing your work while, 18–19, 218–219
  embedding pictures in notes
      (no can do), 327
  finding a misplaced note, 220–221
  forwarding a note, 237–238
  printing contents of a note, 234
  printing list of your notes, 233
  reading a note, 221–222
  selecting a group of notes, 223
  time-saver shortcut for, 219
  tricks for, 220
  viewing your notes, 225–230

• Z •

Zip drive, 339

IDG BOOKS WORLDWIDE BOOK REGISTRATION

Register This Book and Win!

We want to hear from you!

Visit **http://my2cents.dummies.com** to register this book and tell us how you liked it!

- ✔ Get entered in our monthly prize giveaway.

- ✔ Give us feedback about this book — tell us what you like best, what you like least, or maybe what you'd like to ask the author and us to change!

- ✔ Let us know any other *...For Dummies*® topics that interest you.

Your feedback helps us determine what books to publish, tells us what coverage to add as we revise our books, and lets us know whether we're meeting your needs as a *...For Dummies* reader. You're our most valuable resource, and what you have to say is important to us!

Not on the Web yet? It's easy to get started with *Dummies 101*®: *The Internet For Windows*® *98* or *The Internet For Dummies*®, 5th Edition, at local retailers everywhere.

Or let us know what you think by sending us a letter at the following address:

...For Dummies Book Registration
Dummies Press
7260 Shadeland Station, Suite 100
Indianapolis, IN 46256-3945
Fax 317-596-5498

™

...FOR DUMMIES

**BESTSELLING
BOOK SERIES
FROM IDG**